Everything you always wanted to know about...

D1591873

Comparative Government & Politics

2nd edition

STERLING
Education

2   1

ISBN-13: 978-1-9475565-8-4

Sterling Education
6 Liberty Square #11
Boston, MA 02109

info@sterling-prep.com

Published by Sterling Education

 Printed in the U.S.A.

Dear Reader!

Why different countries have different forms of government and political institutions? Why some countries exist as democracies and others are authoritarian regimes? Why are some revolutions successful and others fail? This clearly explained text is a perfect guide for anyone who wants to be knowledgeable about political systems and regimes that affect the lives of people around the world. It elucidates the complexity of various political structures and provides readers with the information necessary to compare governments across the globe.

This book was designed for those who want to develop a better understanding of political cultures, structures, and governmental functions, as well as the relationships between the governments and the governed. The content is focused on a thematic approach and introduces readers to the key concepts, structures and arguments using the examples of six representative countries: Great Britain, China, Mexico, Russia, Iran, and Nigeria.

You will learn about major events that shaped how these governments function, the different institutions of government and political cultures that exist around the world, how branches of governments interact with each other and the governed, and how these institutions may be affected by the input from the populace. Created by highly qualified political science teachers, scholars, and researchers, this book educates and empowers both the average and the highly informed reader, helping them develop and increase their understanding of world politics.

We congratulate you on your desire to learn more about the world's political systems. The editors sincerely hope that this guide will be a valuable resource for your learning.

Our Commitment to the Environment

Sterling Test Prep is committed to protecting our planet's resources by supporting environmental organizations with proven track records of conservation, ecological research and education and preservation of vital natural resources. A portion of our profits is donated to help these organizations so they can continue their critical missions. These organizations include:

For over 40 years, Ocean Conservancy has been advocating for a healthy ocean by supporting sustainable solutions based on science and cleanup efforts. Among many environmental achievements, Ocean Conservancy laid the groundwork for an international moratorium on commercial whaling, played an instrumental role in protecting fur seals from overhunting and banning the international trade of sea turtles. It created national marine sanctuaries and served as the lead non-governmental organization in the designation of 10 marine sanctuaries.

For 25 years, Rainforest Trust has been saving critical lands for conservation through land purchases and protected area designations. Rainforest Trust has played a central role in the creation of 73 new protected areas in 17 countries, including the Falkland Islands, Costa Rica and Peru. Nearly 8 million acres have been saved thanks to Rainforest Trust's support of in-country partners across Latin America, with over 500,000 acres of critical lands purchased outright for reserves.

Since 1980, Pacific Whale Foundation has been saving whales from extinction and protecting our oceans through science and advocacy. As an international organization, with ongoing research projects in Hawaii, Australia, and Ecuador, PWF is an active participant in global efforts to address threats to whales and other marine life. A pioneer in non-invasive whale research, PWF was an early leader in educating the public, from a scientific perspective, about whales and the need for ocean conservation.

With your purchase, you support environmental causes around the world.

Table of Contents

Table of Contents (*cont.*)

Chapter 1

Introduction to Comparative Politics

This chapter introduces the study of politics by explaining how political scientists study politics and why it is important to be informed about politics abroad, emphasizing the utility in distinguishing between normative (or value-related) questions and empirical or factual questions. How political scientists divide up their field of study is clarified through discussion on what comparative inquiry has to offer. Recognizing the interdependent framework of our modern world, themes of globalization and the general political and economic permeability of national borders are brought into consideration. Concepts of state, nation, regime, and government are contrasted to evoke consideration about legitimacy, authority and bases of political power, as well as the differences between these concepts. Thus, it is framed that the "state" is generally used to refer to the political power exercised over a defined geographic territory through a set of public institutions, while the "nation" is articulated as a human community with a shared culture and history. Governments are discussed as collections of individuals who occupy political office or exercise state power, whereas regimes are treated as the sets of rules and institutions that control access to (and exercise of) political power that typically endures from government to government. Regime change, or when these rules and institutions are replaced, is also parsed. The conceptual differences between (and similarities among) varying political systems are explored in detail. Also articulated is how, despite vast differences between economies and regimes types, most countries face similar challenges, including those presented by the natural environment, social and ethnic diversity, economic performance and the delivery of healthcare to citizens.

Purpose and Methods of Comparison and Classification

Comparative politics is a branch of political science defined by its methodological considerations. This means that comparative politics can study almost any topic, as what makes it comparative is the method of studying differences and similarities between two or more distinct concepts. Traditionally, comparative politics has tended to focus on comparing the various workings of countries, such as the form of government or type of economic system. Today, comparative politics just as often focus on *non-state actors*, for example comparing social movements in different countries, or even *super-state actors*, like the European Union or the African Union. As the era of globalization continues, where nothing happens in isolation, it is increasingly important to understand what is happening in other countries to understand how those events might affect one's own country and to understand one's situation by comparing it to the situation of others.

Comparative politics enables political scientists, as well as the general public, to understand issues and events from a broader perspective. Comparing what is happening in other countries with what is happening at home can help evaluate the performance both of the American government and that of other countries. For example, if looking only at the United States in isolation, the sole basis of comparing, for example, economic performance, would be based on the history of the United States. While this counts as comparative politics in some respect, in the era of globalization it can be more informative to compare the economic performance of the United States to other similar countries rather than only comparing it with past U.S. performance. Thus, if one sees that the United States is not doing as well economically as it has in the past, yet is doing much better than other countries, there can be a better basis of comparison for evaluating current economic performance.

Comparative politics is also useful for discovering innovative methods of government that may be useful at home. By studying other countries, one may find a policy implemented in a different and more beneficial way. Thus, comparative politics is essential to understand the world and America's place within it.

There are many methods of comparison that can be used, but *"the most similar"* and *"the most different"* are two of the most common. When evaluating economic performance, it is useful to compare countries which are similar. This means comparing wealthy developed countries in the G7 group with other G7 countries and comparing underdeveloped countries with other underdeveloped countries. Comparing the relative economic performance of Canada and Zimbabwe probably will not say much about the relative strength of either country but comparing Canada with the United States and Zimbabwe with Tanzania could tell a lot.

On the other end of the spectrum, it can be useful to look at comparisons between countries that are dissimilar in certain respects. If one country has a problem with racial violence, it can be useful to compare it to countries with very low levels of racial violence to try to determine what is different that makes one country have fewer problems than another.

The goal of such comparative studies is often to uncover the independent variable. The *independent variable* is the cause of something which explains why it occurs. By comparing multiple countries, one can develop better theoretical explanations of political events.

For example, when looking at gun violence in the United States, it may be caused by a large number of guns per capita. The number of guns relative to population would be the independent variable, and gun violence would be the dependent variable. This hypothesis can be tested by looking at other countries with high gun ownership. If the hypothesis is correct, then the independent variable of high gun ownership should mean that these other countries have high gun violence as well. However, looking at Canada and Switzerland, which also have high levels of gun ownership, they have low levels of gun violence. This means that although gun ownership per capita might be a factor in gun violence, it is not the sole cause of it; therefore, it can be rejected as the independent variable. This means a new hypothesis is needed. If it is comparatively tested and supporting evidence is found, then this independent variable could be developed into a larger theory explaining the issue.

From its year of national independence in 1944 to 2014,
Iceland experienced only a single police-shooting fatality.

Ways to Organize Government

A major theme of comparative politics is to compare and contrast the way that governments in different countries are organized. The idea of comparing different types of regimes goes back to Aristotle, who first devised characteristics of six different types of government based on how many people held power. This first classification remains influential today and divides the regimes into: *government by one person*, *government of the few* and *government of the many*.

Aristotle argued that each of these types of government had a good version and bad version. The good version ruled in the public interest, and the bad version ruled for private gain. For Aristotle, a good one-person government was a monarchy; a bad one was a tyranny. A good government of the few was an aristocracy; a bad one was an oligarchy. A good government of the many was a mixed polity; a bad one was a democracy.

During the 20th century, two new prominent typologies of government emerged and became highly influential. The first one divided the world into *democracy, fascism,* and *communism.* These three ideologies were in many ways a division of the rallying cry of the French Revolution into three parts. During the French Revolution, which overthrew the monarchy, the main slogan was "Liberty, equality, fraternity." The revolutionaries intended for all future governments to uphold these three principles, but in the 20th century these principles diverged and became the basis for three separate ideologies.

Liberty became the basis of democracy, *equality* became the basis of communism, and *fraternity* became the basis of fascism. In this sense, these three systems of government can be compared using these three principles.

Democratic regimes, such as the United States, the United Kingdom, and France, were governed in a way that upheld "freedom" as the highest principle, through having elected governments and civil liberties. Communist governments, such as the Soviet Union, Yugoslavia, and Cuba, believed that "equality" was the most important principle and focused on ensuring that people were taken care of economically. Fascist governments, such as Spain and Germany in the 1930s-1940s, believed that "fraternity" was the most important ideal, and promoted ideas of social cohesion and racial purity.

From a comparative perspective, this classification was very convenient as each of these regimes lacked the key elements of the other two. Democracies had freedom but very little economic equality, as evidenced by widespread poverty, unemployment, and homelessness, and were generally less concerned with maintaining social cohesion. Communist governments had strong economic equality with almost no unemployment or poverty but were dictatorships without freedom. Fascist governments believed that the people must all be unified and that there could be no racial or social differences in the population to ensure a harmonic society; they did this through eliminating both freedom and equality. Before World War II, it was very easy to classify governments into one of these three systems, and during World War II, democracies and communist countries decided to band together to eliminate fascism because Hitler's Germany had become a threat to global stability.

Churchill (left) and Roosevelt (center) meet with Stalin (right) at the Yalta Conference, marking one of the last moments of tentative cooperation before the Cold War saw democracy and communism enter into hostile competition.

After the end of World War II, democracy and communism became the two dominant ideologies and a new three-part typology dominated comparative politics. During the Cold War, the world was divided into the First World, the Second World, and the Third World. This was a ranking system somewhat displaying the bias of Western political scientists who believed democracy to be inherently superior to communism. However, for most of the Cold War, the Soviet Union was considered the second most powerful country in the world and therefore more powerful than most of America's First World allies, so it is less of a ranking system than a descriptive term. The First World consisted of the developed democracies that were generally part of the North Atlantic Treaty Organization (NATO), such as the United States, Canada, the United Kingdom and most of Western Europe. The Second World was the communist states in the Warsaw Pact defense alliance, such as the Soviet Union, Czechoslovakia, Poland, Romania, and East Germany. The Third World was the remaining countries who were not aligned with either side in the Cold War.

The Third World did not have the connotation of being the less economically developed countries that the term tends to mean today. There were major international meetings of Third World Countries, called the Non-Aligned Movement. These meetings were designed to create an alliance of these countries to forge their path independent of both the First and the Second Worlds and incorporate both communism and democracy into a new system of government. The Non-Aligned Third World movement had trouble organizing and agreeing, in part because they consisted of a large number of diverse countries, including Peru, Egypt, India, and Indonesia. The main reason for the failure of this new organization was that the Third World became the battleground of the Cold War, with American and Soviet military interventions frequently getting involved in these countries to try to sway them to their side.

After the fall of the Soviet Union in 1991, new typologies were proposed, focusing on various elements. The level of economic development became a major focus, and the term Third World was repurposed to mean a country that was poor and underdeveloped. Due to the confusion with the prior meaning of the term, most political economists prefer to use the term "underdeveloped" to refer to the poorest countries, "developing" to refer to countries which are mostly poor but rapidly improving, and "developed" to refer to wealthy countries. Thus, under this typology, much of sub-Saharan Africa would be considered underdeveloped, South America would be considered developing, and North America and Europe would be considered developed.

A second typology also emerged after the Cold War which focused on political stability. This largely classified countries into failed states, transitional states, and consolidated democracies. A *failed state* was a situation where the government had broken down, either into civil war or had simply collapsed. Today, Syria and Somalia are failed states; Somalia has no national government and Syria has fallen into a civil war. *Transitional states* are ones who are stable yet still have dictatorships. This term is somewhat hopeful, as it assumes that all dictatorships will one day become democracies. Countries such as Kazakhstan, Jordan, and China would be considered transitional. The United States, Canada and most of Europe are considered *consolidated democracies.*

Normative and Empirical Questions

The method of comparative politics which involves comparing and contrasting different countries, events, and social movements is largely empirical. The empirical analysis looks at data and observations. For example, an empirical comparison of two countries' economies may compare the GDP per capita of each country, the unemployment rate of each country and the balance of trade between the two countries.

Empirical analysis strives to be value-free, which means it simply compares two things without making a judgment or an argument. *Normative analysis*, by contrast, seeks to make an argument or judgment. Neither of these two types of analysis is useful on their own. Comparing for the sake of comparing is not an interesting exercise unless it is part of a wider normative argument. At the same time, a normative argument without empirical data to back it up is simply unsubstantiated and is mere opinion, rather than a developed theory backed by facts and data. In the study of comparative politics, both empirical and normative analysis tend to operate in tandem, as comparing different countries always provides both grounds for empirical analysis and for making a normative argument about how things should be.

As an example, think of comparing poverty rates in different countries. In a purely empirical study, one could compare the United States and Sweden and find that Sweden has much lower poverty levels than the United States. While this is factually true, this empirical analysis is not very useful, as it does not speak to anything other than basic facts. It is not known if one should consider less poverty an inherently good thing, and it is not known if there is anything the United States should learn from Sweden as these are both normative questions. Thus, a normative analysis might argue that poverty is inherently bad, but on its own will not speak to what someone can do about it.

Swedish public housing built in Stockholm's Rinkeby district by the national government through their ambitious Million Programme implemented between 1965 and 1974. Approximately one million dwellings were built during the program's lifespan.

By combining an empirical and normative analysis, one can see what programs Sweden has that might be useful for the United States to emulate to reduce overall poverty levels. Thus, normative arguments are more philosophical and argue how things should be, which is the basis of all political thinking. For these philosophical arguments to lead to policy ideas, political scientists engage in comparative empirical analysis to find data and examples. The philosophical argument that poverty is bad can then be translated into government policy by looking at how other countries have reduced poverty.

Concepts (State, Nation, Regime, Government)

Comparative politics has traditionally had a number of concepts which form the basis of the study. These concepts, such as the state, the nation, the regime, and the government, are today being challenged and complicated by globalization, which is blurring the boundaries between states. Thus, while comparative politics tends to focus on comparing the internal situation of different states and the discipline of international relations has tended to look at how states interact with each other, the boundary between the two disciplines is becoming blurred in the era of globalization.

While these four themes remain as the content of analysis for comparative politics, globalization itself has become an important terrain of study within the field. *Globalization* can be roughly defined as increasing interconnectedness of people, governments, economies, and technologies across the world. The main driver of globalization has been technology. The ease by which people can travel across the world in modern jets and the rapid spread of information and communication connectivity via the internet have ushered in a new era in human history. Globalization has many aspects and cannot simply be reduced to one element.

Early examples of globalization that the popular media picked up on were almost all economic in nature. As the Soviet Union collapsed, most of the world was pushed toward adopting a single model of capitalist economics called neoliberalism. This model, which emphasized privatization, deregulation and increased international integration, was driven by corporations and organizations such as the World Trade Organization (WTO) and the International Monetary Fund (IMF). Many people around the world saw this form of globalization as something negative, as it tended to increase inequality and shift power away from democratic governments and into the hands of corporations. Major protests in the late 1990s occurred, and the popular media labeled these as anti-globalization.

However, the protesters themselves were an example of globalization, as they were an interconnected network of people from hundreds of different countries and different backgrounds supporting different causes. Labor unions joined up with environmentalists, and urban democracy activists joined up with poor farmers. These protests were not anti-globalization but merely opposed to one form of globalization while promoting a different form that focused on uniting people rather than economic systems. Thus, globalization is a complicated and multi-faceted issue which will continue to play a role in each of the four themes that make up traditional comparative politics.

The State

The *state* refers to the governing structure of a specific country. The United States, Nigeria, China, and Iran are individual states. Despite globalization significantly reducing their power, states remain powerful entities and the primary point of comparison for this section's purposes. When one engages in comparative analysis, they are usually comparing differences among states. Different states have different institutional frameworks, which are often the basis of comparison. These frameworks can range from different types of political regimes in the broad sense, including democracy or dictatorship, or can be related to what sort of economic or social system prevails within a state. States are generally the top level of analysis, as the three other themes operate within the context of states.

One of the most important aspects of the current state-based system of global politics is *legitimacy*. The German sociologist Max Weber defined a state as an entity which is capable of maintaining a monopoly on the legitimate use of force. This means that a state is defined by its ability to control its territory via the military and control its people through the police. If there is a piece of territory in which no single entity or state has control of, then the state is not considered legitimate.

Police forces are used by governments to enforce law and project sovereignty.

For example, in Syria the initial protests overran the police forces, and the government's inability to quell the popular uprising led to the dictatorship of Bashir al-Assad being seen as illegitimate. In the following civil war, various factions emerged which control different parts of the country. Under Weber's definition of a legitimate state, there is no true Syrian government anymore because Kurdish groups control the

North and Islamist groups control the interior. Syria is a good example of how states are not natural entities but creations of people which rest on being seen as legitimate by the people and being able to maintain their legitimacy through force. In the case of the Syrian government, it lost legitimacy on both accounts when the people rose up in an attempt to overthrow the dictatorship and when it was unable to defeat other groups during the civil war militarily.

Weber's idea of what a legitimate state consists of is quite controversial, however. According to Weber's definition, if a state can use force to take over another state, then this is considered legitimate. Thus, when Russia recently took over Crimea, which was part of Ukraine, much of the world saw this as an aggressive action that was illegitimate. Weber's theory, however, would argue that so long as Russia was able to control the territory militarily and police the population, their control of the area is legitimate. Therefore, what counts as a legitimate state is a contested notion itself. While taking land from other states is controversial and often considered illegitimate, the authority and base of power of a state still come from its military and police power. Even if one does not like Weber's definition because it legitimizes acts like Russia's annexation of Crimea from Ukraine, his definition holds because Russia continues to control this territory and its monopoly on the use of force in Crimea remains unchallenged, essentially allowing Russia to get away with this land grab.

In the context of globalization, states have lost a significant amount of power because the economy largely operates at a global level, while states can only control what happens inside their borders. Before economic globalization, states were more powerful as economies tended to be national in scope rather than global. This meant that states could regulate and control corporations and generally direct the economy in a way that they were elected to do.

Today, states are simply less powerful; they have trouble passing regulations and directing the economy, as what happens within a single country is a small part of the global economy. For example, if Mexico were to pass laws which required safety and health regulations to be met in low-wage sweatshops, the company that owns the sweatshop can simply move its operations to another country that does not have these laws. This is called the *"race to the bottom,"* as corporations in a globalized world can force states to compete with each other to see which will offer the lowest wages, most minimal workplace safety standards and least regulation to attract global corporations to set up operations in their country.

In many countries, this situation directly undermines democracy. In the 1980s, the people of Argentina elected a government on a platform of fighting poverty, restoring social programs and regulating the economy. The government ended up doing the exact opposite of all of these things because prior governments, including a military dictatorship, had racked up huge debts which forced Argentina to get loans from the IMF to pay interest on its debt. As a condition for these loans, the IMF imposed a "structural adjustment program" which dictated economic policy to the Argentinian government. Even though voters elected a government to do one thing, the government ended up doing the exact opposite because it lacked the power or the will to resist powerful global financial organizations.

At the same time, corporate rights treaties, such as the WTO and the Trans-Pacific Partnership (TPP), included provisions to allow global corporations to sue governments for passing laws that might hurt their profitability. For example, in the 1980s the United States banned the import of tuna that was caught using a method which unintentionally killed dolphins in the bycatch. Mexican companies challenged this environmental protection law at the WTO and won, forcing the U.S. to change its laws. The U.S. lost again after instituting labeling for dolphin-safe tuna when the WTO ruled that this law harm the profitability of fishery corporations. Economic globalization has significantly reduced the authority of states and thus undermined democracy. The global economy can only be regulated at a global level, but states do not operate at the global level, leaving a power imbalance in favor of transnational capital.

The Nation

Nations can be tricky to understand, as in popular discourse nations and states are often taken to mean the same thing. A *nation*, however, is different from a state, as a nation refers to a group of culturally and socially similar people. When states first became dominant in Europe after the treaty of Westphalia, there was an assumption that states and nations lined up one-to-one. Thus, every nation was intended to have its state, leading to the term *nation-state*. This means that France would be made up only of French people, Spain of Spanish people, Germany of Germans, and so on. A nation is a historically constituted group of people with a similar origin and to some extent a shared cultural experience.

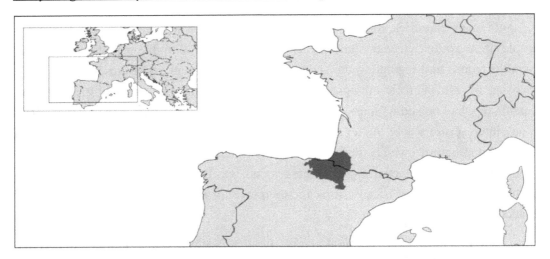

The indigenous ethnic Basque population (shaded) constitutes a nation (of peoples) without a state of their own.

The idea of the nation-state became problematic on two accounts. The first was the existence of Jews as a nation within the states of Europe. At first, Jews were denied basic rights as they were considered to be a foreign national living within a state, even though most Jews had lived in the states of Europe as long as any other person in France or Germany. As Jews eventually began to win political rights, the idea of a state corresponding to a nation began to fall out of favor, as such a situation was ripe for discrimination.

In the colonial period, the idea of a nation-state became even more problematic. As European powers colonized Africa and America, they sought to form new nation-states, which placed the original inhabitants in a subservient position. Could Algeria be a state for the French nation when the vast majority of those who lived there were not French but were Algerian, Berber and Arab? When these contradictions became exacerbated to the point of major ruptures and the colonized states won or were granted independence, new problems arose. After the Ottoman Empire was defeated in World War I, the U.K. and France arbitrarily divided up the Middle East into what they decided would be nation-states. However, these divisions empowered one group of people over the others who lived there, leading to problems of oppression that are still present today. For example, the Kurdish nation, which was formerly part of the Ottoman Empire and which lives in Turkey, Iraq, Syria, and Iran, were not given a state of their own. The Turkish state oppressed the Kurds because they were part of a different nation, and the Iraqi and Syrian Arab states oppressed them as well. Thus, the idea of states being only for one nation of people led to oppression and violence once again.

The idea of a state that was not made up of one nation but of multiple nations did not become widely accepted until the modern era when it was recognized that countries in the Americas, in particular, the United States, Canada, Brazil, and Mexico were flourishing despite having multiple nationalities. Canada was originally half British and half French, but eventually, waves of Irish and Scottish immigrants added new nations to the mix, to the point where today Canada consists of large groups of people from almost every nation on earth. The same is true with the United States and Brazil. Mexico was born of a combination of Spanish and indigenous nations and the mestizos (who were half and a half) who had developed their own historical identity. Thus, in today's globalized context where population migration is the norm, there are almost no nation-states left, as all states encompass many nations, with rights being afforded on condition of citizenship, not according to which cultural nation one belongs to.

Globalization further complicates the idea of *national culture*. The original theorists of globalization argued that the world adopting a single economic model would cause it also to adopt a single culture and lead to the disappearance of nations. In reality, the opposite has turned out to be true, as transnational corporations have adapted themselves to local cultures and tailored their products to meet regional demand. This has resulted, in many cases, in extreme nationalism, as transnational corporations choose to side with nationalist groups which seek to purge minority nations and cultures from their borders.

A good example is India, where upper-class Hindus are supposed to follow a vegetarian diet. As a result, McDonald's has opened vegetarian restaurants in some parts of India to cater to local tastes, while at the same time supporting the policies of the Hindu Nationalist Party. This party promotes international trade and corporate deregulation, but it also promotes policies that many see as discriminatory against non-Hindu minority groups in India. In this sense, globalization has led to the replacement of wars between states with wars between nations within states.

After the fall of communism and the onset of economic globalization in 1991, there was a major increase in ethnic and nationalist wars.

Once unified, countries like Yugoslavia broke apart in the civil war as Orthodox Serbs, Catholic Croats and Muslim Bosnians fought each other. Rwanda faced a civil war where genocide was committed by one ethnic group against another, while the majority ethnic group of Bhutan forced out the minority, creating over 100,000 refugees. Instead of wiping out different cultures and nations, economic globalization seems to be increasing conflict between self-identified groups of people who claim to constitute nations. This leads to the question of the validity of "the nation" as a term of analysis to begin with. Many political scientists prefer to focus on ethnic origin or religious community today, but these are all invented categorizations, or as the philosopher, Benedict Anderson put it, *"imagined communities."*

Map indicating the Croatian, Bosnian and Herzegovinian territory occupied by Serb forces during the Yugoslav Wars (March 31, 1991 to November 12, 2001).

There was a joke in Yugoslavia before its disintegration that a Croat was someone who didn't like the Pope, a Serb was someone who didn't go to church, and a Bosnian was someone who didn't believe in Allah. The differences between the nations and ethnicities that made up Yugoslavia were considered insignificant, but once the civil war broke out, these previously insignificant differences became the basis for violent conflict and ethnic cleansing.

The entire concept of ethnicity is an imagined community which invented the idea of a group of people sharing a similar cultural heritage that makes them incompatible with other nations or ethnicities. There is nothing natural about ethnicity or nationality; it is not something passed down genetically by one's parents, but rather something invented and sustained down through the years for political purposes.

The Regime

A *regime* is the institutional arrangement of a state. Regimes can change, but the state will stay the same. Typologies of states are often based on regime type, so during the Cold War states were classified as to whether they had a democratic or communist regime. A regime is also different from a government, as a government can change while the regime stays the same. When the United States elects a new president, the government changes, but the regime of presidential democracy remains in place.

The most common regime types today are a parliamentary democracy, presidential democracy, and single-party dictatorship. *Parliamentary democracy* is led by a Prime Minister who is the leader of the largest party in the legislature. *Presidential democracy* is a led by a President whose executive function is separate from the legislature. *Single-party dictatorships* usually operate in much the same manner as a presidential democracy except that the leader is chosen from within the ruling party rather than by popular vote.

Canada and the United Kingdom are examples of parliamentary democracy, the United States and France are examples of presidential democracy and China, and North Korea are examples of single-party dictatorships. These differences are not absolute, however, as many countries will have popular elections, but where only one party has any realistic chance of winning. While Russia is a presidential democracy, Vladimir Putin's United Russia is the only party that has any chance of winning. Thus, Russia is something of a hybrid between the Chinese and American models.

Regimes can change in different ways, from total regime change to minor alterations. Regime change became a major buzzword during the U.S. invasion of Iraq because President Bush said that he wanted regime change, meaning replacing Saddam Hussein's one-party Baathist state with a new, democratic regime.

The United States has a long history of attempting to force other countries to engage in regime change. Throughout the Cold War, the U.S. was heavily involved in

Latin America especially, overthrowing regimes in an attempt to transform not just who was in power in a country but also their structure of government.

One of the first such forced regime changes was in 1953 when the United States and the United Kingdom worked together to overthrow the democratic regime in Iran and replace it with a monarchist dictatorship. Both countries were worried about the democratic government controlling Iran's oil supply to the detriment of American and British oil companies, so they intervened to put in power a king they knew would be friendly to British and American oil corporations.

Other examples of American-led regime changes include 1964 in Brazil and Bolivia, where presidential democratic regimes were replaced with military dictatorships, and in 1973, the U.S. overthrew the democratic socialist regime of Salvador Allende in favor of yet another military dictatorship led by Augusto Pinochet.

2007 Brazilian protesters demonstrate the nation's continued skepticism and anti-U.S. sentiments.

Regime change can also be the result of revolution from inside rather than external meddling as in the above examples. Recently, revolutions have changed the regimes of Tunisia and Egypt dramatically. Tunisia began as a one-party dictatorship and is now transitioning to democracy. Egypt's single-party government was overthrown by the people, replacing it with a democracy which elected an Islamist government who set about enacting their regime change. The military then overthrew the Islamist regime, and Egypt remains in the hands of the military pending a possible future transition to another form of regime.

In 1979, Iran underwent a revolution which overthrew the monarchy that the U.S. had put in power in 1953. The regime was changed to a presidential democracy within a wider Islamic theocracy.

In 1959, Cuba had a *revolution* which overthrew an authoritarian dictatorship in favor of a communist dictatorship. Revolutions are much less common but often result in the most dramatic and often unpredictable outcomes. Revolutions are always unpredictable because they are so intensely political, meaning that when large groups of people come together to oppose a regime, they often have very different ideas as to what should replace the existing power structure. This was evident in Egypt, where the revolutionaries wanted democracy but not the Islamic democracy they ended up with, which led them right back to a military government. In Iran, the revolution originally had a very strong communist component, but after the king of Iran was overthrown, the Islamists conducted a violent purge, killing and jailing the communists who helped make the revolution possible for their Islamic vision of Iran to prevail.

While revolutions and foreign intervention result in major changes, regime change can be more minor and less dramatic. For example, Canada underwent a minor regime change in 1984, when it officially adopted its constitution independent of the United Kingdom. While this was a relatively minor change in day-to-day politics in Canada, it was significant in that it meant Canada could now make constitutional changes independent of the United Kingdom's approval.

Bolivian President Evo Morales initiated procedures necessary for a new national constitution to be drafted and ratified by January 2009.

In 2007, a constituent assembly was elected in Bolivia to write a new constitution. The resulting document enshrined unique ideas such as plurinationalism into the constitution, changed Bolivia from officially Catholic to a secular state, changed the voting system and reformed the judiciary. These were relatively major changes, altering significant portions of the structure of the regime, but ones who did not change Bolivia away from a presidential democracy. The new constitution was approved in a referendum, and the President of Bolivia declared that day as a "refounding" of Bolivia.

In the context of globalization, regime differences have come into sharper focus. In 1992, the American political philosopher Francis Fukuyama published an influential book arguing that American-style democratic capitalism represented the final stage of history, and in the era of globalization, all countries would have to adopt this regime type. As communist dictatorships continue to topple in the early 1990s, it looked like Fukuyama was correct and that in the future there would be only one regime type.

However, another American political scientist, Samuel P. Huntington, published a book a few years later which argued that regime type differences would no longer be relevant in the age of globalization, and instead cultural and religious differences would be the cause of much conflict, which would prevent the era of global peace that Fukuyama predicted. Although it seems that Fukuyama was right in principle, as virtually everyone proclaims democracy to be the best form of government, the continuing prominence of ethnic conflict and religious-based terrorism proves Huntington's point.

At the same time, many political theorists argue that there is an increasing convergence between dictatorship and democracy. These theorists argue that democratic countries are simply elected dictatorships, not structurally different from dictatorships; the only difference is that the people get to decide who their dictator will be, rather than the party elite.

Government

The *government* is the current administration in power in a country and is a subset of both the state and the regime. Governments tend to change frequently, while the regime and state rarely do. While it is common to think of governments mostly changing in the context of a democracy (when a new government is elected from a different political party), governments change within one-party states as well. In China, the Premier, who is the leader of the government, serves a five-year term which can be renewed once. Thus, the longest a government will remain in power is ten years. Even though all officials in the government are from the same Communist Party, the government can still change, which can lead to dramatically different policies. Despite being ruled by the Communist Party, the successive governments of China since the late 1970s have transitioned the country's economy to capitalism. Without a dramatic regime change, the country has gradually transformed its economic system through changes in government despite it not being a democracy.

At the same time, many complain that in most democracies elections do not change anything. Given a choice between two parties who are mostly the same, these critics argue that changing governments in a democracy is largely meaningless; it changes the people who are in power but not the policies of the government. Such critics argue that dictatorships (like China) and democracies (like the United States) are not fundamentally different, only procedurally different.

Another example is Iran, in which the government can change through elections, but the Ayatollah (who is the Supreme Leader) has much influence in many areas of government. While the Ayatollah does not control legislation directly, all candidates for the legislative parliament must be approved by the Supreme Leader. Changes in government can change the direction of the country, but not in a significant manner. This was evident in the election of President Ahmadinejad, who took a hardline anti-American stance, while the new President Rouhani (elected in 2013) has taken a much more pro-American position and advocated for peace and negotiation. These are major changes in policy as a result of different governments. However, in 2009, a pro-Reform candidate lost an election that many Iranians claim was rigged in favor of Ahmadinejad by the Ayatollah, who feared that the Reform candidate, Mir-Hossein Mousavi would allow more religious freedom.

Governments can be seen as legitimate or illegitimate for some reasons. Democratic legitimacy comes from winning free and fair elections, however, in many cases the electoral system itself may be problematic. Many Americans saw George W. Bush as an illegitimate president because he lost the popular vote and only won the election because of the Electoral College. Given that more Americans voted for Al Gore than for George W. Bush, his legitimacy was questionable.

Similarly, the electoral system in Canada enabled the government of Prime Minister Stephen Harper to control a majority of the seats in Parliament despite only getting 38% of the popular vote. Many Canadians argued that his government was not legitimate because the majority had voted for the two other opposition parties. Simply having an election is not enough to guarantee legitimacy, something which the Egyptian dictator Hosni Mubarak realized after he was overthrown. He would hold elections where he was the only name on the ballot, then proclaim that he was a democratically legitimate president because 95% of the population had voted for him.

Egyptian protesters gather in Cairo's Tahrir Square
to demand Mubarak's removal from office in February 2011.

Countries which do not have elections have different ways for governments to claim legitimacy. China's one-party dictatorship claims legitimacy by arguing that such a system is best suited for managing the economy. The Chinese government continually points to China's rapid economic growth since it began to transition from communism to capitalism as the source of its legitimacy. Chinese leaders state that if they allowed democracy, the growing wealth of China would be threatened by an unpredictable government.

Another example is North Korea, which is a *hereditary dictatorship*. North Korea claims that the ruling Kim family can directly know and act on the wishes of the North Korean public. Even though North Korea is a dictatorship resembling a medieval hereditary monarchy, it claims democratic legitimacy. This is reflected in the official name of the country, which is the Democratic People's Republic of Korea. Another example is Saudi Arabia, which is a *monarchical dictatorship*. The Saudi government claims legitimacy by appealing to the people's religious beliefs, claiming that the royal family is legitimated through Islam.

Governments have been dramatically affected by globalization, as they have lost authority to transnational financial organizations and often find themselves at the mercy of corporations. The decline in the authority of states means that the power of governments is constrained, for even if the people can change the government (either through elections or revolution), they still have to operate within the framework of a global economy. As a result of the loss of authority over economic matters, there has been a surge in xenophobic rhetoric in Europe and the United States, which is symptomatic of the decline in the authority of states and governments on economic matters. Unable to control the economy, governments have turned to exercise their authority over what they can control, namely people. In many European countries, new far-right movements which focus on limiting immigration or even promoting deporting recent immigrants have gained popularity.

Process and Policy

When engaging in comparative politics, one of the major questions that continue to arise has to do with definitions and how they tend to differ across countries. For example, most of the world's governments would define democracy as requiring elections at its most basic level. However, North Korea officially considers itself to be a democratic people's republic. So, what does democracy mean? Moreover, at a higher level, what is politics? These are questions that are more often dealt with in political philosophy, but they are somewhat relevant to comparative politics as disputes over terminology often arise when comparing countries.

What is *politics*? This is a question that most people find very hard to answer. Often it is simply posited that government is politics. However, if politics consists only of governance, then this means that a revolution or a protest would not be considered political, even though they most certainly are. Furthermore, if politics means government, then voting in an election would not be politics because this is choosing a government rather than governing. Politics is more than simply the exercise of governance. Lately, it has become fashionable to state that everything is political. However, does this make sense? Is walking to school political? Is playing soccer political? These are not political acts, so not everything is political. What is political? This is a question which should form the basis of all political philosophy but has rarely been taken up

The question of what is politics did not become a major point of consideration by political philosophers until the 20th century. The German philosopher Carl Schmitt was one of the first to approach the question systematically, arguing that politics is that which involves friends and enemies. Thus, when a state allies with another state, it acts politically by siding with a friend, and when it condemns another state's behavior, it acts politically by criticizing an enemy. Later philosophers have expanded this notion of meaning that politics by definition is about conflicts and disputes over which there is no clear or obvious answer. Thus, politics comes into it when a decision needs to be made on an issue where the decision is a matter of picking one side over another without any objective method to decide which side is correct. As long as people disagree, politics is needed to arrive at a decision. Politics must involve debate between multiple opposing sides and a final decision. When that final decision is subject to popular participation (e.g., debate in the legislature and the press), this form of politics is called democratic. When authoritarian regimes attempt to silence opposition and prevent multiple sides from publicly debating an issue, they are not just acting anti-democratically, but also anti-politically.

The United Kingdom is famous for its tradition of engaging in open, passionate and sometimes raucous political debates.

Democracy is also a tough term to define. Some political theorists argue that politics is democratic when decisions have public legitimacy and input, while others argue that politics must always be democratic or it ceases to be political in the first place. Democracy meant "rule by the people" in ancient Greek, and this has been interpreted in some ways. Communist dictatorships argued that elections were not needed for democracy, as "the dictatorship of the proletariat" was a means for the people to rule directly. (Every citizen was a "comrade.") They argued that elections in capitalist countries were not democratic because they resulted in rule by the rich, not by the ordinary people.

The flip side of this is that countries that hold elections argue that without public input into who the leaders of a country will be, the communist dictatorships cannot claim to have any democratic legitimacy. However, there are also many political theorists who argue that representative democracy is an extremely weak form of democracy and hardly deserves the name of democracy. Deliberative democrats argue that voting in elections is not enough to have a democracy, but that there must also be public forums for people to discuss and deliberate on important issues. Without such public forums, the elected officials will simply act on their own, rather than representing what the people want. Going even further, participatory democrats argue that democracy should mean direct participation by the people, not just in deliberations but on decisions of government.

At yet another level deeper, one can think about what the purpose of government should be. Again, this is a highly debated question, with different schools of political thought having different answers. In ancient Greece, where politics first arose, the philosophers argued that government existed to promote virtue and excellence in the citizens. The purpose of government was to enable its citizens to reach their full potential and perform great public-spirited deeds and speeches. By fostering individual virtue, the city would be virtuous as well.

After the fall of the Roman Empire and the enforced dominance of the Christian church in medieval Europe, the purpose of the government changed to having a religious function. The government, in the form of a king, was considered the divine representative of God on Earth and obeying the government was seen as a religious duty equivalent to obeying God.

During the Enlightenment, when religious belief started to wane, and the legitimacy of monarchies was challenged, new theories of government arose. English philosopher Thomas Hobbes argued that the government existed for security purposes, as without a government everyone could kill everyone else. He argued that the purpose of government was to be an ultimate authority which could keep everyone under control because it was the most powerful entity in existence. Later another English philosopher, John Locke, argued that the government's primary job was protecting private property.

The Scottish philosopher Adam Smith took this a step further and argued that the primary purpose of government is economic in nature. Thus, there is a major difference between ancient and modern conceptions of government, with the ancients seeing the purpose of government as promoting virtue among citizens, and the modern view which sees the purpose of government as promoting economic well-being.

Today most countries have adopted the modern view of government as economic stewardship, but depending on the country and philosophical viewpoint, this is not the only role of government. In many countries, the government still has an explicitly religious element, and the purpose of government is seen as upholding religious morality and sentiment. In some countries, the government is seen as having the purpose of maintaining social cohesion and harmony, either through promoting social programs that help disadvantaged groups or minorities or by trying to push these groups out of the country. In many places, the economic role of the government is seen as being an advocate for business, while in others the government's purpose is seen more as to help those who are being "left behind" by capitalism.

1940s United States Housing Authority poster is decrying the blight of slums.

There are many different philosophical and practical approaches to what people think the purpose of government is. It is necessary to keep these in mind when comparing different countries who may have completely different approaches to what the purpose of government should be, what they think democracy is and even what politics consists of. The fundamental method of comparative politics is to compare and contrast similarities and differences between the domestic situations of various countries. To do this effectively, all of the above must be considered. The key question of comparative politics is not merely what are the differences and similarities, but why are these countries different or similar. The choice of which countries to analyze in comparison must take into account all these factors.

While comparative politics emphasizes finding differences and trying to explain them, the entire field is only possible because of similarities. Despite all the different types of political systems, government ideologies and forms of political economy, all countries face a common set of problems. Comparative politics is possible because, for example, the environment is a global problem which all countries need to deal with.

Comparative politics analyzes how different countries all approach this same issue. It looks at how different conceptions of government and regime type lead to different approaches. In this sense, comparative politics is more of a methodology than a field of its own. If one is interested in environmental politics, then using comparative methods would be extremely useful in looking at the differences in environmental policy between China, the United States, and the United Kingdom.

Those who study issues related to culture and religion also find comparative methods extremely useful. As countries become more diverse and less nationally homogenous, tensions between cultural, ethnic, racial and religious groups have been on the rise. Using a comparative method to study how different countries approach this same issue is highly informative. For example, why are Aboriginal people in Canada much worse off than they are in Bolivia? What is different about these two countries that leads to many different outcomes on the same issue?

Those who study the politics of religion find comparative methods essential, as they can look at the differences between secular countries and religious ones, or between countries with many religions and countries with just one religion and draw conclusions about what sorts of policies work best at promoting certain aims. The issue of multiculturalism and diversity especially lends itself to comparative study; some countries are much better than others at integrating people from a variety of backgrounds, leading to comparative studies to try to find out why this is the case.

Economic well-being, poverty, and unemployment are problems that affect every single country in the world, and political economists tend to be predominately comparative in their approach. Political economists often look at similarities as much as differences, as they look at two countries with similar political systems but which have different economic situations and ask what factors cause these differences. Political economists are also keen to compare regime types and look for economic policies prominent in one regime but not in another, to find new ways of promoting certain economic goals.

One of the key questions that a comparative political economy has looked at is the relation between democracy and economic development. Does having a political democracy lead to economic development, or does having a developed economy lead to democracy? Comparisons of China, South Korea, India, and Nigeria are important, as all four countries represent different situations. China is rapidly developing without democracy, Nigeria has a democracy but is not developing, India is developing as a democracy, and South Korea developed as a dictatorship but switched to democracy once it became more developed.

Political economists also increasingly focus on comparing not just countries but different *supranational trade blocs*. They might look at the differences between NAFTA,

MERCOSUR in South America and the European Union and attempt to see which forms of economic treaty work best for the countries concerned.

Healthcare is another important field that relies heavily on comparative politics. Almost every country has a different healthcare regime, but most people only know about how the one in their own country works. By engaging in comparative studies, one can find what works in other countries and try to determine if those successful policies would work here. America's private health insurance system is often contrasted to hybrid systems (as in France) and completely public systems (as in Canada). Comparative researchers look for the advantages and disadvantages to each of these systems and try to determine if there are policies from one country that might make another country better. Rarely is one country simply the best, as there is always something that can be learned from others to improve the domestic situation of a country.

Chapter 2

Sovereignty, Authority, and Power

This chapter addresses the nature of power in politics. While modern political understanding holds that power is territorially organized into states (or countries) that more or less control what happens within their borders, which is to say that they exercise sovereignty, the world has not always been structured as a system of states. These modern nation-states first emerged in Europe in the seventeenth century. Today, there are some challenges to the sovereignty of the nation-state in the form of increasingly emerging supranational systems of governance, such as the European Union (EU) and the Economic Community of West African States (ECOWAS). Sovereignty can be affected by internal divisions over power and its distribution as well.

Across national borders, the sources of power that are the foundation for politics vary in importance, and these different sources affect the construction of the rules of politics. These rules, which generally take the form of constitutions, need to be understood in this context. Constitutions define both the role of and the constituent parts of a government and the limits and obligations of government concerning the rights of citizens. Different types of political regimes, from forms of democracy to the various nondemocratic forms, greatly determine how states strike a balance between citizens' rights and government power. The exercise of power requires justification, and political scientists use the concept of legitimacy to refer to the popularly accepted use of power by a government. Political legitimacy (and the loss of it) is recognized differently according to the type of states in question.

State power is exercised within the context of specific economic systems. The scope and role of government in the economy are important factors. Equally important are the belief systems that might form the foundation for claims to legitimacy. Ultimately, both the belief systems that strengthen the legitimacy of the political system and the structures of the economy will have an impact on governmental effectiveness, capacity, and control over state resources.

Political scientists are interested in political culture, core values and beliefs, and how these values are fostered and disseminated through the process of political socialization. Such values are often organized in specific ideologies that influence the direction of the exercise of power. The differences among political values and beliefs are explored. In some instances, religious belief systems play an important political role. In other instances, more overt political agendas and ideologies are central.

Political Culture, Communication and Socialization

The historical evolution of a country plays a major role in the type of institutions and form of government that has developed. This historical development of a country's situation is called its *political culture*, and it plays a role in determining what sources of power and authority are considered legitimate. The political tradition of a country may date back a long way or be relatively short. Different countries also have differences in terms of how important the political tradition is in shaping current political attitudes.

When referring to the political tradition of a country, political scientists usually call it the political culture, which encompasses both traditional and contemporary beliefs, attitudes, values, and practices people have with respect to government. For example, a political culture of gun ownership has developed in the United States which did not develop in the United Kingdom. Thus, the U.K. has more legal restrictions on gun ownership than the U.S. This difference can be traced to the political culture that has developed, as Americans care more about guns than British people.

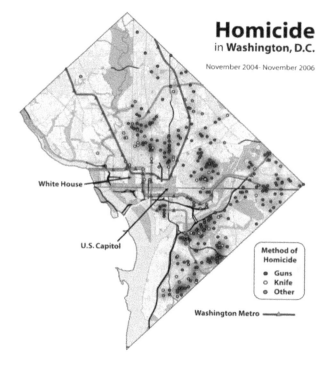

Map of Washington, D.C. indicating homicides by gun,
knife or other means between November 2004 and November 2006.

For comparative purposes, political cultures are often divided into two types: consensual and conflictual culture. A *consensual political culture* is one where it is assumed everyone generally agrees with how the country is run and trusts its leaders to make decisions in the best interests of the public. By contrast, *conflictual political culture* is one where people are not afraid to openly disagree with and critique both the actions of politicians but also openly criticize the institutions of government. Depending on one's point of view, one of these may seem better than the other. Advocates of consensual political culture view it regarding social harmony and a lack of division among the population, which bestows legitimacy on the government. They view conflictual political culture as full of strife and disunity and as a threat to the stability of the government. Advocates of conflictual political cultures argue that conflict and dissent are the highest expressions of political freedom. They see consensual political cultures as inherently oppressive because to maintain consensus; dissenting voices must be silenced or marginalized.

While it can be difficult to simply divide up countries and place their political cultures into one basket or the other, there are general trends which have emerged. Consensual political cultures have come to be favored in some form in most of the world. In the United Kingdom, developing a consensual political culture was an explicit goal of Prime Minister Tony Blair when he was elected in 1997. Blair was a member of the traditionally left-wing Labour Party but transformed his party according to Third Way principles. The Third Way was a political theory developed by Anthony Giddens who stated that after the end of the Cold War, British political culture needed to drop the divisions between left and right and rule from the center. As Prime Minister, Tony Blair transformed the left-wing Labour Party into a more centrist party by adopting the right-wing neoliberal economic policies of the previous Conservative Prime Minister Margaret Thatcher in combination with a few left-wing policies, such as supporting environmental regulation and supporting gay rights. Blair also pushed through some laws imposing fines for anti-social behavior, which were meant to strengthen social cohesion.

Blair's goal was to create a new consensual political culture in Britain in which both the traditional left and right would support him and his New Labour Party. Blair was initially a very popular leader because he did appeal to people on both the left and the right, but eventually, he alienated many of his supporters on the left for supporting President Bush's war in Iraq and for his right-wing economic policies. Many of his supporters on the right eventually turned against him because of his support for multiculturalism and gay rights. Blair's experiment in creating a new consensual political culture was something of a failure, as many critics complained that he was introducing forms of soft authoritarianism to try to quell dissent from both the left and the right. What Blair's experiment demonstrated is that politics is inherently conflictual, and to create consensus dissent must be eliminated, which is all but impossible without resorting to authoritarianism.

If the United Kingdom had something of a culture of conflict that Tony Blair tried to change, Mexico is an example of a country with a history of political consensus that has more recently become conflictual. A single party, the Institutional Revolutionary Party, is known by its Spanish acronym of PRI, ruled Mexico from 1929 until 2000. PRI emerged after the Mexican Revolution, which overthrew the dictatorship of Porfirio Díaz. PRI's political ideology was based on the centrist ideals of corporatism. *Corporatism* means that politics is treated like a body whose parts must work in harmony. PRI sought to establish a form of government that created a harmonic society in which government, labor, and corporations all worked together for the good of the country. Their explicit goal was to create a consensual political culture in which everyone agreed this was the best form of government and that PRI was the only party that could run it.

While Mexico did have national presidential elections beginning in 1929, PRI won every single one of these elections until they were finally defeated in 2000. According to PRI, they won because Mexican political culture had developed a consensus that PRI was the only party fit to lead. In reality, PRI engaged in widespread electoral fraud, rigged elections and violently suppressed potential opposition movements. During the Olympics of 1968 which were held in Mexico City, student protests broke out at the biggest university demanding economic justice for the poor and more political freedom. PRI responded by arresting 1300 people and breaking up one major demonstration by firing on crowds of protesters, killing around 40 people in what is today known as the Tlatelolco massacre. PRI finally lost a close election in 2000 to Vicente Fox's National Action Party (PAN), a pro-democracy conservative Christian party who had long opposed PRI's stranglehold on the political system.

In the 2006 elections, PAN and Filipe Calderon won the presidency in an extremely close race against the Party of the Democratic Revolution (PRD)'s Andrés Manuel López Obrador. While many hailed this election as historic because it saw PRI fall to third place, there were allegations once again of vote fraud, this time potentially caused by PAN, and large protests broke out after the results were announced. In 2012, PRI returned to power after voters turned against PAN's inadequate response to emerging drug cartels and violence.

Former Mexican President Vicente Fox

The 2012 election was also marked by irregularities, with PRD claiming that PRI was again guilty of voter fraud. Either way, since 2000 Mexican elections have become competitive, with each of the three main parties having a chance to win. By comparison, before 2000, PRI often won with over 80% of the vote, even getting a very unbelievable 100% in the 1976 elections. Many political scientists argue that this demonstrates how Mexico has shifted from a consensual political culture in the 1900s to a conflictual one in the 2000s.

If Mexico switched from consensual to conflictual, and the U.K. moved from conflictual to consensual, Iran and China are examples of somewhat persistently consensual political cultures in their modern history. The Chinese Communist Party remains the only legal party in China and has controlled the government since the revolution in 1949. The party is no longer communist, having shifted to capitalism in the late 1970s, and its ideology has changed to one that promotes social and economic harmony.

The Chinese government argues that China has a consensual political culture. It also claims this culture is the basis of its legitimacy and strength, and internal divisions would tear the country apart. As such, China has been eager to crack down on dissent in the name of preserving consensus. As in the case of PRI in Mexico, maintaining consensus requires the elimination of dissent through oppression. A similar claim to consensus is at work in Iran. The government argues that it upholds the ideals of Shia Islam, which is a matter of consensus among the Iranian people. This consensus is maintained through religious police who crack down on those people who choose not to follow Islamic traditions.

By contrast, Nigeria has long had a conflictual political culture owing to the division between the North and the South of the country. The North's majority is Muslim, and the South's is Christian, with an almost even population split between the two religious groups. The conflict between these two groups had shaped Nigerian political culture since the 1980s when religion increasingly became a major identifying factor and source of conflict. Since then, violent skirmishes and protests have broken out between those in rival religious groups, as each group fears the other might take over the government and oppress them.

While neither of Nigeria's two political parties is aligned with one religion over the other, the 2015 election was a major test because one party ran a Christian candidate and the other a Muslim candidate. Many religious leaders called for people to vote based on the religion of the Presidential candidate rather than his platform, which caused fears of a renewal of the religious unrest that killed 800 people after the 2011 election. Eventually, the candidate from the Muslim North won. This caused religious tensions within the Muslim North, as the extremist group Boko Haram, which is aligned with the Syrian ISIS group, engaged in terrorist violence because they saw the new president as not sufficiently Islamic, even though he was Muslim.

Nigerian police and military are deployed to keep the peace during the inaugural transfer of presidential powers after the 2015 election.

Nations and States

Today, states are still some of the most powerful entities in global politics, despite their relative decline in the age of globalization. While corporations and suprastate organizations are increasingly powerful, states are still the primary point of study in comparative politics. The challenge to the authority of states from other non-state actors on the global political stage requires a clarification of terms. *Authority* can be defined as the top-down ability to impose one's will. In the case of states, authority relates to having a monopoly on the use of force. This means if a state cannot control its borders militarily or its people through the police, then the state lacks authority. States can have authority, but so can corporations, terrorist groups or supranational organizations such as the World Trade Organization (WTO). The authority that is exclusive to states is called sovereignty. *Sovereignty* is defined as the ability of a state and people to control their territory and affairs. In this sense, sovereignty is specifically the authority of states, as a corporation does not control territory directly.

Power is a much more complicated idea. While authority is top-down, power is more bottom-up and is derived from the people. Thus, state sovereignty tends to be derived from a combination of power and authority, in that the people who live within a state must support the state government for it to remain legitimate. When a state lacks power, meaning popular support, its authority is undermined; any coercive action is seen as oppressive rather than as simply enforcing the law. Power can be found in movements and groups which lack authority altogether, such as in a popular protest or revolutionary movement.

Today, state sovereignty continues to be important, although the idea that states should be able to do what they want inside their borders without interference from other states is an idea that is falling out of favor and practice in the era of globalization. In many cases, internal human rights abuses led to calls for an invasion, which violates state sovereignty to protect the people being abused by their government. Corporations increasingly leverage their global power to make state governments do what they want, and suprastate organizations such as the European Union often commit member countries to act on certain issues, ignoring any claims to state sovereignty. The world currently lives in a transitional period where many states retain their sovereign power, but this power is being challenged, both theoretically and in practice, in some ways.

Protesters in the U.S. capital demonstrate against the increasing influence of corporations

In the context of this transitional period brought on by globalization, it is useful to look back and see how the international state system came to be. The idea of different states and nations exclusively controlling territory is a fairly recent invention in human history. The idea of state sovereignty, in which countries agreed not to meddle in the internal affairs of other countries, stems from the Peace of Westphalia, which was a series of peace treaties signed in 1648 to end the Thirty Years War and the Eighty Years War. These were religious wars between Catholics and Protestants, two of the most destructive wars in European history.

To end the religious wars between the various Christian denominations, the idea of Westphalian state sovereignty was created. It set out the idea of national self-determination and religious tolerance. This system is credited with ushering in the modern state system. It ensured that secular state sovereignty was the highest authority in the land, not a religious authority, which had caused nothing but war in the pre-Westphalian era. Before the Peace of Westphalia, Spain had occupied the Netherlands and Belgium to impose Catholicism, and the remnants of the Holy Roman Empire had attempted to impose religious uniformity despite religious differences in its national territories.

Out of the treaty of Westphalia, the idea of the nation-state emerged. This meant that nations were meant to have self-determination as states. Thus, the Dutch were no longer to be ruled by Spain, and the Holy Roman Emperor would no longer rule the various German principalities. There was an assumption that each state would correspond to one nation, which corresponded to one religion. State sovereignty was designed to ensure that one ethnic/cultural group with one religion would correspond to a state. For example, Spain would no longer be allowed to politically control the Netherlands and force them to be Catholic instead of Protestant. However, the idea of states having one nation and one religion resulted in internal fissures later on, when it became all too clear that states had several (or many) different religions, nationalities, and cultures.

Eventually, state sovereignty evolved to be more secular and no longer related to nationality or culture. Today the concept of state sovereignty is rarely invoked in relation to the right of religious or national authority, but it more generally refers to the control of geographical borders by a state. To put it simply, today a state is sovereign when it can exercise the authority to control its geographical boundaries against incursions by another state and when it derives power from the support of the population. Some states have more authority and power over others and could threaten their sovereignty in practical terms, but the questions of whether states should invade and violate the sovereignty of other states militarily are usually considered part of the field of international relations.

Comparative politics tends to be less interested in how states interact on an international level, instead of focusing on comparing and contrasting the internal workings of state authority, power, and sovereignty. Nigeria is a good example of a sovereign state which, for the most part, has control over its geographic boundaries, and the population largely supports the concept of Nigeria as an independent state. Nigeria, however, is made up of two religions and at least two nationalities. In modern terms, Nigeria is still considered to have sovereignty despite these internal divisions.

Supranational Governance

As the world becomes more globalized and power has shifted away from individual states, supranational governance structures are beginning to emerge. Since comparative politics is interested in contrasting and comparing the internal workings of different political entities, the field has increasingly shifted toward examining and comparing the operation of the European Union, MERCOSUR in South America, the African Union and other suprastate organizations such as the WTO and IMF. *Suprastate organizations* are not properly sovereign, as they do not have full control over their geographic boundaries, but they do have the ability to impose decisions on member states somewhat.

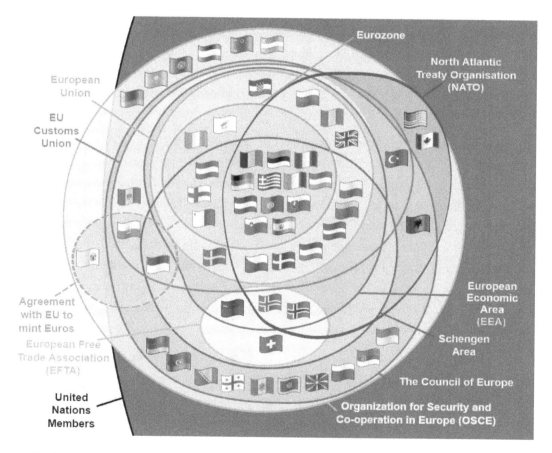

Euler diagram of European supranational organizations and their member states.

For example, when Greece went bankrupt and needed a bailout from the European Union, the EU was able to attach a number of conditions to this bailout that

Greece had to meet. Greece had to accept these conditions, even though they were punitive in nature, or risk being kicked out of the European Union. Suprastate organizations are an evolution of authority, and as such, the concept of sovereignty does not apply to these unions. Each of these suprastate governance entities tends to be very different as well, with some primarily focused on economics, some being a blend of political and economic union, and some being primarily military and strategic in orientation.

The European Union is an interesting example because unlike NAFTA, MERCOSUR, the WTO and many other suprastate organizations; it attempts to be more than just an economic union. The EU works like a very weak federation, almost in the way the Anti-Federalists desired the United States to operate when the Constitution was being developed. The EU government is a combination of an elected parliament with members from each EU state and a large bureaucratic governing structure. Each country is expected to follow resolutions passed by the EU Parliament but still retain state sovereignty. Thus, even though the United Kingdom is part of the EU, it still uses the British pound and not the euro as its currency. Each country still passes its laws but is expected to follow the general directives of the European Parliament, which is largely limited to economic matters.

As it stands, the EU is a somewhat confused entity with questionable status and many critics. Critics from the left claim that the EU is nothing more than an economic union and that the European Parliament has no power, thus making it anti-democratic. Critics from the right also see it as anti-democratic because they do not like the Schengen Zone agreement allowing people to travel freely between all EU states without a passport or visa. Some countries also see the EU as being dominated by stronger countries, such as Germany. During its bailout proceedings, Greece complained that Germany was simply dictating the terms of the EU agreement rather than being the consensus of all EU members. Despite all these problems, most countries seem to want to stay in the EU, but many members also want changes to how the EU is run.

One of the biggest issues with the EU is the common currency union. Monetary policy, which controls the relative strength of the euro currency and sets interest rates, is controlled by the European Central Bank for all countries. If Germany is doing well and Greece is not, monetary policy for both countries will be the same, which means that one country is going to lose out from the European Central Bank (ECB) decisions. If the ECB decides to raise interest rates to prevent a bubble forming in Germany, it could cause a recession in Greece. If it lowers interest rates to stimulate the Greek economy, it risks causing a bubble in Germany, leading to problems there.

Unlike in a federal state where the government can compensate for uneven effects of monetary policy changes through spending, in the EU spending is controlled at the state level. Problems such as this lead to many criticisms, but much of these problems are a result of the fact that these organizations are still relatively new, leading to problematic power imbalances. While the EU simply becoming a single country would solve all of the above problems, none of the member states want to give up their sovereignty.

While problems such as refugees and climate change transcend national borders and are better addressed by suprastate political entities, there tends to be a democratic deficit in these organizations. They focus on economic relations and do not give people any input into their proceedings. The creation of global economic treaties which take authority away from elected governments and put it in the hands of corporations has been criticized by many as eroding democracy for the sake of "economic efficiency." Treaties such as the North American Free Trade Organization (NAFTA), for example, give corporations the right to sue governments for passing laws that might harm their ability to make money. In cases like this, the government will usually simply repeal the law, allowing global corporations to overrule the sovereign authority of the state and the democratic will of the elected government.

While these suprastate economic organizations continue to grow in power, the idea of a suprastate political organization has gained less traction. States are willing to give up economic authority to global corporations so long as they can maintain their control over other domestic issues. Given that economic governance is now largely in the hands of suprastate corporations and organizations, many argue there is a need for suprastate democratic organizations, which would allow people across the world to directly have a say on international issues that affect them regardless of geographic state boundaries.

One attempt to create such a democratic suprastate organization is the World Social Forum (WSF). First held in Brazil, the goal of the WSF was to promote a democratic version of bottom-up globalization. They intended to create a suprastate political entity that would empower people from around the world to have a democratic voice in global issues, which are increasingly becoming the exclusive domain of elites. While the WSF began as a motley organization combining various protest movements from around the world, it is increasingly gaining legitimacy and is now endorsed by the United Nations. While it has a fair bit of popular support, it lacks the authority to impose any of its decisions on states like the WTO and IMF can do.

World Social Forum rally in Brazil.

Sources of Power

Power in the proper sense is always bottom-up, which means power must always come from the people. Power can manifest itself in multiple ways. In relation to states, power is largely derived from the consent of the governed. In democracies, consent is indicated through popular participation in elections. In the United States, the United Kingdom, Mexico, Nigeria, Russia and Iran, the state's basis of power is that people willingly participate in electing the government of these countries. The government is then empowered to act as it sees fit, having received a mandate from the people. In China, which does not have elections, the idea of consent and power is more complicated. The Chinese government argues that, as a developing country, China needs to have a steady government to manage the growing economy and the best way to do this is through a single-party system without elections. The power of the Chinese state is directly tied to its ability to improve the economic well-being of citizens. China claims that so long as the people feel that their lives are gradually improving economically, the government retains the consent of the population.

Power can also be used against the state. Protest movements that have wide public support can become very powerful and threaten the state's authority. In 1989 in China, major protests broke out in the capital Beijing, with protesters demanding a socialist democracy rather than a dictatorship that was transitioning from communism to capitalism. Students organized the protests, and the general population of Beijing was very supportive. The Chinese government was threatened by the power generated by these protests and cracked down using military force against the protesters. In this case, the authority of the state, which is top-down in nature, was stronger than the bottom-up power generated by the protesters. However, the protests were powerful enough for the Chinese state to see them as a legitimate threat. In the Arab Spring protests in Egypt and Tunisia which began in 2010, the power of the people was so strong that it overthrew the governments of those countries.

When governments lose the support of the people, and the people organize their power against a government, the state relies on the *coercive authority of force*. This means that governments can have authority while lacking power. A powerful government does not need to resort to violent force to get people to comply because the public supports a powerful government. Sometimes governments can have power but lack authority.

Dubbed the "Tank Man," this iconic image shows an unidentified man non-violently blocking a column of tanks from deploying to the center of democracy protests in Tiananmen Square.

In 1953, the democratically elected government of Iran was powerful in that it had public support, but due to the relatively weak military, it lacked the authority to fend off a coup d'état which overthrew the government. To reiterate the point from the previous section, a government is sovereign when it has both top-down authority through the use of force and bottom-up power derived from the consent of the people.

Other than elections and economic prosperity, how do governments remain powerful? This is the question that much of comparative politics seeks to answer, and it will be outlined in the following sections. These sources of power include a constitutional framework setting out limits on government and establishing the rule of law, the ability for the state to promote a certain belief system that most people endorse, such as a religion or ideology, and maintaining a general air of transparency so that the government is viewed as acting in the best interests of the people. When at least some of these conditions are met, the state will retain the support of the people and hold power. When a state is powerful, its citizens are willing to join the military and police force to provide the state with the authority of force.

Constitutions (Forms, Purposes, Application)

One of the primary sources of state power, authority and therefore sovereignty is its *constitutional framework*. The constitution sets out the role of government, the rights of citizens and the general political framework of a country. A constitution enshrines the rule of law and ensures that governments must act within the constitutional framework to maintain legitimacy. For example, the United States Constitution sets out a two-term limit for the president. If a president tried to run for a third term without first winning public support to change the Constitution, such a candidate would be considered illegitimate by the public. If such a candidate were elected, the government would lose legitimacy, and many people might organize protests to kick the illegitimate president out of office.

A constitution is meant to have more power than any individual government that might hold power in a state. In the six countries that are being studied here, constitutions play different roles and have different levels of legitimacy. From an American perspective, the constitution is considered the highest law and must not be violated by a government, but this is not the case in other countries.

Like the United States, the constitution is considered the highest law in China, setting out the role of the government and the duties and responsibilities of citizens. In China, however, the constitution is often subject to major revisions. For example, the 1982 version of the constitution places political authority in the hands of the Communist Party, who are described as an alliance between the working-class and the peasant class. The 2004 revision, by contrast, sets out legal protections for the right to own private property and contains clauses protecting the rights of citizens which did not exist previously. These revisions are much more than just amendments as they tend to significantly revise aspects of the political and economic structure of the country. However, unlike the United States, China does not have a Supreme Court that can enable citizens to challenge the current government's interpretation of the constitution. The government, which is expected to follow the constitution, is also the entity that can enforce it, so it is extremely rare for the government to be found in violation of the constitution.

Usually, constitutional violations in China are a result of the central government finding a local official in violation, rather than the central government being in violation. Citizens have no legal recourse against the central government, but they do have a significant ability to petition the central government to remove corrupt local officials. Local officials who are found in violation of the constitution by the central government often face harsh penalties, sometimes including the death penalty.

Zhou Yongkang, a former top Chinese domestic security official,
was arrested in 2014 as part of an emerging anti-corruption movement.

The United Kingdom is an interesting case because unlike most countries it does not have a written constitution. The constitutional framework of the U.K. is based on a *constitutional convention*, which means that the traditions of the country form the legal framework. In the case of the U.K., these conventions date back as far as the Magna Carta of 1215, which is the basis of British due process. The U.K. is also based on the practice of *parliamentary supremacy*. Any law passed by Parliament forms a basis for future legal precedent. Parliament cannot pass a law that is unconstitutional, as every law they pass is essentially the basis of future legal decisions.

Unlike the United States and other countries with a codified constitution, there is no separation of powers between the legislative and judicial branches, so citizens cannot legally challenge the validity of laws passed by Parliament. This can be problematic because there is no check on the power of the British government. Parliament has supremacy over both the judiciary and the Queen, who is the official head of state. The only thing that could stop an act of Parliament would be a revolution from below or a foreign invasion. Despite these issues with the unchecked authority of the British government, by tradition, the government has acted moderately. Advocates of an unwritten and evolved-over-time constitution argue that it makes positive change easier as there is no complicated procedure for amending laws. Critics point to potential avenues of abuse by unchecked government authority.

Iran presents another interesting case. Its written constitution stems from the 1979 revolution and is a hybrid of elements of democracy and Islamic theocracy. The

Iranian constitution speaks in favor of democracy but claims that religious leadership must guide and ground the actions of government. Iran has a functional democracy embedded inside an Islamic theocracy. The constitution states that sovereign authority is derived directly from God, who endorses the popular election of the Iranian President and the Majlis, the Iranian legislature.

These democratically elected bodies are overseen by the religious authority of the Ayatollah and the Guardian Council, who are meant to provide religious guidance to the elected President and the Majlis. In many ways, the Ayatollah, who is called the Supreme Leader, acts as a kind of religious check on the power of the Majlis. If the Supreme Leader believes that the Majlis has passed a law that violates Islamic principles, he has the power to overturn that law after a meeting of the Guardian Council. In this sense, the Ayatollah and the religious-based Guardian Council do not rule Iran because the government is democratically elected, but they regard the Quran as the ultimate source of law and act as a form of Supreme Court for religious matters. The democratically elected government is free to do as it wishes, so long as they do not do anything, the Guardian Council deems to be contrary to Islam. Of course, what is contrary to Islam is open to interpretation, and there have been different levels of involvement by the Ayatollah and the Guardian Council in different Iranian governments since 1979.

The Mexican constitution of 1917 is in many ways the opposite of the Iranian constitution, as it was explicitly adopted to constrain the power of the Roman Catholic Church over the Mexican political situation. In this sense, the Mexican constitution is very similar to the American constitution in that it outlines a separation of powers, representative government, a federal political system and the secular supremacy of the state over the church.

The Russian constitution, adopted in 1993, is similar to the American constitution as well. It outlines a federal government with different powers for regions, adopts a bill of rights for citizens and sets out the operation of the President, the Federal Assembly, and the judiciary. Across much of the world, the American constitution has been extremely influential. As with the United States, these constitutions are also open to interpretation. For example, Vladimir Putin is seen by many as violating the Russian constitution. After serving two terms as president, Putin then was elected Prime Minister, which is constitutionally supposed to be a less powerful position than the president. Putin continued to essentially lead the country as Prime Minister because the president acted on Putin's wishes. After serving a term as Prime Minister, Putin was elected for a third term as president, arguing that the term limits in the constitution only applied to consecutive terms. There were major street protests and accusations of electoral fraud, but Putin retains power and remains fairly popular.

A 2013 anti-Putin procession marches towards Trubnaya Square in Moscow.

Nigeria has had a series of constitutions since its independence from the United Kingdom. Initially, Nigeria adopted a British model with the Queen as head of state. After the military overthrew the government in 1966, the country was ruled without a constitution and largely based on the whims of the military. In 1979, Nigeria adopted a new constitution, this time based on an American-style presidential system. The military again overthrew the first elected government under this system in 1983. A new constitution was proposed in 1993 by the military government to transition to democracy, but the military did not like the results of the election and simply annulled the results and canceled the new constitution. This caused political chaos and violence which kept the military in power until 1999. Finally, in 1999 Nigeria returned to democracy with a new constitution modeled on the 1979 constitution, adding protections for civil rights.

Regime Types

Regime types of modern states do not fit into easy classifications. For purposes of simplicity, political regimes can be categorized into three main types. A *presidential democracy* places in the role of the executive a single person in charge of the government and the state. Presidential systems generally have a separation of powers, with the legislative and judicial branches acting as checks on the power of the president and each other. The United States, Nigeria, and Mexico are presidential systems. Russia is constitutionally supposed to be a presidential system, but after the recent term of Vladimir Putin as Prime Minister, Russia has moved to more of a hybrid system where sometimes the head of the legislature can have as much power as (or more than) the president.

Parliamentary democracies are systems in which the head of state is a largely ceremonial position with no real authority, and the leader of the government, the Prime Minister, is the person with the most power. The Prime Minister is the head of the largest party in the legislature, and there is no separation of powers between legislative and executive branches. The legislature is theoretically a check on the power of the Prime Minister, as the legislature can toss out a Prime Minister at any time through a no-confidence vote, but this is very rare because the Prime Minister usually comes from a party that controls the majority of the seats in parliament. In a parliamentary system, the main check on power is the judiciary, which in countries other than the United Kingdom has the power to overturn laws as unconstitutional. Finally, a *one-party state*, such as China, is a situation where there are no elections, and the government's leadership is chosen only by members of the ruling party. In these countries, the ruling party tends to hold all the authority and cannot be held in check by courts or opposing political groups.

The type of regime is also increasingly less a source of power or authority itself. During the Cold War, the Soviet Union claimed that its "dictatorship of the proletariat" was a direct representation of the will of the common people and that corporations and elites dominated the Western democracies. In turn, the Western democracies pointed to the Soviet Union's system of elite control and argued it excluded the common people they allegedly represented. Today, regime types tend to be a mixture of elements of a single party state, a presidential democracy or a parliamentary democracy. For example, while in theory, Russia is the Presidential Republic with democratic elections, in practice these elections are dominated by a single party which easily wins every time. This makes Russia resemble a Chinese-style single-party state with no elections more than most democracies. At the same time, China's policy of changing governments and leaders every five years appears more democratic than Russia, where Putin has been in power since 2000.

*A 1911 Industrial Worker (newspaper) illustration is depicting
their criticism of capitalism's hierarchy.*

In today's context, regime type is largely only a source of illegitimacy rather than the basis on which a government claims to hold power. For example, the United Kingdom does not claim that a constitutional monarchy with a powerful parliament is the best form of government, and therefore this is where the power of the British state is derived. Instead, they point to issues other than regime type for the basis of legitimacy.

However, as was the case in the recent Arab Spring revolutions, single-party states can become a source of illegitimacy, leading to people-power protests which overthrow them. Many of the protesters in Egypt and Tunisia wanted an end to the one-party dictatorships in those countries to have more political freedom. The regime type itself was a source of frustration rather than the specific policies of the government. By contrast, the Euromaidan protests in Ukraine in 2013 and 2014 overthrew a democratically elected government. Their complaints were not with democracy itself but with that specific government. In this case, the Ukrainian President could not simply rely on the fact that his regime was an elected democracy as a source of legitimacy.

Types of Economic Systems

In the modern era, perhaps the most important role of the state is administrating the economy. The interaction between states, markets, and corporations is called the political economy. *Political economy* differs from economics in that political economy recognizes that there are different types of economic systems and that people may not always act rationally. Traditionally, all economic study was the political economy, such as the work by David Ricardo and Adam Smith. Since World War II, economics has become its discipline outside of political science and has largely operated within a rather narrow set of assumptions which political economists criticize as not properly reflecting the real world. In many cases, the administration of the economy by the government is cited as the primary form of legitimacy. If the economy is doing well, governments claim this gives them the right to hold power, and when the economy does do not well, people often demand a change of governments.

The economy has a complex and interdependent relationship with the political system. During the Cold War, many simply linked democracy to capitalism and dictatorship to communism; however, this was a simplistic reduction. There were many democratic communist governments, such as in Chile in the 1970s and Greece in the 1940s, and capitalist dictatorships, such as in South Korea in the 1970s and in Chile in the 1980s.

In a single-party state such as China, the economic system is built into the constitution and is not meant to be easily changed. Ironically, China has undergone a sweeping transformation from an agrarian-based communist economy into a situation of state-driven capitalism. At the same time, in a democracy, the elected government is theoretically supposed to be able to implement whatever economic system it has promised the electorate, but the reality is that economic systems are very rarely changed through democracy. Thus, there is the paradox of major economic change coming about through a single-party state which was designed to prevent economic change and no economic changes coming about through open democracies which are designed to allow broad economic changes with new governments.

In the post-Cold War era, political economists have identified neoliberalism as the dominant ideology of state policy toward the economy. *Neoliberalism* was initiated by Margaret Thatcher in the United Kingdom and is premised on avoiding deficit spending, reducing government spending on public welfare programs, broadening the tax base through consumption taxes, liberalization of trade, deregulating financial markets and industries, privatizing state-held companies and increasing legal protections for private property. The point of these policies was to dismantle the welfare state, which was the primary form of capitalist economies during the Cold War.

The *welfare state*, often called Keynesianism, believed that the role of the government in the economy was to assist those left behind by capitalism through social spending programs. The welfare state era also positioned the government as a countercyclical agent in the economy. If there were a recession, it would be the government's job to try to stimulate the economy to get out of the recession. If there were a bubble, it would be the job of the government to try to cool off the economy to prevent a crash. Neoliberalism, in contrast, sees the role of the state as facilitating maximum corporate growth, usually accomplished by reducing the role of government in the economy.

New Deal Era Social Security benefit poster

After the end of the Cold War in 1991, the belief in neoliberalism was very strong. Not only had communism been defeated, but the more moderate version of welfare state capitalism had been sent into retreat as well. Neoliberal economics became something of a global ideology; it was now posited as the only valid approach to political economy by major countries such as the United Kingdom and the United States. It also became the dominant form of economics promoted by suprastate economic organizations such as the International Monetary Fund and the World Trade Organization. The International Monetary Fund, in particular, is notorious for forcing countries to change their economic systems to neoliberalism in exchange for financial assistance. These conditions on financial assistance were called Structural Adjustment Programs, and the IMF believed (or said it believed) that they would fundamentally improve the long-term health of the indebted countries. In reality, these reforms often made the economic situation worse, leading to a series of economic crises beginning in the late 1990s with the Asian Financial Crisis.

In the Asian Financial Crisis of 1997, countries such as Thailand and Indonesia opened their borders to foreign investment and adopted neoliberal frameworks at the urging of the IMF and WTO. This led to a hands-off approach to governing the economy. As a result, foreign investment flooded into the country, drawing yet more investment and creating a bubble which sent stock prices soaring. The problem was that most of the investments were not being allocated efficiently. As developing economies, Thailand and Indonesia needed money to develop their basic infrastructure, such as roads and sewage, for the economy to grow.

However, foreign investment focused on financial firms and most of the money went into banks and financial services, creating a huge demand for office towers. Eventually, people started to realize that most of these foreign-funded financial firms were not profitable. Office towers were sitting empty because they lacked sewage disposal and proper road connections. This caused the bubble to burst, and foreign money quickly drained out of the economy. Thailand and Indonesia were left worse off than before they opened their borders and adopted neoliberal economics. Many claimed that this financial crisis was an attack on the sovereignty of these two countries, and the governments of both have become more authoritarian in recent years.

When the Soviet Union collapsed in 1991, it needed an entirely new economic system. Once again neoliberalism was proposed as the best method. Instead of gradually shifting away from communism and slowly making capitalist reforms in the manner that has worked quite well for China, Russia was prodded into adopting what was called *neoliberal shock therapy*. It was to transition from a centrally-planned communist economy to a radically capitalist economy overnight at the urging of American economists, the IMF, WTO and with support from then-President Boris Yeltsin. The shock therapy plan was a complete disaster, and the economy became worse than it was under communism. Prices skyrocketed, and major industries went bankrupt. The average life expectancy of a Russian male went from 65 in the 1980s under communism to just 57 in 1993 a few years after shock therapy.

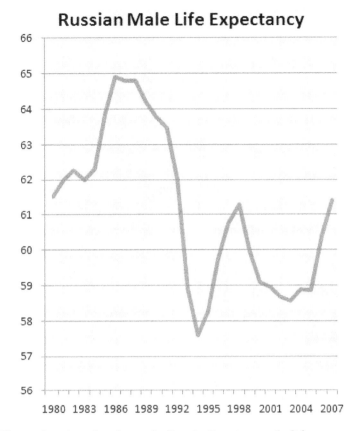

Russian Male Life Expectancy

Chart showing the sharp decline in Russian male life expectancy.

By the mid-1990s, Russia's economy was in a severe depression. The country went from a major economic powerhouse to an underdeveloped state with high levels of poverty and a dramatic decline in GDP. During this time, economic power concentrated in the hands of a select few, who became known as the Russian *oligarchs*. These were usually high-ranking officials from the Soviet Era who took advantage of shock therapy privatizations to take control of entire industries that were once owned by the state. Massive industries once owned by the Russian people were now making a select few former Communist leaders immensely wealthy, and amidst this corruption, the Russian economy suffered a sharper decline than the U.S. did in the Great Depression of the 1930s. The public became extremely distrustful of the Russian political system.

Russia suffered a further major financial crisis in 1998 when the price of raw materials Russia exported dropped dramatically due to the Asian Financial Crisis. The Russian government increased the interest rate to 150%, and the IMF began to give Russia emergency loans. Amidst this severe economic decline and crisis, the people of Russia lost all faith in the Russian government. Against this backdrop of economic trouble, Vladimir Putin ran for president on a campaign of cracking down on the oligarchs, rebuilding the economy and implementing some stability. In his first term, Putin accomplished much of this, and although he failed to restore Russia to its former economic glory, his ability to stabilize the economy led to massive public support.

Meanwhile, China's strategy of slow reforms to transition from communism to capitalism has put them on a path to surpass the United States as the world's largest economy within the next few years. China began its reform process by implementing *Special Economic Zones*, which were small capitalist areas designed to export goods to the rest of the world. Having achieved some measure of success in the special zones, China then gradually expanded these zones and introduced more market reforms over the period from 1976 until now. The Chinese government continues to play a strong role in managing the overall direction of the economy, which allows it to prevent the chaos that occurred in Russia. China slowly privatized certain state-owned enterprises. Although these often went into the hands of Communist Party officials, China's reforms have decreased poverty, while Russia's reforms dramatically increased it. The corruption at the high levels of China's economy and the creation of a new ultra-wealthy capitalist class is more tolerated in China since the average person sees their economic fortunes improve. China also abolished price controls on a large number of goods to allow the market to determine prices. China did this in a gradual manner which maintained price stability, unlike Russia where hyperinflation set in and people had to turn to the black market and organized criminal enterprises to secure basic needs.

State Building, Legitimacy and Stability

As is clear from the economic transition examples of Russia and China, legitimacy and stability are keys to state building. *State building* refers to the establishment of a new regime of state. It can occur following the collapse of an old regime, as was the case with Russia and with Nigeria after the military gave up power. State building can also occur within the context of a newly formed state. A new state needs to start from scratch in building institutions of authority and building power by winning support from the people through legitimate government.

After the collapse of the Soviet Union, some new states were created, such as Ukraine, Kazakhstan and Slovenia, which had to build entirely new systems to create a functioning state. Many of these new countries continue to be unstable because they are plagued with legitimacy issues. If a state apparatus that combines authority and power cannot be maintained, there is potential for it to become a failed state. A *failed state* is a country where there is no single central government with legitimate power or with enough forceful authority to control an entire territory. Examples today include Somalia and Syria, where different factions control different parts of each of these countries, and anyone claiming to be a central government is viewed as completely illegitimate.

In comparative politics, the most influential theory of political legitimacy comes from German theorist Max Weber, who defined legitimacy in terms of a government having public support and not needing to use coercive force against the people. *Legitimacy* is a measure of power: the more legitimate the people view a government to be, the more powerful it will be. Weber classified three types of legitimacy that are still widely influential today: traditional, charismatic and rational-legal.

Max Weber

Traditional legitimacy rests on the authority of tradition and history. It is an example of traditional legitimacy when people argue that a government is legitimate because it has always ruled. The monarchies of the Middle Ages rested on traditional legitimacy, as do governments today who appeal to religion or ethnic origin. *Charismatic legitimacy* is when people widely support a popular leader despite an otherwise weak or undeveloped state. In such situations, when the charismatic leader is removed from power, the state tends to lose legitimacy. *Rational-legal legitimacy* is derived from a codified set of laws and a constitution, in which people believe that the state is legitimate because the legal framework constrains any potential government misdeeds.

To provide examples of these three different types of legitimacy, six comparative countries can be contrasted to the United States. The U.S. is based on rational-legal legitimacy; people generally see the government as legitimate so long as it obeys the Constitution, even if they disagree with the political decisions a government makes. China is a complex example; under the Communist leadership of Mao Zedong, it was based on the charismatic legitimacy of Mao. After Mao's death, China has been transitioning to a rational-legal framework with appeals to Chinese tradition. China today relies on a combination of traditional and rational-legal legitimacy. Traditional legitimacy focuses on the legacy of the Communist Party as the traditional authority and the rational-legal legitimacy of a capitalist economy.

The United Kingdom also rests on a combination of traditional and rational-legal legitimacy. Like the United States, the U.K. has a system of strong legal protections for individuals. However, it lacks a written constitution and instead relies on the traditional authority of past legislative acts. Without the legitimacy of tradition, the British Parliament could become authoritarian because the force of tradition is its only real check on power.

Iran is an even more complex example because it relies on a combination of charismatic, traditional and rational-legal legitimacy. At the most outside layer of the Iranian political framework is the Supreme Leader, Ayatollah Ali Khamenei, whose religious popularity maintains the traditional legitimacy of Iran, which is based on the principles of Islamic Sharia. Within the outside religious layer is a democratically elected government that is limited by both the constitution and religion, thus presenting a measure of rational-legal legitimacy. Iran is structured like an onion, with charismatic legitimacy as the outer skin represented by the Ayatollah, the traditional legitimacy of Islam as a middle skin, and the rational-legal constitutional framework in the center.

Grand Ayatollah Sayyid Ruhollah Mūsavi Khomeini

Mexico too has evolved its basis of legitimacy. While Mexico has had a strong constitution since the revolution of 1917 until 2000 it was dominated by a single party. PRI justified its position as being the one true defender of the principles of the Mexican revolution, giving it traditional legitimacy. With the move to a competitive multi-party state in 2000, Mexico transitioned to a rational-legal legitimacy. However, this rational-legal legitimacy is currently under stress as Mexican drug cartels flaunt their ability to get away with extreme forms of violence and easily break out of prison. The legal system is unable to control these cartels, and the rational-legal legitimacy of the Mexican state is currently in question.

Russia is currently a classic example of charismatic legitimacy. The Russian state derives almost all of its legitimacy from the personal popularity of Vladimir Putin. If Putin were to be removed from office or resign, it is likely that a legitimacy crisis would erupt in Russia. Putin also demonstrates the inherent problem with charismatic legitimacy, in that when the popular leader sticks around for too long he inevitably becomes more heavy-handed and people start to turn against him. To combat his diminishing charismatic appeal, in his third term in office, Putin has been promoting the traditional legitimacy of the Orthodox Christian Church and using such religious appeals to traditional authority as a means of trying to maintain his legitimacy.

Nigeria has had a long history of charismatic legitimacy. A series of military dictatorships from the 1960s until 1999 retained power through force and personal charisma. President Sani Abacha was initially welcomed as a charismatic leader whose legitimacy stemmed from his ability to use the military to quell unrest and restore stability. Eventually, he fell out of favor and democracy returned to Nigeria after his death. The country fell into religious-based violence as both sides, Muslim and Christian, demanded a government based on the traditional legitimacy of their religion. President Goodluck Jonathan was unable to maintain religious peace, and in the 2015 elections, a former military dictator was elected to power on a promise of once again using military force to put down unrest. The new president, Muhammadu Buhari, will have to appeal to his charismatic legitimacy to maintain power. His history of military rule prevents him from appealing to rational-legal legitimacy, and his desire to unify the Muslims and Christians prevents him from appealing to the religious traditions of either side. Given how tenuous charismatic legitimacy can be, the Nigerian state will likely continue to be plagued by instability and a lack of legitimacy.

Belief Systems as Sources of Legitimacy

Perhaps the most effective mechanism of legitimacy is *ideology*. If a government, regime or state can get people to believe it is the best form of government, then legitimacy can be easily maintained, even in the face of major misdeeds. While the word ideology can be used to refer to regime types such as communism, fascism or democracy, political scientists use ideology to refer to a concept through which the state socializes the public to believe in certain ideas to get the people to accept the legitimacy of the state. One of the most influential theorists of ideology was the French philosopher Louis Althusser, who defined ideology as "the imaginary relationship of individuals to their real conditions of existence."

THE IDEOLOGICAL AXES

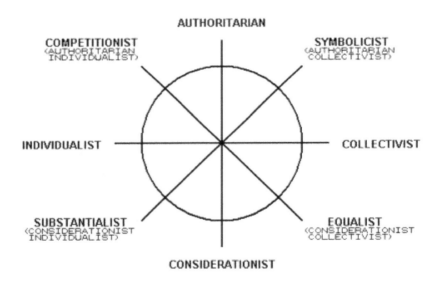

Axial chart of ideologies

Ideology can make people believe things that are not true, and the state can maintain legitimacy by shaping the beliefs of the people. For example, in North Korea, the state ideology makes its people believe that the U.S. is continually on the verge of invading the country, and this is used as a justification for North Korea's poor economy. The government can get away with abuses because the people will think it is justified in the context of an impending military invasion.

Ideology is something akin to propaganda but much more complex and embedded into society. German philosopher Georg Hegel outlined three major types of ideology that had been used historically by various structures of authority to get people to accept their subjugated place in society. Hegel sought to explain why slaves and "bondsmen" (people who were dominated and controlled by others) throughout history had for the most part simply accepted their subjugation and had not constantly and violently rebelled, making such conditions of oppression impossible. Hegel first identifies Stoicism as a slave ideology, meaning that the slave will accept being unfree if he believed himself to be mentally free. Eventually, this ideology became inadequate, and the slave becomes a skeptic, saying that freedom does not exist or matter, and maybe even the external world itself does not exist, just what is inside one's mind. In both of these cases, ideology is an excuse to justify the use and abuse of oppression. Finally, the slave adopts religion as the final ideology, believing that if he tolerates non-freedom and oppression on Earth, he will be rewarded with eternal life in heaven.

As it becomes apparent, ideology is a set of beliefs that people adopt, sometimes on their own and sometimes at the urging of the authorities, which paint a fantasy to deceive themselves about the reality of their situation. When looking in from the outside, people who are dedicated believers in ideology, like the North Koreans, seem to be almost insane. However, ideology is extremely powerful, especially when it operates at a society-wide level. Althusser argued that the modern state recognized the power of ideology and sought to establish institutions which reproduced ideological beliefs in its citizens to get everyone to believe the state was legitimate. Althusser pointed out that the repressive elements of the state, such as the police and military which relied on sheer force to control people, were inadequate in maintaining popular legitimacy. People are less likely to see a government as legitimate when it uses violence to keep them in line. Instead, the state uses ideology to essentially shape the beliefs of people and manufacture legitimacy. Althusser argues that people adopt the state's ideology through the socialization process of attending church, going to school, from family life, and the workplace. All these elements work together to reinforce an ideology that teaches people to accept the state as the only legitimate means of political authority. Ideology is then a means to cover over injustices and abuses of power with false belief.

Comparative politics examines ideology to explain seemingly irrational sources of legitimacy. For example, an ideological operation was present in Iran when Mahmood Ahmadinejad was elected President. He appealed to the ideology of Iran as a bastion of Islam under attack from the U.S. to win votes, which covered over the fact that he was a largely incompetent president whose saber-rattling harmed the economy and led to economic sanctions from the rest of the world. Ideology is a mechanism which leaders and states use to trick people into acting against their interests by fostering beliefs on some other topic. Ideology can come in many forms, ranging from religion, ethnicity, history or regime type. These will be explained in more detail below with respect to each of the six countries under study.

Religion

Religious ideology is one of the oldest ways to generate political legitimacy and control the beliefs of the populace. From the earliest period of human history, people have created stories to explain what they did not understand and invent a higher authority capable of keeping people in line. Each religion has a system of rewards and punishments which can be used by political authorities to appeal to the public for support. Christianity and Islam promise either punishment or reward in the afterlife for what happens on Earth. Hinduism and Buddhism rely on notions of karmic justice which will lead to receiving rewards or punishments in the next life. States or leaders who appeal to religion can often convince people to support them by claiming they represent the true form of the religion and threatening eternal punishment for not supporting them. At the same time, religion can also be a bottom-up ideology which people adopt to explain their situation of oppression and justify inaction.

Keith Ellison, elected to Minnesota's 5th congressional district in 2006, becomes the first Muslim congressman in the U.S. and gets sworn in on a copy of the Quran owned by Thomas Jefferson.

Religion as a mechanism of ideological, social control dates back at least to Plato, who wrote about the need for the ideal state to create a new religion which would foster certain beliefs and attitudes in the population to prevent them from rebelling against the government. In the wake of the Peace of Westphalia, religion became less important to states, and in the early modern era of the 19th century, states rarely appealed to religion as a source of legitimacy. By the outbreak of World War II and the Cold War, religion had been almost completely superseded by political ideologies as a mechanism for instilling certain beliefs in the population to maintain legitimacy. After the fall of Communism, however, religion made a major comeback as a source of ideological control and manufactured legitimacy. As political ideologies became less forceful, states and people often returned to religion to look for explanations about the world and to ground political authority.

This recent political history of religion as a state ideology is important to consider in the current context. Today there is continual violent conflict between Christians and Muslims in Nigeria; there is a constant threat of religiously-motivated terrorism, and there are states such as Iran who base their entire existence on their religion. This is all a very recent phenomenon. Even though religion itself dates back thousands of years and religion as the basis of governing authority was the norm during the Middle Ages, even countries in the Middle East rarely made appeals to religion from the late 1800s to the 1970s. While religion-based governments and terrorist organizations may seem like groups who have not advanced through history, they represent a very recent development in the history of political authority.

A good example of this recent upsurge in religious-based ideological legitimacy is Iran. After emerging as a somewhat independent country in the 1920s (after colonization attempts by the British and Russians upon the discovery of oil), Iran was ruled by Reza Shah as a monarchy (Shah is the Farsi word for king). Reza Shah had no interest in Islam, and his goal was to modernize Iran by bringing in new technology and social norms. His government created something of a cultural revolution, and the influence of Islam significantly declined. During this period, from the 1920s to the 1940s, women did not wear the hijab head covering and freely mixed with men publicly. During World War II, the Soviets and the British both invaded Iran to try to secure its oil. This resulted in a treaty establishing the modern borders of Iran and setting its government to be a constitutional monarchy with true power lies with the democratically elected Prime Minister. Prime Minister Mohammad Mosaddegh continued the trend of modernization, and in 1951 he moved to nationalize British-controlled oil companies in Iran. This prompted a joint British-American plot which eventually overthrew Mosaddegh and reinstalled the Shah as the sole source of power in Iran. During this period, Mosaddegh was hugely popular among the Iranian people, but the Shia Muslim religious establishment opposed him.

After Mosaddegh was overthrown, Shah Mohammad Reza Pahlavi took power. He ran an extremely oppressive government which included a secret police force that captured and murdered most of the remaining left-wing supporters of Mohammed Mosaddegh. Despite Shah Pahlavi's oppressive government, Iran continued to modernize socially, and the influence of religion declined even more in the 1960s. In the late 1970s, the Pahlavi monarchy had lost all legitimacy because it had been put into power by foreign invaders and because of its violent oppression. The Iranian people rose up in 1979 and overthrew the government. At this time, Islamic groups re-emerged as a major force in Iranian society precisely because Shah Pahlavi had violently eliminated nearly all other opposition groups. When some students started to organize a Communist Party during the 1979 revolution, the Shia Muslim groups violently attacked the students and eventually took power after the revolution. They reversed Iran's course of social modernization by imposing Islamic laws that had not been observed in Iran for more than 80 years.

Iranian revolutionaries take refuge behind makeshift barriers in 1979.

Iran's turn to religious ideology is an extremely recent move that is not rooted in the history of the country. Since 1979, the government has used Islam as an ideological basis to get people to support diminishing social rights. Most people still considered themselves Muslims even though the average Iranian was not an observant Muslim during the 1950s and 1960s, and the appeal to religious ideology carried weight. In the same manner that church attendance in the United Kingdom is at an all-time low, the majority of British people still consider themselves Christians, even if they do not practice the religion.

Russia has had a similar resurgence of religion, which in their case is Orthodox Christianity. The Soviet Union was officially a non-religious state, and churches were often closed down, and religion repressed. In the 1960s and 1970s, most Russians considered themselves to be atheists. Today the Eastern Orthodox Church is gaining political power, and President Putin is increasingly appealing to religious ideology to provide cover for his authoritarian tendencies. For example, to silence journalists who were critical of his policies, Putin passed a law restricting freedom of speech. He framed this law as protecting the Orthodox Church from blasphemy. While most Russians supported freedom of the press, they went along with the law because they did not want people to be able to criticize the Church publicly.

Why did a country where most people were atheists just 50 years ago suddenly become so religious? The answer lies in ideology; as the shock therapy period after the fall of communism threw the country into chaos and economic decline, people looked for a belief system to explain their poor condition and promise hope if they just accepted the deterioration of their once powerful country. They found this ideology in the Orthodox Christian Church. This is in stark contrast to the United Kingdom, where atheism is on a dramatic upswing while the country has enjoyed relative stability for the last two hundred years. Any time there is a dramatic change in regime type, such as in the ex-communist countries or with the revolution in Iran, people look to new ideologies of legitimacy; this has sparked a return to religion in the recent era.

Another interesting example of religious ideology at work is Nigeria, which is divided almost equally between Muslims in the North and Christians in the South. Nigeria became a country in 1914, and Christians and Muslims had lived in the area for hundreds of years without any major problems. Nigeria's history of religious violence only dates back to the 1980s, except for a few occasional skirmishes in the 1960s. In the mid-1980s, there were a number of clashes in border towns where Muslims burned churches and Christians burned mosques after claiming one side was trying to convert members of the other side. These small-scale events were largely put down by the military dictatorship, and this prevented a wider outbreak. Then in 1991, a German evangelical preacher named Reinhard Bonnke started a riot in the northern city of Kano after calling for a Christian crusade against the Muslims of the North. About 20 people were killed before the military once again intervened.

These were relatively small-scale events until major troubles began in 1999 with the transition to democracy after the death of dictator Sani Abacha. Once again, a period of regime change led to an increase in religious sentiment. Islamic groups in the North imposed Sharia law, with each side worried that the other might take control of the government. Violence continued throughout the 2000s, and in July 2009 an Islamist group called Boko Haram started an uprising that killed over 1,000 people. By 2012, nearly 8,000 people had been killed as a result of the Boko Haram insurgency by the Boko Haram insurgents themselves, by the government forces and by Christians carrying out retaliatory attacks. As with the other countries in question, Nigeria went from virtually no religious troubles in the first half of the 20th century to be on the verge of a religious-based civil war. People feel so strongly that religious ideology must be the legitimating factor in any government, and Nigeria risks becoming a failed state due to internal religious violence.

The aftermath of a Boko Haram bombing

China is something of a special case when it comes to religion, ideology, and legitimacy. China is officially an atheist state, but recognizes five official state religions: Buddhism, Taoism, Islam, Protestantism and a non-Roman variation of Catholicism. The Chinese state, which is supposed to be officially atheist, recognizes these five religions as legitimate and cracks down on any religion other than these five or any form of the heresy of these religions. China uses religion as a means of ideological legitimacy by protecting the five major religions that support the government because of its willingness to suppress any deviations or other religions, such as Falun Gong. It is a strange case of an atheist state that defends and protects the religious integrity of five religions, rather than trying to get rid of religion altogether or create a secular state. Even officially atheist states can use religious ideology as a source of legitimacy.

Ideology

In contrast to the resurgence of religion as a legitimating political ideology, the old ideologies of communism, capitalism, and fascism have been decreasing in power. With the end of the Cold War and the advent of neoliberal economic globalization, some combination of democracy and capitalism emerged as essentially the main forms of ideological legitimacy in government. With the end of the sharp divisions of the 20th century between different regime types, the importance of these political ideologies gave way, and religious ideology has taken their place. Now, for example, very few people would get worked up if one claimed to be a communist or a socialist, but during the Cold War people in the U.K. and the U.S. were thrown in jail for their political allegiances. Today religion is emerging as a major source of contention that people will get upset about, and not just in places like Iran or Nigeria but in the United States as well.

Despite the decline of clashing political ideologies, these ideologies are still in play in terms of shaping people's beliefs to allow the state to get away with abuses of power and maintain a manufactured legitimacy. *Capitalist ideology* promotes the idea that everyone is free and all the people have to do is work hard, and they can become anything they want. The ideological opponents of capitalism believe that it creates structural inequality and poverty. Similarly, communist ideology taught people that economic equality was the path to prosperity. This was meant to make people accept the fact that communist governments were authoritarian in nature.

During the Cold War, states worked hard to indoctrinate the public with each of their respective ideologies to win legitimacy for their government. People in the United States believed capitalism was superior and that the United States government was legitimate because of this. People in the Soviet Union believed the Soviet government was legitimate because communism was superior. In reality, both systems were riddled with problems, and ideology was a mechanism that distracted people from the real problems of each system.

American Cold War propaganda

The same ideological apparatus can apply to socialism, fascism, liberalism, and conservatism as well. Each ideology promotes a sort of internal mythology, much like a religion, to avoid internal criticism. *Socialist ideology* would create a situation of paranoia, where any criticism of socialism is seen as an outside infiltration. This sort of socialist paranoia was evident in many social movements which ended up splitting apart internally among accusations of spies and infiltrators. *Fascist ideology* attempted to create the fantasy of racial purity and blame immigrants and Jews for a country's problems to make people accept as legitimate a totalitarian form of government. *Liberalism* and *conservatism* are also ideological mechanisms which create fantasies for people to believe in, to obscure the reality of their situation. Liberals promote the illusion of personal freedom and progress   and conservatives promote religion and "traditional values" as a means of keeping people from being aware of the internal problems of capitalist democracy.

Given that no political system is or ever could be perfect, political theorists tend to promote the idea of the critique of ideology. This means that political theorists want each person to try to think independently and critically as much as they can, rather than simply aligning themselves with an ideology and letting the false ideological beliefs cloud reality. The basis of critiquing ideology means questioning basic assumptions. This means critiquing and questioning what is held to be true. If one thinks that the best political regime is liberalism, or socialism, or conservative capitalism, then one must spend most of their time critiquing their own beliefs.

This form of self-questioning can allow individuals to develop their own opinions, even if it might be impossible to escape ideology completely. For simplicity, people always group up with others that have similar political views, and those similar views can have an ideological effect on us. However, if someone develops a habit of thinking critically about his or her views, they can resist the forces of ideology and be less inclined to follow the herd simply. Such herd behaviors in politics are extremely dangerous; the rise of Adolph Hitler and fascism in Germany demonstrated how people who were otherwise normal and even somewhat philosophically sophisticated could get taken in by a dangerous ideology that led to massive violence. If more people were critical of the ideology, they would be less inclined to defend it violently, and situations such as Nazi Germany, the Cold War, and the current religious conflicts would be less likely to occur.

Governance and Accountability

The final source of legitimacy is *accountability*, which means that the government explains to citizens what it is doing and why it is doing it. Related to accountability is transparency, which is a major principle of democratic legitimacy. If a government is to be a democracy, it must represent the people. For this to happen, the people must know what it is doing so they can hold it accountable. If people cannot hold a government accountable because the government does things in secret, then the government can no longer claim to have democratic legitimacy. Even governments with fair elections can act in a non-transparent manner which prevents the people from holding them accountable, and even the most advanced democracy can lack democratic legitimacy.

After Edward Snowden revealed that the U.S. government was secretly spying on all Americans internet activity, the U.S. government lost legitimacy. If the government is not transparent, then the American people will not know if it is doing anything bad, and it cannot be held accountable. Voting a government out of office for doing a bad job becomes impossible when the voters have no idea that the government is doing a bad job. China faces similar problems of a lack of legitimacy because it is not transparent and not accountable to the citizens. Mentions of the protests in Tiananmen Square in 1989 are still censored in China today because the government does not want to be held accountable for its violent suppression of student activists. It attempts to cover up these facts by preventing transparency.

CCTV surveillance cameras on Wall Street

All governments owe citizens the right to know what the government is doing and why they are doing it. When governments act in secret, all claims to legitimacy are lost. Regardless of what other mechanisms the government uses to legitimize itself none of those mechanisms can be evaluated, and the government cannot be held accountable. The Chinese government claims legitimacy through its ability to spread economic prosperity, so when the government enacts an economic policy in secret, there is a problem. If the citizens cannot verify whether or not the government is doing something to enhance economic prosperity, the government's claim to legitimacy is empty.

In the United Kingdom, the existence of the House of Lords is a continual problem as many argue that it lacks accountability and undermines the legitimacy of the government. The House of Lords is the upper chamber of the British legislature, equivalent to the American Senate. However, it is entirely appointed: 26 seats are given to the Lords Spiritual, who are high-ranking members of the Church of England, 92 Lords Temporal inherit their place in the House of Lords from their father, and the remaining seats are appointed by the Prime Minister, allowing the Lord to sit for life. Since the House of Lords can essentially veto the House of Commons, a motley crew of religious leaders, aristocrats and lifetime appointees can overrule the democratically-elected House.

The existence of the House of Lords dramatically undermines the democratic legitimacy of the British government. It is entirely unaccountable because there is nothing anyone can do to remove a member from the House of Lords. Even a mature democracy such as the United Kingdom has a major source of illegitimate government as part of its governing structure. The House of Lords continues to exist through the power of ideology and tradition; people in the U.K. are socialized from an early age to believe the House of Lords is a necessity for a functioning government and are taught to believe that it must continue to exist since it has existed. To people outside the U.K. who do not share this ideological upbringing, it simply seems undemocratic and illegitimate.

The same is true for Iran; most observers feel that the outer layer of theocracy undermines the inner core of democracy within the Iranian state. However, within Iran, people are taught that democracy uncontrolled by religion leads to decay and foreign invasion. In China, the unaccountable one-party government is ideologically supported for bringing economic prosperity because Chinese citizens are continually reminded of the disaster that happened in Russia after its quick transition to capitalist democracy.

In Mexico, people believed for a long time that only the PRI political party had the legitimacy to rule Mexico, and this belief persists with their recent election victory. When comparing and contrasting different countries, it is found that people are ideologically pushed into believing things that people in other countries would consider completely illegitimate. It is important to think about what forms of ideological legitimacy a government is pushing on its people that people in other countries might think is completely illegitimate. The goal of comparative politics is not just to compare how other countries operate, but to make individuals think about how their own country operates and why it may have problems that may not even be recognized as problems.

Chapter 3

Political Institutions

This chapter addresses the formal structure and workings of states and governments, including overviews about different authority systems and government structures. The powers that correspond to each level of authority varies widely according to the national context. Some countries keep most policymaking at the national level, while others distribute powers more widely to regions and localities. Depending on the country, some authority is now passing to supranational organizations such as the European Union (EU) as well.

Overviews of the six countries' branches of government and how these branches relate to one another are provided; included in this are explanations of the different arrangements of executive power, legislative structures and the models of executive-legislative relations. Basic concepts such as parliamentary and presidential systems and the separation and fusion of powers are defined, characteristic advantages and drawbacks of different institutional arrangements are explored, and methods toward understanding how the executive and legislative policymakers interact with other branches of the state apparatus are provided. Some countries, such as the United Kingdom, have independent court systems, while China and others do not. Often, these judicial features depend on the roots of the legal system — whether the system uses code or common law, ideology, custom and traditional authority or religious codes. The implications of whether a country has judicial review and whether it operates through an independent national court system, theocratic oversight or supranational courts are addressed.

In these endeavors, the chapter goes beyond purely addressing constitutional arrangements, patterns, and procedures since politics has both formal and informal components. Included in this is an overview of how political elites are recruited and how political preferences are aggregated. Major electoral systems, as well as one-party systems, dominant-party systems, and multiparty systems, are covered in detail. Also addressed is how the number of political parties in a particular country is usually connected to the country's social cleavages as well as its electoral system. Explorations in how interest groups exercise political influence, as well as the effects of corporatism and pluralism, are undertaken.

Examples among the six studied countries of how the exercise of real political power often does not correspond to the model implied by formal political structures are provided and discussed. The composition and recruitment of political elites and how they are linked to other elites in society reveal much about informal political power.

The bureaucracy is a crucial part of the political system. Technical experts advise and administer a policy that, in principle, is fashioned by political leaders. The ideological sympathies and traditions (e.g., professionalism) of the bureaucracy and its channels of recruitment influence its political role. The military also affects politics in many countries through informal pressure, as in China and Russia, or through periodic seizures of power, as in Nigeria. The professional or political role of the armed forces and the nature of civilian control over them varies across countries and time. The intelligence community or secret police can be an additional locus of coercion. Similarly, the judiciary plays a variety of roles in the six studied countries; in some places, it exhibits important levels of autonomy, and in other countries, it is used to establish religious or ideological domination. Further, familiar with how the judiciary does or does not exercise independent power and how it shapes public policies and political practices of citizens as well as of the state is established.

Levels of Government

By comparing the internal institutions of government in different countries, it can be understood what the advantages and disadvantages of each of these institutional arrangements are, as well as why different countries have different arrangements. An institutional arrangement that works best for one country may not work well in another country because of differences. The first of these institutional differences is the relative power of different levels of government. In the United States, citizens are used to having a strong federal government under which state governments have much room to make their laws. Other countries, however, have evolved different systems, which can be compared with the American example to evaluate the relative strengths and weaknesses of these systems, both in their context and how they might operate in America.

Supranational / National / Regional / Local

The United Kingdom provides an interesting example for looking at the relative power of different levels of government because it has an interesting mix of powers. Although the U.K.'s governing system is based on the supremacy of Parliament, as a member of the supranational European Union some aspects of public policy are decided by the EU rather than the British Parliament. In most EU countries, one of the major areas where the EU has more authority than national governments is over economic policy. EU member countries using the Euro as their currency have no control over monetary policy, which is set by the European Central Bank.

The U.K. is an exception in this case because it retains its currency, the British Pound, and maintains its ability to control monetary policy. As in the United States, however, monetary policy is not controlled by the government but by the bureaucracy. The U.K. is a member of the EU's trade bloc, which means that external tariffs and import taxes are controlled by the EU and not the U.K. The U.K. is also a member of the Schengen zone, so other EU citizens are free to move to and work in the U.K. and vice versa. The EU controls this form of free internal movement within the Eurozone, and member governments do not have the authority to restrict internal movement from other Eurozone countries.

The EU has also established a cooperation framework to enable the police forces of each country to cooperate and generally controls issues related to fishing. The EU can put quotas on the amount of a certain type of fish that can be caught, and U.K. fishermen must obey these regulations.

Resolutions passed in the European Parliament also limits the national government of the U.K. The EU parliament, however, only has authority on cross-border issues. For example, it passed legislation which significantly reduced the roaming charges incurred on cell phone usage when outside of one's home country. It would not have the authority, however, to legislate on cell phone contracts inside a single country. The national government of the U.K. has broad authority to pass legislation on all other issues not covered by the EU that affect the whole country.

Unlike the United States, the U.K. does not have strong sub-national governments equivalent to the American states. Instead, some of the powers of the national parliament have been "devolved" (beginning in 1999) to the governments of the countries that make up the United Kingdom. Beginning in 1999, Northern Ireland, Scotland and Wales were given room to pass their legislation in their parliaments on certain issues. The U.K. did not become a federal state at this point because the central government still retains the right to overrule or even dissolve the rights of the national parliaments. This is in contrast to the United States where the authority of the states is built into the constitution. *Devolution* is different from federalism because the U.K. remains as a unitary state with smaller national parliaments having been granted powers only at the discretion of the U.K. national parliament, not as a legal structure.

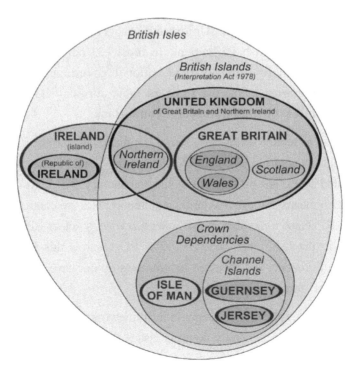

Euler diagram of the many overlapping relationships of the British Isles

One interesting quirk that emerged from devolution is that England did not receive devolved powers and did not have its national parliament. This is a strange situation because the United Kingdom is made up of North Ireland, Wales, Scotland, and England, with only England not having devolved authority. Many people in England argue that this leaves them worse off because they lack the autonomy to set their policy in the way Scotland and Wales can. At the same time, some people in Scotland, Wales and Northern Ireland point to the lack of devolved power for England as evidence that the national government of the U.K. is really just an English government that rules in the interest of only one part of the U.K. The issue of devolution remains highly contentious in the U.K., especially in the light of the recent failed vote in Scotland on becoming an independent country.

Local governments in the U.K. are somewhat more powerful than their American equivalents. The City of London has devolved power, and the London Assembly is extremely powerful for a city government. The mayor of London is a figure equivalent to the First Minister of Scotland or Wales. For example, the city of London has a congestion charge on vehicles entering the central city during working hours on weekdays. This is part of the city's control of environmental and transportation policy, and it is evidence of their ability to raise their forms of taxation. A similar scheme in the United States would have to be approved by the state government because municipal governments lack the autonomous authority for such sweeping legislation. While other city governments are less powerful than the Greater London Authority, they still retain limited tax-raising powers and the ability to pass their laws with minimal interference from above.

China's constitution sets out three sub-national levels of government, but in contemporary practice, there are five sub-levels. The first is the provincial level, which includes twenty-two provinces, five autonomous regions, four municipalities, two special administrative regions, and one special case. According to the Chinese constitution, provincial governors are to take their orders directly from the central government, but in practice, provincial officials have a great deal of independence. Beginning in the 1990s, provinces started to develop their own formal sets of political institutions which mirrored the structure of the central government.

Since the 1990s, China has been increasingly taking on the characteristics of federalism as provincial governments gain more and more powers. In addition to the twenty-two provinces with top-level sub-national authority, five autonomous regions have the same power as provinces. These autonomous regions are places where there are a large number of people from ethnic minorities who are given their legislative authorities. These regions include Tibet and Xinjiang, which are sites of periodic rebellion by Buddhists and Muslims, respectively. Constitutionally, these regions are supposed to have more autonomy than a province, but their powers have been scaled back recently in light of religious and ethnic tensions. The four municipalities that are given provincial powers are the four biggest cities, and the two special administrative regions are Hong Kong and Macau, which used to be controlled by colonial powers and have developed a tradition of autonomy. The special case is Taiwan, which in practice is its own country completely independent of China, but the Chinese government claims it as part of China.

Map indicating the five (named) autonomous regions of China.

Given the massive population of China, more levels of government are necessary to manage a large number of people involved. Below provinces, prefectures have been created to give more power to larger cities within a province or to areas where there is a majority of people from one of the protected ethnic minorities. Below prefectures are counties, many of which date their boundaries back to 100-400 B.C.E. Below counties are townships, which include large rural areas and medium-sized towns. At the bottom level are villages, which include both actual villages and also neighborhoods in some larger cities.

The Communist Party controls all these regional levels of government. Since each local level of authority is accountable to the central government, people have had success in removing unpopular sub-national governments by appealing to the central government and arguing that their local official had become corrupt. Even though there is only a single party which controls all these levels of government, they do not operate with a single ideology or method given the massive number of local politicians. Dissent and protest against local authorities in China are much easier and more tolerated than questioning the central government.

Iran provides yet another contrast. Its primary levels of government are national and local. The Iranian constitution states that all cities and towns should have an elected council which governs for a period of four years, and these city councils are, along with the national government, the "decision-making and administrative organs of the State." This aspect of the constitution was not implemented until 1999 when the first local elections for city councils were held. In practice, the local councils are relatively weak compared to the national government, despite the constitution placing them in tandem.

Mexico is similar to the U.S. as a federal system with strong state governments. However, city governments are constitutionally the third level of government and not simply administrative creations of the state. City councils and mayors in Mexico are very powerful, and the constitution backs their broad legislative autonomy on local issues.

Unitary / Federal

In comparative politics, states can generally be divided into two types of systems regarding the division of powers. A state is considered *unitary* when the central government is the ultimate authority, and any sub-levels of government have only as much authority as the central government delegates them. By contrast, a *federal* state is a union of semi-autonomous, sub-level governments whose own political authority is constitutionally guaranteed.

The key to understanding the difference between a unitary and a federal state is not how much sub-national power governments have, but the constitutional arrangement. In a unitary state, the central government can unilaterally abolish the political authority of any sub-level governments; in a federal system, this is impossible. For example, the United Kingdom is a unitary state, but the Scottish Parliament is given a fairly large amount of autonomy and political power. While the Scottish Parliament has more political autonomy than other regional governments in a federation such as Germany, the authority of the Scottish Parliament is exercised solely at the will of the British Parliament. By contrast, in Germany, the local, regional governments are constitutionally protected.

Map indicating the world's unitary states (dark) and federal states (light).

Unitary states are much more common around the world, with 165 of the 193 UN-recognized states being unitary rather than federal. However, of the ten most populated countries, six of them are federations. Of the ten largest countries regarding land area, eight are federations. Of the six countries under study, Mexico, Nigeria and Russia are federations, while the U.K., Iran, and China are unitary states. China and Nigeria, however, are exceptions. China has been moving toward more of a federal system, and many scholars consider it a hybrid system. Nigeria is constitutionally a federation as of its most recent constitution, but it tends to switch to a unitary state when the military controls the government or when religious tensions increase.

This leads to the question of which form of state is better, a unitary or a federal one. This is one of the founding questions that vexed the United States; there were deep disagreements between the Federalists and Anti-Federalists at the constitutional conventions. Despite their names, the Anti-Federalists accused the Federalists of essentially favoring a unitary state that would take away too much autonomy from the states; the Anti-Federalists in early America were, in today's terms, more like extreme federalists than anything else. This problem arose again at the time of the Civil War because the Southern states argued that the federal government did not have the right to abolish slavery across the country.

The contrast between federalism (or how much of it there should be) and unitarism is evident in other states as well. Before devolution in 1999, the Scottish, Northern Irish and Welsh argued that the U.K.'s unitary system denied national self-representation to those groups. They argued the U.K. should move toward a federal model, with devolution being a compromise. In Russia, the federal system was inherited from the Soviet Union but became controversial as many regions attempted to become their own countries altogether. In Russia, separatist wars broke out in the Muslim regions, spurring the question of whether these regions would be better controlled via limiting their autonomy by adopting a more unitary model or by giving them more autonomy.

Nigeria has been plagued with similar religious tensions. The recently adopted federal system has enabled the northern Muslim regions to adopt Sharia law and other hardline Islamic positions while the Southern regions have entirely different sets of laws. This has spurred religious tensions and led to questions of national unity, with many Nigerians calling for adopting a unitary state to keep Nigeria from splitting in half. While the general trend is that larger and more diverse countries have preferred federalism to allow a measure of self-government for distinct regions, the same problems have spurred separatist movements in countries such as Russia and Nigeria.

In the loosest federations, such as Belgium and Canada, there have been serious debates about whether such countries should break apart. Belgium is divided into a French-speaking half and a Dutch-speaking half, and many argue that the federal government adds nothing to the mix, especially in the context of Belgium being a prominent member of the EU. The same question arose in the recent Scottish independence vote: being a member of the EU, would it matter if Scotland was a semi-autonomous region of the U.K. or an independent country still under the supranational authority of the EU?

Québécois parade goers participating in Saint-Jean-Baptiste Day, a holiday increasingly expressing separatist instead of religious sentiments.

Canada as well has been plagued by separatist movements. Quebec has had two referendums on becoming an independent country, and many in Newfoundland and Alberta argue that the Canadian federation only hurts the people of their provinces.

Despite its lack of democracy, China's hybrid system might be a model for the future. China is increasingly granting constitutional autonomy to its various sub-levels of government, but the central government retains the ability to remove officials it deems corrupt. The existence of local governments is protected and cannot be abolished centrally as in a pure unitary state, but unlike in a pure federation, corrupt individual politicians can be removed by the central authorities.

Centralization / Decentralization

Within the wider context of whether a state is unitary or federal is the much more relevant question of how centralized or decentralized it is. A state can be a loose federation constitutionally, but if the real authority is centralized in the national government, then the sub-national governments will lack authority. At the same time, a state that is unitary may pursue decentralization and willingly give great amounts of autonomous authority to sub-regional governments. In this sense, the U.K. can be thought of as a decentralized unitary state, and a country such as Venezuela as a centralized federation. So even though the U.K. is a unitary state, the regional governments have more power than the regional governments of a federal state like Venezuela. When comparing states and attempting to determine how much authority sub-national government entities have, it is not enough to determine if the country is unitary or federal. Its actual practices must be examined to determine whether it is centralized or decentralized.

Economically, there had been a push toward decentralization in the 1990s driven by the dominance of neoliberal economics. This economic ideology believes in small government and accordingly pushed governments to delegate authority to lower levels that were smaller in size and much less powerful. While the justification for this was "to bring government closer to the people it served" because a citizen is likely to have more contact with his or her provincial government than with the national government, the actual effect was to cause budget crises and dramatically reduce government spending.

In Russia, President Putin pushed for and signed legislation in 2013 that drastically restructured and centralized how regional governors come into the office. Instead of determining governors by direct public elections, they are now appointed by regional legislatures from an approved list of candidates developed by the presidency. Putin defended the move by claiming this new procedure helps to protect ethnic/religious minorities in regions where elections might become highly contentious and even violent. He also supported his decision by claiming it would encourage national cohesion in light of recent terrorist attacks. The opposition, however, attacked the centralization as undemocratic and intended to aid the dominant United Russia Party to avoid popular vote defeats. Mexico, on the other hand, saw a prominent movement led by the Institutional Revolutionary Party (PRI) in 2009 to decentralize their politics by devolving powers previously held by the federal government to the state level. Support for this goal centers on the argument that it will establish a bulwark against previous institutional errors that were expensive. Critics of this move say it leads to inefficiency and that the increased discretion and spending abilities of governors are intended to be used for campaign reelection promotion. Such debates about centralization and decentralization continue to play a large role in comparative politics. The advocates of centralization focus on the economic benefits of economies of scale provided by national spending programs, and the advocates of decentralization focus on arguing for the benefits of empowering the lower levels of government that people have more direct contact with.

Executives

A major point of comparison among countries is how executive authority is exercised and what its relation to the legislative branch is. In the contemporary comparative political analysis, systems of government are divided into nine general types based on the form of executive and legislative authority. These nine subtypes to be used for the next three sections are: *presidential republic* (USA), *semi-presidential republic* (France), *parliamentary republic with an executive chosen by parliament* (South Africa), *parliamentary republic with a ceremonial executive* (India), *constitutional monarchy with the prime minister as executive* (Canada), *constitutional monarchy with a monarch exercising executive authority* (Morocco), *absolute monarchy* (Saudi Arabia), *military dictatorship* (Thailand) and *one-party state* (China). These nine government system types can be divided into three broader sub-types, depending on whether the executive authority is in the hands of a president, a prime minister or a combination of the two.

Single or Dual

A *single executive system* is one where executive power is solely in the hands of either a president or a prime minister. For example, the United States and the U.K. both have a single executive: the president and the prime minister, respectively. A single executive system can be either a presidential or a parliamentary system. The more complex arrangement is a *dual executive system*, more commonly called a *semi-presidential system*. This is a system of government in which a president exists alongside a prime minister and a cabinet.

Photograph of Russian Prime Minister Dmitry Medvedev (left) and President Vladimir Putin (right), dual executives of Russia in 2008.

The president of a semi-presidential system is elected and appoints the cabinet. Unlike in a full presidential system, the cabinet is responsible to parliament, meaning that parliament and the prime minister can force the cabinet to resign. In a *full presidential system,* the legislative branch has no authority over the cabinet, and a semi-presidential system adds another layer of checks and balances that do not exist in a full presidential system. A semi-presidential system also differs from a parliamentary republic because in a parliamentary republic the president is usually a ceremonial position appointed by the government with no actual power.

Russia is an example of a semi-presidential or dual system, but it is not a good example. Russia's constitution sets out a dual executive system in which the president is the dominant authority with real executive power. In Russia, the president has broad authority over the legislative branches and can even dismiss them and call for new elections. The president also has the power to pass decrees which have the same status as laws passed by the legislature.

Even before Vladimir Putin's rise to power, many within Russia criticized the position of the president as too powerful with respect to the prime minister. They called for a more balanced semi-presidential system where the legislature and prime minister could hold the president to account in the style of France's government. However, after Putin served two terms as president and was barred from running for a third term, he won the election as prime minister of Russia. As prime minister, he exercised real executive authority and transformed the President into essentially a ceremonial position.

Finishing his term as prime minister enables Putin to be once again elected as president, and he returned true executive authority to the office of President. According to Russia's constitutional semi-presidential system, Putin's powers as prime minister should have been extremely limited. Putin was able to get away with this largely as a result of his charismatic authority and personal popularity.

China is once again something of a special case. The executive branch of the Chinese government is the State Council, with the president as head of state. Constitutionally, the Chinese President is a ceremonial position without any real powers. The Chinese President is chosen by the legislative branch and serves a five-year term with a two-term limit. While the Chinese President holds no power on his own since the 1990s the person chosen to be president has also been appointed the leader of the Communist Party and Chairman of the Central Military Commission. While these two positions are not formally linked to the president, they are positions of real influence and power. As a one-party state, being in charge of that one party carries a great deal of power, and the head of the Central Military Commission is equivalent to being a commander-in-chief. Even though the actual position of president holds no real power in China, the system has evolved to the point where being president also leads to being appointed to other powerful positions. This situation has led some to describe China as a de facto semi-presidential system.

Constitutional executive authority in China is in the State Council, which is equivalent to the American cabinet. It consists of fifty heads of bureaucratic departments and is headed by the Premier. The president chooses the Premier on the advice of the Communist Party senior leadership (which recently has also been the president). The Premier is considered the head of the bureaucracy. While the Premier is not in charge of the military like a traditional executive, their duty of managing the economy and bureaucracy is seen in China as being of primary importance. China has something of a dual executive system with some powers in the hands of the Premier and some in the hands of the head of the Communist Party and Chairman of the Military Commission (which is not necessarily the president, but by recent tradition are positions filled by the president).

President

In a *full presidential system*, the president is both head of state and head of government. This means that executive power is separated from legislative power. In a presidential system, the president is not held to account by the legislature and usually does not have the power to dissolve the legislature and force new elections. Presidents usually have veto power over the legislature, meaning they can over-rule any piece of legislation they choose. They also usually serve fixed terms. In a presidential system, the members of the cabinet are appointed directly by the president and are not members of the legislature.

In addition to the United States, Mexico, Iran, and Nigeria all have presidential systems. In Mexico, the president is also the Supreme Commander of the Armed Forces, and the president is only allowed to serve one six-year term. During the period of single-party dominance by the PRI from 1917 until 2000, the outgoing PRI president was tasked with authority to choose the incoming president, who would then be elected in general elections of questionable validity.

The president during this era had sweeping powers, including the ability to appoint people to government positions right down to the lowest level, essentially giving the government control over the entire structure of the civil service. This period in Mexican presidential history was called the "perfect dictatorship" because the sweeping powers of the president were shrouded with democratic legitimacy. Since 2000, successive presidents have taken measures to roll back the authority of the Mexican president. The current Mexican President is Enrique Peña Nieto of PRI.

Although Iran is more of a full presidential system than a semi-presidential system, it does have aspects of a dual executive. The Supreme Leader (the Ayatollah) is the head of state and generally is expected to stick to religious matters and not get involved in politics. However, the position does carry some executive authority. The Supreme Leader appoints the top ranks in the military, the director of the state-run TV and radio outlets, all major religious leaders and the top judges in the country. The Supreme Leader also has veto powers and the ability to prevent certain candidates from running for office. The Supreme Leader can declare war, but this requires a two-thirds majority vote supporting the declaration in parliament. Second in the overall command structure is the president, who exerts political executive authority while the Supreme Leader is more like a religious executive.

Two Iranian men attest their having voted in the 2013 presidential election by displaying their stamped index fingers.

The president of Iran is popularly elected and must first be approved to run by the Guardian Council, which is led by the Supreme Leader. As head of government, the

Iranian president is responsible for appointing the cabinet, making executive decisions and determining the legislative agenda of the Iranian parliament (the Majlis). Since the Supreme Leader must first approve the president, the Supreme Leader generally does not interfere with the government, and the president acts as normal executive authority. The only major difference is that although the Iranian President appoints the cabinet, including the Defense Minister, he is not the commander of the military and cannot declare war. The current Supreme Leader of Iran is Ayatollah Ali Khamenei, and the current president is Hassan Rouhani.

Nigeria's system is purposely and directly modeled after that of the United States. It has a separation of the three branches of power, and executive authority is in the hands of a popularly elected president. The current president of Nigeria is Muhammadu Buhari. Nigeria is interesting because they had previously been a parliamentary democracy, having been colonized by the United Kingdom.

Prime Minister

The U.K. is the most obvious example of a parliamentary system with executive power in the hands of the prime minister. In the U.K., the prime minister as an office exists based on tradition rather than on a constitution, but the PM has a large amount of executive authority. The PM appoints the cabinet and is the head of government, but they appoint cabinet ministers only from those who have been elected to parliament. The PM is a position which combines executive and legislative authority. In the modern era, the power of the PM as an executive has increased dramatically in countries such as the U.K. and Canada. Formally, a parliamentary system meant that the prime minister was simply first among equals, and before World War II cabinet ministers enjoyed much more influence and power than they do now.

After World War II, successive prime ministers have begun to concentrate more and more authority into the hands of the PM. Many scholars of British political history have argued that the prime minister in the modern era has acted more like a president. The PM has carved out more territory as the exclusive domain of executive decision-making is not subject to parliamentary votes. While this runs against the intention of parliamentary systems, it is a general trend across all systems of government that the executive branch has sought more political authority. The modern political era is one where democracy seems to prevail, but in reality, legislatures are being diminished in authority at the hands of the single person who leads the government.

One of the major differences between a prime minister and a president is that the PM is still accountable to parliament. In the U.K., there is a daily Question Period where members of parliament can ask the government questions (often phrased more as scathing critiques than as questions) about what the prime minister and government are up to. In many cases, the inability to properly answer these questions or refute criticisms can be a major source of embarrassment for the prime minister. Also, the prime minister is merely the leader of the political party, which maintains the confidence of the House of Commons. If parliament turns against the prime minister and their government, they can pass a motion of no-confidence which only needs a majority to pass. If a no-confidence motion passes the House of Commons, the government falls, and new elections are triggered.

The prime minister can also be ousted if their party turns against them. If the prime minister's political party controls a majority in the House of Commons and does not want to pass a no-confidence motion, they can get rid of the prime minister by choosing a new party leader. This has recently happened twice in Australia, which uses a British-style parliamentary system led by a prime minister. In 2010, Australian Prime Minister Kevin Rudd's Labor Party turned against him and replaced him with Julia Gillard. Then in 2015, the Australian Liberal Party replaced their own Tony Abbot as prime minister with Malcolm Turnbull. The prime minister must retain the confidence of both a majority of the members of parliament and the confidence of their political party, or they risk being replaced before their term in office is over.

Israeli Prime Minister Shimon Peres reacts to
the Knesset's plenary session no-confidence motion.

Legislatures

The *legislature* is the law-making body of government, and it is usually made up of a large number of people whose job is to debate and deliberate on various bills before deciding on what to pass into law. The legislature is usually called a chamber or a house in general terms, but each country tends to have a different name for its legislative chamber or chambers. Each country also has a different arrangement of power in the legislature, with some countries having legislatures which have much more power than others. The institutional arrangement also differs from country to country, depending on whether it is a presidential or parliamentary system. Legislatures in parliamentary systems tend to have much more power and influence than in presidential systems.

Unicameral / Bicameral (symmetric / asymmetric)

There are generally two arrangements of legislative chambers. *Unicameralism* means there is one legislative chamber, and *bicameralism* means there are two. The United States, with a House of Representatives and a Senate, is a bicameral legislature, while Iran has a unicameral legislature with just one legislative chamber, called the Majlis. Unicameral systems tend to be more democratic and more efficient, as legislation only needs to pass one chamber of government which is usually meant to represent the people of the country directly. In contrast, the principle behind bicameralism is that there has to be a second chamber to represent the interests of some group other than the people.

In the United Kingdom, which is bicameral, the upper chamber is called the House of Lords, and it is meant to provide representation to religious leaders, large hereditary landowners, and generally wealthy people. In this sense, the upper chamber is intended to represent the upper classes, and the lower chamber, called the House of Commons, is meant to represent the common people or lower classes. Most of the countries with two chambers instituted an upper chamber out of a fear of the democratic will of the people and to provide some means of representation for the established elite that could allow them to overrule the popularly elected legislature. This system evolved at a time when voting rights for common people were relatively new, and the established elite was wary of what might happen should they allow the "uneducated" and "unsophisticated" commoners to choose their representatives.

Mexico also uses a bicameral system with the Chamber of Deputies as the lower house and the Senate as the upper house. The primary role of the Mexican Senate is related to developing foreign policy resolutions, but it also has the authority to approve and deny presidential appointments. The Senate was originally meant to provide geographical representation, with each Mexican state having two members, but this representation scheme was dramatically changed in reforms in the 1990s. The question of why Mexico needs an appeal to tradition usually answers two chambers. Seeing that the Senate has limited duties that could just as well be carried out by the Chamber of Deputies, the Mexican Senate continues to exist more out of inertia and a lack of will for change.

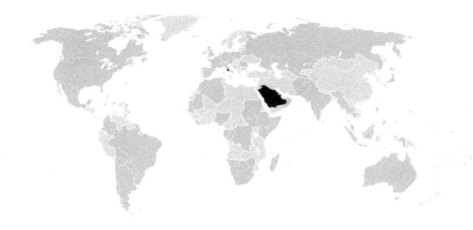

World map indicating nations with bicameral legislatures (gray),
unicameral legislatures (light gray) and no legislature (black).

Like Mexico, Nigeria has a bicameral system consisting of a Senate upper house and a House of Representatives as the lower chamber. Nigeria is directly modeled on the U.S., and its Senate is elected based on state representation rather than geography. Russia has a more explicit purpose for its bicameralism. The lower chamber, called the State Duma, deals with legislative issues, and the upper house, called the Federation Council, exists to represent regional governments directly. The Federation Council is not elected, but provincial governors appoint representatives. The Federation Council focuses mainly on issues that affect the regional territories, such as changing borders and dealing with issues related to the power of the president. The Federation Council is more of a formal power structure, with the real authority lies with the State Duma and the president.

The continued existence of upper legislative houses remains a contentious issue; in most countries, their role is either somewhat limited, redundant or has changed dramatically since the upper chamber was created. Advocates of democracy argue that unicameralism is superior to bicameralism because the legislature should directly represent the people, not religious leaders, landed elites or sub-national territories. In most countries which are federations and have a bicameral system, one of the justifications for an upper house is that it represents the disparate geographic regions of the country by providing representation for state or provincial governments. In practice, this is almost never the case. Most federations have mechanisms whereby provincial or state governments can get together and speak directly with the prime minister or president.

Except Russia, most upper houses that claim to be based on representing sub-national territories have no contact with the lower house governments. In Nigeria and the United States, Senators do not meet with and take orders from the governors of the states they represent but instead vote according to their political party's position. In practice, most bicameral systems end up simply being redundant since both houses are elected and vote according to party lines. Advocates of unicameralism argue that having two legislatures tasked with performing largely the same tasks only induces deadlock and slows down the legislative process.

Due to the increased emphasis on democratic representation in the legislature, many countries have moved to abolish their upper chambers. In Canada, the provincial governments have all abolished their Senates, and the question of whether or not to abolish the federal Senate remains a hot topic. New Zealand eliminated its unelected upper chamber after deciding that making it elected would only create redundancy. Croatia, Denmark, Greece, Hungary, South Korea, Peru, Portugal, Sweden, Turkey, and Venezuela have also all abolished upper houses in favor of a unicameral system. By contrast, there are no countries which were once unicameral and then decided to create an upper house.

Organization

Legislatures generally consist of seats, which can be assigned based on election or appointment. Seats are assigned in a number of ways, depending on whether they are elected or appointed. Elected seats usually represent either a geographical territory or a section of the population. Appointed seats can be by some qualifications, such as religion, wealth or expertise. In unicameral systems, the organization of the legislature is relatively straightforward, as a bill requires a majority of votes to pass. In bicameral systems, the organization of the legislature can be more difficult. In Russia, the upper house is mostly symbolic in nature and generally does not block legislation, but in countries such as Nigeria and the United States, the upper chamber may take an active role in blocking or rewriting legislation from the lower house (which must also be passed by the upper house). The rules of the legislature are governed through constitutions, parliamentary procedure, and informal traditions.

Memberships (representation)

In most countries, a member of parliament or representative is expected to represent the interests of the constituents they represent directly. This is the basic idea behind representative democracy, but in practice members usually, represent the interests of the political party to which they belong. Depending on the level of party discipline, representing the interests of constituents can often get politicians in trouble if it causes them to vote against the party line. At the same time, if a politician claims to be representing a group of people and that group disagrees, then the constituents can become angry with the politician. Representatives generally follow the party line to avoid such troubles. This may make representation much less democratic, but at the same time, it resolves the inherent contradiction of trying to represent groups of people who frequently disagree.

Illinois Governor Daniel Walker greets Chicago constituents
at the 1973 Bud Billiken Parade.

Parliamentary and Presidential Systems

The presidential system has many advantages as compared to a parliamentary system. The first of these is that in a presidential system the president is directly elected by the people. This means that the executive branch is directly chosen and accountable. In a parliamentary system, the prime minister is not directly elected but is simply the leader of the party that holds the majority of parliamentary seats. Advocates of presidential systems also point to the separation of powers inherent in a presidential system, which introduces a series of checks and balances between executive, legislative and judicial power. Having a single executive authority who is not accountable to the legislature can also speed up decisions because they do not need to be approved by parliament. Presidents also provide more stability; they usually serve a fixed term, whereas their party can dismiss prime ministers or lose the confidence of parliament at any time.

On the other hand, there are also major critics of presidential systems who argue that it is not a good system of government at all, let alone the best. These critics tend to focus on how the position of the president has a built-in tendency toward authoritarianism, as the legislature does not control the president's power. These critics argue that the president is essentially an elected dictator, which in the case of Mexico in the PRI years was certainly an accurate assessment. Critics of presidential systems also point to the fact that they tend to produce gridlock. The executive and legislative branches can be controlled by different parties, pitting the two branches of government against each other for partisan reasons. Critics also point to presidential systems introducing stagnation and corruption since it is difficult to eliminate a failed president before they serve out the full term.

Parliamentary systems have the advantage of unity between the executive and legislative branches, so the government can pass legislation in a timely fashion without having to worry about what the legislature might do. It also ensures that there is less gridlock. If the prime minister cannot pass legislation, new elections are held, and that government does not remain in power, unable to do anything. The parliamentary system also tends to promote more of a spirit of compromise and cooperation between parties. In most European parliamentary democracies, no single party will win enough seats to control a majority, so coalitions between parties are formed to create workable compromises to get legislation passed.

Another commonly cited advantage of parliamentary systems is that they tend to provide a much larger role for the opposition. In the United Kingdom, the second biggest political party is referred to as Her Majesty's Official Opposition, and they have the official role of questioning every decision the government makes. The prime minister must continually defend the merits of all legislation since they will face open and public criticism during the Question Period. In contrast, there are no official means for representatives to question and debate the president in a presidential system. Advocates of parliamentary systems argue that this makes parliamentary democracy more democratic than a presidential system.

Some of the disadvantages of a parliamentary system involve the lack of a clearly defined role for the prime minister. Since the PM's powers are largely a result of tradition and evolution, they are only limited by what parliament and their party will allow. As long as the PM has the support of their party and a majority in the House, they are largely free to pass any legislation they wish. In countries that have an independent Supreme Court, such as Canada, the PM's power is limited by the courts. The British PM is limited only by tradition and can get away with anything on issues for which there is no precedent. The lack of clear rules, even in constitutionally defined parliaments, can often lead to prime ministers taking more power than has been traditionally afforded to them.

The indirect election of the PM can also be an issue. Since the PM is the leader of the party that wins the confidence of the House of Commons, the people do not directly vote for the prime minister. Instead, they vote for the prime minister's party or a local representative of the same party. In the U.K., this can cause problems. Sometimes people like the local candidate of a party but do not like that party's leader. In that case, they must vote for the preferred local candidate, who will support a prime minister they do not like, or for a local candidate they do not care for to support that party's leader. This can also create the unique situation in which a party may win a majority of the seats in parliament, technically making its leader the prime minister, but the PM loses their local district and is then unable to become prime minister. While this is rare, it has happened. On the other hand, this can allow the people to support a political party without supporting its choice of party leader.

Until recently, in countries such as the U.K. and Canada, when a government's term in office was up after 4 or 5 years, the government was free to choose the date of the election. This was a tremendous advantage for the government. In Canada in the 1990s, Liberal Prime Minister Jean Chretien called an election only three years into a four-year term because his popularity was so high. He won the election, thereby extending his term another four years. Because of such abuses, both the U.K. and Canada now have fixed election dates to prevent the sitting government from deciding to hold an early election to take advantage of then-favorable polling numbers.

Japanese Prime Minister Ryūtarō Hashimoto faced
a highly contended 1996 home district election, which, if he had lost,
would have resulted in the selection of another head of state.

Institutional Relations

In a parliamentary system, the main institutional arrangement is the combination of executive and legislative authority. Usually, judicial authority remains separate, but this varies from country to country. The separation of the three branches categorizes presidential systems to ensure a system of checks and balances. However, in practice, neither of these institutional arrangements tends to operate according to its theory. A parliamentary system would be expected to have a weaker executive since the prime minister must always maintain the confidence of the legislature. In practice, prime ministers have carved out huge amounts of executive authority that allow them to act like presidents and ignore legislative authority.

Similarly, the institutional arrangement of a presidential system is supposed to guarantee a strong executive, capable of making resolute decisions untrammeled by the partisan bickering that happens in legislatures. In reality, most presidents find it hard to get anything done if they do not have all but unanimous support of the legislature; this can lead to presidents trying to carve out more power and weaken the system of checks and balances. The general trend of more powerful executives undermining the institutional relations of government is again on display here. The U.K. is an example of a parliamentary system with an increasingly powerful executive, and Russia is an example of a presidential system where any checks and balances on executive authority are being undermined.

Elections

The next section will go into detail on the different types of electoral systems, so this section will focus on how the six countries of this study implement their versions of these general systems.

Presidential

U.S. President Obama casts his 2012 ballot in Chicago.

Presidential elections are the simplest form of the election because only one person can win. There are two main ways to implement a presidential election. The first is to use the *first-past-the-post* method, and whoever gets the most votes wins, even if they do not get 50%. The second method is to hold the *second round of voting*, in which all but the top two candidates are eliminated. A two-round system, used in France, works so that people can vote for a third party candidate without feeling their vote is being wasted.

Like the U.S., Nigeria uses a simple *plurality system* for presidential elections, meaning that whoever gets the most votes is the winner, even if the amount is less than 50%. Such a system discourages third parties and perpetuates Duverger's Law since voters are encouraged by the system to vote only for one of the two biggest parties or risk having their vote count for nothing. Iran also uses a single-round, winner-take-all system; however, presidential candidates must be approved by the Guardian Council, which tends to limit the scope of debate in Iranian presidential campaigns.

Mexico also uses a single round system, which has proven to be very controversial since Mexico became a three-party state in 2000. The 2012 elections were won by Enrique Peña Nieto, who received only 38% of the vote. Given that Peña was the PRI candidate, a party which has a long history of electoral fraud throughout the 20th century, there were many claims of fraud and calls to move to a two-round system. By contrast, Russia uses a two-round system, in which if no candidate receives more than 50% of the vote in the first round, the second round of voting is held in which only the top two candidates run. This system encourages a multi-party system. However, in the case of Russia, the dominance of Vladimir Putin's United Russia Party has resulted in more of a single-party system.

Parliamentary

The United Kingdom uses a standard first-past-the-post, single-member plurality system to elect seats in the House of Commons. Each seat corresponds to a single district, and whoever gets the most votes wins. Nigeria elects both its Senate and House of Representatives using the same system like the U.K. Parliamentary elections in the other countries are more interesting, as they have adopted the general systems that will be discussed in Section F for local use. For elections in the Iranian Majlis, the country is divided into districts, some of which elects one member and others more than one.

In the single-member districts, if no candidate gets at least one-third of the votes, then the second round of voting is held with only the top two candidates. In the multi-member districts, voters get one vote for every seat available. After the votes are counted, seats are assigned to the candidate with the most votes who received over one-third of the votes. Any seat or seats left unfilled because not enough candidates got more than one-third of the votes go to a second round in which double the number of candidates are allowed to run, compared to seats available; if a district has three seats available, and after the first round of voting one candidate gets more than one-third of the votes, then that candidate gets a seat. The second round of voting would then be held with the top four candidates to fill the remaining two seats.

In China, the national legislative body, called the National People's Congress, is elected through indirect elections. With China's complicated system of six layers of government, only the lowest layer of government, the most local, is directly elected by the people. Those elected to a local council are then given the ability to vote for who should go into the next level of government, all the way up to the national legislative body. Local governments in China are democratically elected, and higher levels are less democratic because lower-level representatives only elect them. Each level of government gets less democratic, with the national legislature being the least democratic and local governments the most.

Mexico also has a unique electoral system which resembles Mixed Member Proportional (MMP) with less proportionality. The lower house, called the Chamber of Deputies, has 300 seats which are filled by single-member plurality districts: whoever gets the most votes wins. The remaining 200 seats are elected by proportional representation and are divided into five constituencies of forty seats each. Since the seats elected by Proportional Representation (PR) are assigned without concern for the overall representation in the legislation, the Mexican system is called parallel PR rather than pure MMP.

The upper house in Mexico, called the Senate, uses a parallel system with a twist. For Senatorial elections, each of the thirty-two Mexican states elects two Senators from the party that wins the most votes. These two senators run as a pair. The party that gets the second-highest number of votes in each state also chooses one candidate out of their pair to send to the Senate. Also, thirty-two seats are elected based on nation-wide proportional representation. If a party gets 50% of the overall votes in the Senate races, that party will get sixteen of the nation-wide PR seats. Russia used a similar parallel system to Mexico until 2005 for the State Duma. Half of the seats were elected in single districts, and half were elected by proportional representation. This changed to just proportional representation in 2005, but it will change back to a parallel system for the 2016 election.

Parliamentary

Referendums are a means for people to vote directly on government policy, instead of simply leaving it up to representatives to decide. The most prominent system of referendums is in Switzerland, where any piece of legislation passed by parliament can be sent to a yes/no referendum if 50,000 signatures are collected. Referendums are a highly contentious topic in democratic theory. Advocates of referendums argue that this is a form of direct democracy that allows people to have a say in legislation without the mediation of representatives, who may ignore the wishes of their constituents.

Washington D.C. canvasser collects signatures for the marijuana-legalizing Initiative 71.

Critics argue that the general population is often uninformed, do not properly deliberate on issues and are easily swayed by the media to vote a certain way. Due to its referendum tradition, Switzerland was one of the last democratic countries to allow women the vote because legislation authorizing it kept getting defeated in referendums. In other countries, referendums are mostly used by authoritarian governments as a means of manufacturing the illusion that the people support the government. Since referendum questions set by the government can be manipulated to generate a certain response, military dictatorships have relied on them as a means to claim democratic legitimacy.

Noncompetitive

Noncompetitive elections can happen within the context of many different electoral systems and political frameworks. Russia is a current example, with the United Russia Party dominating most elections, and PRI in Mexico from 1917 to 2000 is a historical example. Noncompetitive systems can develop due to fraud and coercion (as in

Mexico), one party being genuinely much more popular than others (as in South Africa), or some combination of fraud and popularity (as in Russia).

Noncompetitive elections, even in countries where there is no fraud or coercion, are problematic. Even if the vast majority of the population supports one party, the lack of visible opposition in parliament can lead to complacency and even corruption. In the British system, the second biggest party, even if they were to win only one seat in Parliament and the governing party was to win all the others, is given special privileges as Her Majesty's Official Opposition. Having a structure which provides privileges and benefits to the opposition, no matter how small, ensures that parliament can fulfill its role in keeping the government honest. Also, this structure enables the leader of the opposition a high level of public visibility since they have the right to publicly question the prime minister every day during the Question Period.

Electoral Systems

The type of electoral system a country uses can have a dramatic effect not only on how democratic the country is overall but also in terms of what type of party system is produced. If democracy can be measured by how much political input into government a citizen has, then a wider range of choices during an election means that a country is more democratic. Thus, countries with more political parties are more democratic since voters have more options from which to choose.

The electoral system plays a dramatic role in determining how many political parties are competitive. French political scientist Maurice Duverger found that countries using single-member plurality districts tend to produce two-party systems where only two parties have a reasonable chance of forming the government. This idea is widely cited, and it is called *Duverger's Law*. However, this "law" does not always hold, and it is more of a tendency that can sometimes be offset by the individual circumstances of a country.

In many countries, there have recently been pushes toward electoral reform to rethink how politicians are elected and make the system more democratic. Many countries have used the same electoral system since they were founded, and these countries have not incorporated any new ideas about how elections should work and how to make them more democratic. Usually, these reform efforts are aimed at countries with a single-member plurality system, commonly called first-past-the-post. Reform efforts focus on switching to a form of proportional representation to ensure that parliament will accurately reflect the democratic will of the citizens.

Occupy London sign demanding worldwide democracy and electoral reform.

Studies have shown that countries with a version of proportional representation tend to have more parties represented in parliament, so voting in these countries is more meaningfully democratic. Studies have also shown that countries with some form of proportional representation tend to have a higher voter turnout than those which use first-past-the-post (FPTP). The higher voter turnout is explained by the fact that there are more parties to choose from, decreasing the number of people who choose not to vote because they feel that none of the parties represent them. Proportional representation ensures that everyone's vote counts equally.

Opposition to electoral reform tends to come from the political parties that have been the traditional beneficiaries of the old system. Since changing the electoral system requires the government to initiate the process, it can be very difficult to spur reform when the established parties are satisfied with the status quo and have the most to lose.

Some countries have had a successful reform process and have modernized their electoral systems. New Zealand is the most recent example; it switched from first-past-the-post to a form of mixed-member proportional representation. In countries such as Estonia, reform of the electoral system was driven by new technology. In 2007, Estonia became the first country to allow citizens to vote online. In the recent 2015 parliamentary election, 30% of Estonians cast their ballot online. Increasingly, calls for changing the electoral system are tied to calls to adopt new technologies. These technologies would make voting easier and more accessible to the general public and combat the general decline in voter turnout most countries have experienced over the last fifty years.

Proportional Representation

Proportional representation is not an electoral system in itself but a general concept which applies to some specific implementations. The basic idea behind proportional representation is that parliament should reflect how the population voted and the primary purpose of representation is representing people, not geographic territory. As such, in most proportional systems, the goal is to translate the popular vote to an equivalent number of seats in the legislature as closely as possible. If a party gets 20% of the votes, the principle of proportional representation states that it should have close to 20% of the seats. By comparison, in a *single-member district system*, seats are assigned based on geographic districts rather than votes. The party that gets 20% of the votes in a single-member system could end up with anywhere from 0% to 30% or even 40% of the seats in parliament. By maintaining proportionality, PR systems prevent wild distortions that occur as a result of having a single-member district electoral system.

Proportional representation systems can be divided into three broad categories, each with subcategories and regional differences in implementation. The first is *Party List Proportional Representation* (List PR). In this system, voters are presented with a list of candidates from each political party, and they vote for their preferred party. If the party gets 30% of the votes, they get 30% of the seats. For example, in a 100-seat legislature, this party would get 30 seats, and those seats would be filled by the first thirty candidates on the party list. This is a relatively simple form of proportional representation and tends to work best in small countries without major regional differences, such as Israel and the Netherlands.

German ballot for the 2005 (proportional) federal elections.

There are two primary implementations of List PR, open list and closed list. In a *closed list system*, the order of the candidates on the list is set by the political party, and voters vote for a party. In an *open list system*, the voters can choose the order of the list which determines which candidates will be selected for office. In some open list systems, voters can vote for specific candidates within the party list rather than simply for the party, and the final order of the list is determined by who in each party got the most votes. Sometimes the order of the list is determined in primaries, when either all voters or only those registered with that political party, vote on the order of the party list before the election. Generally, open list systems are considered more democratic because they allow voters to have more input into who gets into parliament. Closed list systems tend to ensure that party elites fill the seats of the legislature rather than people the voters choose.

The second method of proportional representation is *Single Transferable Vote* (STV). This system is less proportional than List PR, but it comes very close to full proportionality. In an STV system, there are very large districts in which anywhere between two to five individuals will be elected, depending on the population. Voters rank the candidates in order of preference, marking 1, 2, 3, etc., rather than a simple X on the ballot. The preferential votes are then tallied and the two to five candidates who are most preferred win a seat. If ten candidates are running, when calculating the preferences, the last place candidate regarding first choice preferences is eliminated each round. So, if only 2% of people vote for a candidate as their first choice, those people's votes will then transfer to whatever candidate they marked as number 2. This process of transferring and eliminating continues until it is determined which candidates are the most preferred by voters.

This system works best in small countries with little geographic and population diversity since to maintain proportionality all districts should have similar populations and elect the same number of members. One of the major benefits is that it allows people to rank candidates rather than simply choosing one. One of the major drawbacks is that it causes candidates from the same party to run against each other. If a district elects four individuals, then a political party will run four candidates in that district with the hope of winning all four seats. Members of the same party will often be campaigning against each other in close races, which can cause internal strife within a political party. Many voters do not see this as a problem, however, as they like to have the ability to pick and choose among both political parties and candidates. Someone may pick three candidates from their preferred party as his or her first three choices and choose a candidate from a different party as their fourth choice if they do not like all the candidates from their preferred party. Currently, this system is used for national elections in Ireland and elections to the upper house in Australia, India, and Pakistan.

The third major proportional system is called *Mixed Member Proportional* (MMP) and is a hybrid of first-past-the-post and List PR. In an MMP system, there are a large number of single-member districts in which whoever gets the most votes wins, but there is also a second set of seats elected based on proportional representation. Voters get two votes; they vote for which local candidate they want to win in their district and which political party they want to win the national election. This empowers voters to be able to vote for a local candidate who is different from the overall political party they support.

Once the winners of the single-member districts are determined, the proportional seats are assigned in such a way that ensures the number of seats each party has in parliament directly corresponds with the party vote totals. If a party has 20% of the seats after the single-member districts are counted but got 30% of the national party vote, they will be assigned enough proportional seats so that their overall total of seats in parliament is 30%. This makes this system exactly proportional.

Voters like this system because it allows them to maintain their local regional representative while also having the benefits of proportional representation. Voters can also vote for exceptional local candidates who may not be members of their preferred party and still vote for their preferred party to win the national election. This has the effect of removing the problem of safe seats. A safe seat is a district that always votes for a certain party, which allows the party to run a candidate who is a member of the party elite or chosen by them, even if they are locally unpopular.

In an MMP system, all local candidates must be popular in their district, or they will not win, even if they represent the most popular overall party. Most political scientists consider MMP to be the best electoral system for large countries with a diverse population and geography. MMP combines both the regional representation of first-past-the-post systems and the proportionality of PR systems. In this sense, it is the best of both worlds. Currently, MMP is used in Germany, New Zealand, Hungary, Venezuela, and Russia, among others. It is also the main proposed electoral system for Canada, should it switch away from FPTP, and for Thailand, should the military restore democracy.

Single-Member District

Single-member district systems are the oldest and least sophisticated electoral systems. This system represents the geographic territory in the legislature, rather than people, and it tends to result in a major imbalance between how people vote and how many seats a party gets in parliament. The most common single-member district system is called *first-past-the-post* (FPTP), in which whoever gets the most votes in a district wins that seat. This system is designed for a situation in which there are only two parties, and it ensures that the majority party will win the seat. Once more than two parties are running for a seat the system breaks down entirely, and the winner of a seat may only get 30% of the votes in a district.

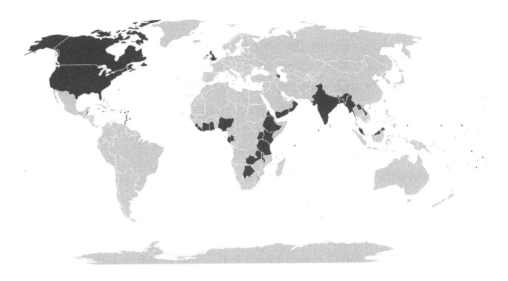

Nations that use first-past-the-post electoral systems (black).

In a situation with five competitive parties (such as in the 2015 elections in Canada), certain candidates could win a seat with the support of just 25% of the votes in the district. In the Canadian example, a candidate was elected with just over 25% because there were four other strong candidates in the district, each of whom got close to 20%. Many people argued that this was a distortion of the will of the people since 75% of the people in that district did not vote for the eventual winner. They argue that democracy is supposed to mean majority wins, which was not the case with this FPTP electoral system.

FPTP can introduce very large distortions on the national level when it is much more important for political parties to concentrate on appealing to voters in specific regions rather than appealing to people across the whole country. An example of such a distortion was the 2015 national election in the United Kingdom, conducted using an FPTP system. The Conservatives won a majority government, so they had more than half of the seats in Parliament with just 36.8% of the votes. The vast majority voted for other parties, but because of the electoral system's lack of proportionality, the party with only minority support formed the government and could pass legislation unopposed. The results were even more distorted for the other, smaller parties running. The U.K. Independence Party (UKIP) got 12% of the votes but only won a single seat, which is 0.15% of the seats in Parliament.

By contrast, the Scottish National Party, which received 4.7% of the popular vote, ended up with 56 seats for 8.6% of the seats in Parliament. Due to this broken electoral system, a party which got more than double the votes of another party ends up with 50 times fewer seats in Parliament. Political scientists have calculated that under an FPTP system, a party which receives 49% of the votes in an election could end up with zero seats in Parliament. In the same scenario, two other parties which get 25% and 26% each could end up splitting the rest of the seats. An FPTP system could lead to a majority government supported by only 26% of the population while a party with almost 50% support could get no representation in Parliament whatsoever. For reasons such as this, there are strong movements toward electoral reform in most countries still using the FPTP system.

A variation of the single-member district system is called *Alternative Vote* (AV) or, less commonly, instant runoff voting. This system is like FPTP except voters rank the candidates in order of preference instead of voting for a single candidate. AV has the advantage over FPTP in that it corrects the problem of distortions at the local level. Consider the example from Canada above where a candidate wins a local election with just 25% of the votes.

In an AV system, the votes of eliminated candidates would transfer to the second choices of those voters, ensuring that the most preferred candidate won the district. For example, if there were three liberal parties and one conservative party, under FPTP, the conservative would win if the conservative party got 25% of the vote and the liberal parties only got 23% each. This would be a problem because even though the conservative got the most votes, the vast majority of voters would likely prefer one of the three liberals to the conservative. By using AV, a district can ensure that a candidate does not win simply because of vote-splitting among the opposition. AV fixes the problems with FPTP at the local level, but it still does not address the national distortions that would arise, such as with the U.K. example above. For this reason, MMP or STV are considered superior systems by most political scientists. Today, Australia is one of the few countries that use AV, as it is used in their lower house elections.

Political Parties

The next section will deal with political party systems in a general sense so that this section will look at the framework of parties in each of the six countries. China is generally considered a one-party system because the Communist Party dominates the entire political landscape. Formally, however, China allows multiple political parties and independent candidates, as long as they join the ruling coalition headed by the Communist Party. In this sense, China has multiple parties without any opposition parties. This is unusual because separate political parties are often oppositional in nature.

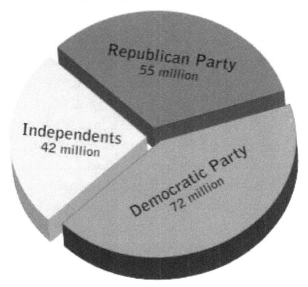

Americans' affiliation by political party circa 2004.

An analogy can be made using the Tea Party and the Republican Party in the United States. Although the Tea Party is not a formal party, it exists as a subset of the Republican Party with slightly different views on issues. This is how the party system works in China; smaller parties are permitted so long as they are broadly subservient to and aligned with the Communist Party. Independents are also permitted to run if they join the Communist Party-led United Front. Parties unwilling to join the National Front or considered by the Communist Party as too deviant to be allowed to join the National Front are generally suppressed, and their activists can be jailed. Exceptions are Macau and Hong Kong, former colonial possessions of Portugal and the U.K. Now that these areas are once again part of China, the central government allows them more leeway for multiple parties because both of these colonies have a long history of more open party systems.

The United Kingdom is a multi-party system with two dominant parties. The Conservative Party is the current governing party and has traditionally alternated in power with the Labour Party. The Conservatives remain conservative in their ideology, but Labour's ideology has been changing in recent years. Traditionally, it was a left-wing social democratic party that represented the working class. In the late 1990s, party leader Tony Blair led the party to jump to the right of the economic spectrum by adopting neoliberalism. Recently, the party has elected a socialist as a leader and seems likely to jump back to the left for the next election. Labour became the primary opposition to the Conservatives in the 1920s when the British party system undertook a major change.

Before the 1920s, the Liberal Party was the main opponent that rotated power with the Conservatives. Since this time, the Liberals, who became the Liberal Democrats in 1988 when they merged with the Social Democratic Party, have become an outsider third party that is competitive but has little chance at winning government. This was an interesting realignment. Labour was more left-wing, with the Liberals (and later, Liberal Democrats) as centrists and the Conservatives on the right. With Labour changing ideology in the 1990s, the Liberal Democrats (as a centrist party) became the most left-wing party. All of these major changes in the party system were confusing to voters, as many people had always voted for the same party regardless of its changes in ideology. The transformation of the party system in the 1990s also led to the creation of two parties on the far right, the British National Party (BNP) and the U.K. Independence Party. While the BNP was short-lived, UKIP has become a national party, winning more than 10% of the votes.

The U.K. is also interesting because of the power of regional parties that only run candidates in certain areas. The Scottish National Party only runs candidates in Scotland and generally seeks to represent Scottish interests in the national parliament. Wales and Northern Ireland have similar regional parties as well. Due to their ability to concentrate their votes in a few districts, these regional parties win disproportionate numbers of seats in Parliament even though their popular vote totals are extremely low.

In the 2015 election, another shakeup of the party system occurred. The Scottish National Party won more seats than the Liberal Democrats, making them the third place party. Part of the reason was that voters were angry at the Liberal Democrats for forming a coalition government with the Conservatives. Most people thought the Liberal Democrats got nothing from this coalition. Usually, in a coalition government, which happens when one party does not control more than 50% of Parliament, the smaller party is given concessions in exchange for supporting the government. These concessions are usually in a few key policy areas and a few key minister positions.

First Minister of Scotland Nicola Sturgeon is the leader of the Scottish National Party.

In Iran, there is a multitude of parties who are broadly grouped into two coalitions: the Conservative Alliance and the Reform Alliance. Since all parties and candidates require approval from the Guardian Council, all parties in Iran profess to be Islamist in nature. However, reformers seek to loosen the control of religion and liberalize Iranian society. The Green Movement protests shook Iran after the 2009 presidential election, which many believed the Reform candidate lost due to electoral fraud. In 2010 the Guardian Council banned all Reform candidates and parties, claiming they are foreign spies.

As a result of this 2010 decision, the Reform movement is attempting to remake itself as the Moderate movement. It is seeking to re-establish a political party capable of competing in elections approved by the Guardian Council. As a result of banning the Reformers, the 2013 presidential election was easily won by Hassan Rouhani, leader of the Moderation and Development Party. Rouhani's party promotes a centrist and moderate approach that opposes both the reform movement and the hardline conservatives, such as former president Mahmoud Ahmadinejad.

President Rouhani has initiated some major shifts in Iranian foreign policy, such as seeking to work with the United States rather than demonizing it. The Iranian party system is in constant turmoil due to the Guardian Council frequently stepping in and banning parties. This causes internal recompositions of parties as supporters try to set up a new party that aligns with their thinking. As a result, Iranian policy tends to undergo dramatic shifts. Elections in Iran are extremely important, even if the theocratic Guardian Council tightly controls them.

President Mohammad Khatami, who was in power from 2001 to 2005, was a Reformist; the Reformist party is now banned. The election of Ahmadinejad after him was a sweeping change to a more conservative Iran. The president before Khatami was Akbar Hashemi Rafsanjani, who was part of the Conservative Alliance, but he has since been banned from all political activity in Iran for supporting the protesters in 2009. Iran's political situation is extremely complicated and constantly changing.

Mexico is now a multi-party system, having made the transition away from being a dominant party system in 2000. Mexico is currently ruled by PRI, which is the traditionally dominant party in Mexican politics. PRI is a centrist party whose ideology is best described as corporatism. They seek social, political and economic harmony by trying to combine labor, corporations and the state into one institutional unit. The second party is PRD, a moderate leftist party that endorses social democracy. PRD's main concern tends to be ensuring the Mexican elections are fair and democratic; they have been strong critics of the way elections have been conducted, even after the 2000 transition to competitive multi-party elections. The third party is now PAN, a conservative party that first broke the PRI's control of Mexican politics by getting elected in 2000. PAN began as a pro-democracy party but, unlike the PRD, they believed that winning the 2000 election meant democracy had been achieved, and PAN began to focus on right-wing economic policy.

Logos for Mexico's Institutional Revolutionary Party (PRI), National Action Party (PAN) and Party of the Democratic Revolution (PRD).

Two other significant parties exist in Mexico: the Ecologist Green Party and the New Alliance Party. The Ecologist Green Party tends not to run its own candidate for president and instead endorses one of the candidates from the three major parties. It only runs for seats in the legislature. The Ecologist Green Party is somewhat unique in that it is a right-wing environmentalist party which was first aligned with PAN and now with PRI. The New Alliance Party won 2% of the votes in the 2012 Presidential Election, and it is a centrist party that split from PRI in 2005. Having a largely similar ideology to PRI, New Alliance's ten Deputies and one Senator tend to be informally aligned with PRI.

Nigeria is largely a two-party system, although a plethora of small parties exist and run candidates that get little to no support. The 2015 election was remarkable for Nigeria because it was the first time power transferred from one party to another through an election. Previously, all such transitions were a result of military coup d'états. The current governing party is the All Progressives Congress (APC), which is a "big tent" party. It seeks to incorporate a large number of differing political views into its platform. As a result, the APC tends to support center-left economic positions, favors government regulation of the economy and even supports some social democratic positions. It also endorses right-wing positions on social issues, such as strong opposition to gay rights and support for the traditional influence of religion.

In particular, the APC is supportive of weak federalism, which grants strong autonomy to the northern states and allows them to implement Sharia law. Like most "big tent" parties, the APC is full of strange alliances; it wins support from religious fundamentalist Muslims in the North who support APC's social conservativism as well as support from the Yoruba people in the South who support left-wing economics. The main opposition is the People's Democratic Party, which is also socially conservative and favors the authority of religion. However, it takes right-wing neoliberal economic positions. Since both parties are very socially conservative (although Christians tend to favor the PDP and Muslims the APC), their main difference is on economic issues.

Russia is a dominant-party system. Vladimir Putin's United Russia easily wins elections, and the opposition parties do not have a realistic chance of winning in the near future. Given that Russia is a relatively new democracy, having held its first open election in 1991, the party system is still developing. In addition to United Russia, there are three other parties with seats in the State Duma who ran candidates for the 2012 Presidential Election. United Russia was only created in 2001 (Putin originally ran as an independent) but has quickly become dominant. The party tends not to run on a platform and instead tries to promote a big tent image where any patriotic Russian is welcome. Practically speaking, it combines centrist economics with social and political conservatism. The party officially rejects both right-wing and left-wing ideologies and sees itself as a pragmatic centrist party.

United Russia also claims to be rooted in the traditional authority structure of Russia, claiming its lineage to both the Tsarist era and the Soviet era. There are questions about whether United Russia can last as a political party without Vladimir Putin as its charismatic leader. Since the party has no real platform or ideology to tie its supporters together, it tends to rely on the personal appeal of Putin simply. If Putin should retire from politics, the party could split up into rival factions and throw the party system of Russia into disarray.

The three smaller parties are much less popular than United Russia. Before the 2011 legislative elections, Putin changed the rules and made it harder for parties other than United Russia to register for elections. After severe criticism, these new restrictions have been dropped for the 2016 elections. Currently, the second biggest party in Russia is the Communist Party, receiving 17% in the 2012 presidential election and 11% in the 2011 legislative elections. The Communist Party is a left-wing party that seeks to create a modernized version of socialism, rather than return Russia to the Soviet Union days. It promotes a mixed economy that allows small businesses to flourish, while also seeking to re-nationalize major industries.

A Communist Party of the Russian Federation rally in Moscow.

The Communist Party is not the same as the one that ruled Russia in the Soviet era (former President Boris Yeltsin banned that party), but it is an immediate successor. Just Russia is another left-wing party. At one point it attempted to merge with the Communists, but it was rejected. Just Russia tends to consider itself something of moral conscience to Vladimir Putin. While it has many times expressed support for Putin's policies, the party believes Russia should have more internal criticism, and it seeks to position itself as a sympathetic critic of Putin. The party is fairly small, usually winning 5% to 13% of the votes.

The fourth party is the Liberal Democratic Party of Russia (LDPR), which despite its name is a nationalist far-right party with post-fascist tendencies. The party tends to promote an imperialist foreign policy and authoritarian political positions. The party received 22% of the votes in the 1993 Duma elections, giving it the most seats of any party, albeit far short of a majority. Its electoral fortunes have since declined, receiving 11% in 2011 and only 4% in 2012.

Party Systems

The concept of a party system refers to the relative influence of certain arrangements of political parties within a country. The concept is used comparatively, both internally and across country borders. As every country has had its history and evolution of different party systems, it can be difficult to speak of party systems as a general concept. However, five basic types are identifiable. A *dominant-party system* is when a single party easily wins all elections, and there is no reasonable prospect of that party being defeated in the near future. Examples include Russia and South Africa.

A *non-partisan party system* is when there are elections without political parties. This type of party system is very rare. Representative government becomes nearly impossible without some form of party allegiance on which voters can decide which platform, rather than which candidate, to vote for. Some very small countries in the South Pacific such as Tuvalu and Palau use non-partisan systems. However, given the exceedingly small population and a limited number of representatives, these systems are more like one-person political parties. Canadian municipal elections are nominally non-partisan, but in reality, candidates run either as unofficial members of a party that operates at the provincial or national level or as part of political alliances that form de facto political parties.

The other three general classifications of party systems relate to the number of competitive parties. A *one-party system*, such as in China, ensures that only a single party is represented in government. A *two-party system*, such as in the United States, is a system where two parties have a realistic chance of winning and tend to alternate control of the government.

A *multi-party system*, such as in Mexico, is when three or more parties have a competitive chance of winning government. In some cases, there are a number of competitive parties, but only two ever form a government. The U.K. is an example of this. Labour and the Conservatives are the only two parties who have formed governments, but the Liberal Democrats are competitive players who win a significant number of seats. Situations like this are harder to classify, and they are a reason why the analysis of party systems tends to focus more on analyzing specific cases and less on these five general categories.

Leadership and Elite Recruitment

In more democratic countries, leadership and recruitment into the elite is usually a result of volunteer activism within a party and the money to influence the party establishment. Despite being democratic, money tends to be the dominant factor regarding who rises to senior positions of party leadership. When outsiders can penetrate this framework of elite recruitment, there is often a realignment in the party system. President Eisenhower's winning the 1952 general election is regarded as the last time a significant Washington, D.C. and party outsider secured the White House. Eisenhower, having never held elected office, was extremely hesitant to announce his candidacy. Widespread public adoration and the grassroots Draft Eisenhower movement eventually persuaded him, however. When Eisenhower did successfully win the Republican primary and secured the nomination, he named Richard Nixon as his running mate to appease the Old Guard of the GOP and gain the party's further support.

Dwight D. "Ike" Eisenhower is campaigning in Baltimore, Maryland.

A similar event occurred in Canada in the 1990s. The Conservative Party got taken over by traditional outsiders who completely rearranged the party's ideology and elite recruitment mechanisms, leading to a shakeup of the structure of party politics in Canada.

In less democratic systems, elite recruitment tends to occur through family and traditional ties. In China, for example, a vast network of connections (often through family) to the senior ranks of the Communist Party is needed to get nominated and internally elected. An enthusiastic peasant who devotes his life to the cause of the Communist Party would be unlikely to move up beyond the lower level, not for lack of money but a lack of family ties and traditional connections to the network of ruling authority. In both systems, there are major obstacles for an ordinary person who does not have the money or connections to become important in politics.

Interest Groups and Interest Group Systems

Interest groups and lobbying largely work similarly across the world. The major difference is the degree to which lobbying, in general, is tolerated. In countries such as the U.K. and Mexico, where the government's democratic legitimacy rests on appealing to the people for support, lobbying efforts are extremely influential. In countries with more authoritarian governments, lobby groups are much less powerful because the government is uninterested in what citizens have to say. The notable exception is through corruption. While it may be difficult to get Vladimir Putin's or Xi Jinping's ear, both countries have been accused of corruption since officials can be bribed. Corruption is a big issue in Nigeria as well, especially since many lower-level politicians and bureaucrats are relatively poor and can often be more tempted with bribery.

Bureaucracies

Some countries tend to rely more on government power and others on bureaucratic expertise. China, for example, is an extremely bureaucratic country where technocrats have a large measure of authority. A *technocrat* is an appointed official in the bureaucracy capable of making major decisions and who also has technical expertise. Many supranational economic organizations, such as the IMF or the EU are run by technocrats whose lack of democratic legitimacy is made up for by their legitimacy as experts in their field. Unlike the U.K., China values expertise and technocracy over democracy, believing that experts are better able to make decisions than representatives of the people.

By contrast, Russia and Nigeria tend to have somewhat corrupt bureaucracies where bureaucrats tend to demand something in exchange for the provision of state services; rather than valuing expertise, money becomes the primary motivator. Since bureaucrats are paid relatively low salaries in these two countries, corruption becomes more attractive. One of the primary means to eliminate such bureaucratic corruption is by increasing the salary of civil servants. If people can make a good living honestly doing their job, they will be less tempted by corruption.

Bribery and interest groups can influence policy decisions that run contrary to public opinion.

The U.K. has a unique bureaucratic creation called a *Quango*, which stands for quasi-autonomous non-governmental organization. Such bureaucratic organizations operate at arm's length from the government and are more independent in their decision making. While the Ministry of Defense, for example, has to follow the government's orders, a Quango in the U.K., such as the Forestry Commission, is largely free to make its policy on forestry-related issues. At the same time, if the Forestry Commission did something extreme, the government would be able to step in and stop them.

Iran also has unique semi-bureaucratic institutions, called *bonyads*, which are charitable trusts that distribute religiously donated money to various groups and run various social programs. Since the government does not directly control these programs, it leads to inefficient funding patterns and rampant corruption. Many critics in Iran claim the bonyads are a failure at providing services to the poor. The government tends to underfund social programs, claiming the bonyads will take care of it.

Military and Other Coercive Institutions

Military involvement in government tends to be viewed as radically anti-democratic, and Nigeria provides a classic example due to the military overthrowing the government multiple times. For the most part, this is true. However, in some rare cases, the military has overthrown elected governments in the name of preserving democracy. This is a somewhat self-defeating claim, as overthrowing democracy in the name of democracy is a contradiction, but sometimes anti-democratic political parties get elected. In 1991 in Algeria, after Islamists won the national election and declared their intention to cancel democracy and rule as a dictatorship, they were overthrown by the military. The military, however, did not restore democracy. Instead, it held onto power in the resulting civil war. The same situation happened in 2013 in Egypt. The military overthrew the democratically elected Islamists, arguing they were a threat to long-term democracy.

One of the key indicators comparative political scientists use to determine the role of the military in government is its relation to the police. If the military is subservient to the state, it should be used to protect the country from external threats, whether a foreign invasion or some national disaster. On the other hand, police are meant to protect the people and the state internally. When a state uses the military against the people, it is considered military intervention in politics. This demonstrates that the government has lost power and is resorting to extreme measures. The temptation to use the military on domestic dissenters must always be resisted. Otherwise democracy becomes endangered due to the politicized role of the military. An example of this is the massacre in Tiananmen Square in China in 1989. The Chinese government sent the military in, including tanks, to break up a protest by students demanding a more democratic version of communism.

While in most states the military is meant to be commanded by and subservient to the government, Iran has a unique relationship between government and the military. In Iran, the military is commanded by the Supreme Leader and the Guardian Council, which leaves the president with no independent ability to mobilize the armed forces. This arrangement is a double-edged sword: while it prevents an elected government from mobilizing the military to put down the opposition and retain control of the state, it also enables the Supreme Leader to mobilize the military against the government in a legal manner, undermining the subordination of the military to government.

Immigrant textile workers on strike in Lawrence, Massachusetts are surrounded by mobilized National Guardsmen with fixed bayonets.

Judiciaries

Judiciaries can serve different purposes depending on the country. In places with standards of civil rights, the judiciary exists to uphold the rights of citizens against the government. By contrast, in situations dominated by customary or religious law, the judiciary's primary concern may be protecting the status of the tribal or cultural group or upholding the dominance of religion. Depending on different political views, the judiciary can be a source of protection against government abuse or a source of oppression.

Degrees of Autonomy

One of the primary considerations in the comparative study of judiciaries is how independent it is from the government. If the judiciary's job is to uphold the law, meaning it may have to overrule the government, it must be independent of the government. In the case of China, the judiciary is largely controlled by the Communist Party and is extremely unlikely ever to rule that the government has violated the constitution. In Mexico, the court system is independent of the government, but Supreme Court justices are appointed by the president, giving them a political taint which may make them less likely to rule against the person who gave them their job.

Due to the principle of the supremacy of Parliament, the United Kingdom did not have a Supreme Court system until 2009. Unlike Mexico and the United States, Supreme Court judges in the United Kingdom and Canada are appointed by a committee of legal experts and are not politically aligned. In the case of Canada, this has led to Supreme Court justices actively rebuffing government legislation that violates the constitution in an even-handed manner, regardless of which political party is in power. In Iran, the judiciary exists to uphold Islamic law and is independent of the elected government but subservient to the Supreme Leader and Guardian Council. Russia is somewhat in between Mexico's relative autonomy and China's lack of autonomy. While Russian courts are supposed to be independent, in practice they are large instruments of the government. There is very little legal precedent in Russia given its recent political transformations.

Judicial Review

Due to the principle of parliamentary supremacy, the newly created British Supreme Court is somewhat limited in its ability to review legislation. It is mainly tasked with upholding human rights and resolving matters in a dispute related to the 1999 devolution of powers. The British Supreme Court can also rule that legislation passed by Parliament violates the EU's human rights declarations, but it lacks the authority to enforce EU law on Parliament. Instead, Parliament is required to simply review the legislation; final authority is left in the hands of the U.K. Parliament.

While the EU does not have a court that can overrule local governments, the European Convention on Human Rights (ECHR) does function as a court system that allows individuals to bring cases to the ECHR against a member state of the EU. The ECHR can force a state to pay the penalty in the event an individual's rights are found to have been violated, and it has the power to extract this payment from a state. This compromise system allows for compensating individuals whose rights have been violated without infringing on state sovereignty by forcing member states to change their laws.

Types of Law

There are four predominant types of legal systems around the world: civil, common, customary and religious law. *Civil law* is based on a framework of codified laws passed by the government which serves as the primary source of law. *Common law* relies on the precedent established by judges. *Customary law* is based on the traditions of a community. *Religious law* is derived from the principles set out in holy books. Common law originated in the U.K., and it is used primarily in countries originally colonized by the U.K., such as the U.S., Canada, Australia, and New Zealand. Civil law dates back to the ancient Romans in tradition and is the predominant system in Latin America, Europe, and Russia. China uses a combination of civil law and customary law. Nigeria uses a combination of religious law in the northern Muslim areas, customary law in certain parts of the country and common law as a general framework. Iran uses religious law, in particular, Islamic Sharia.

Chapter 4

Citizens, Society, and the State

Politics is not confined to the internal workings or the institutional underpinnings of states alone but rather hinges on the interactions between state and society. Through featured case studies, it is explored how certain kinds of cleavages, such as ethnicity, religion or class, become politically relevant. Some regimes, like those in China and Iran, have formal arrangements for representing social groups such as ethnic or religious minorities. A country's political patterns are influenced by the characteristics and demands of its population. Institutions can either ameliorate or exacerbate cleavages in society.

This chapter, by featuring conceptual and country-specific analysis, endeavors to impart an understanding of civil society both conceptually and within countries to provide useful tools to explore how state power is mediated and how the power of citizens can be enhanced. Much of politics is affected by the extent and nature of citizen organizations independent of the state. Interest groups and social networks can assist in the generation of social capital and mobilize political forces. The interaction between the type of regime and these patterns in civil society is often crucial. The range of ways that a citizenry can act politically, through both traditional means such as voting and more forceful political action (e.g., strikes, insurgencies), is investigated. Examples of citizenry agitation for empowerment can range from Iran's 1979 revolution to China's 1989 Tiananmen crisis to Mexico's 1994 Chiapas revolt. The attention is also paid to how much of politics is affected by the extent and nature of citizen organizations independent of the state, including interest groups and social networks that assist in the generation of social capital and mobilize political forces. A crucial factor is often the interaction between the type of regime and existing patterns in civil society. How the emergence of global civil society, such as transnational networks of human rights and environmental groups, exerts a significant effect on government-citizen relations is also covered.

Discussions on how the media plays an important part both in the national and global context are included with special attention paid to the relationships between the various media and the state as well as the techniques in which it can influence and shape public perceptions, beliefs, and practices.

As discussed, citizens participate in politics in a variety of ways. A significant form of political behavior in most societies is political participation. Concept definitions and descriptions for how political participation can either support or undermine a political system are given. This participation can further be either voluntary or coerced, as evidenced in examples of the studied countries. Extreme participation, such as regime overthrow, is also parsed.

Further, this chapter distinguished between individual and group forms of participation. In political science, citizen participation is often framed by social movements as well as by more organized interest groups. Exampled contemporary social movements among the studied countries — ranging from anti-globalization to environmental issues, civil rights, and enfranchisement claims — are included to highlight the specific forms and particular methods employed. Lastly, connections are established linking interactions and collaborations among social movements, interest groups, and elected representatives.

Cleavages and Politics

While each country will have its specific cleavages in a society that divide people up into different groups, there are some common cleavages that exist in many countries. These are ethnic, racial, class, gender, religious and regional cleavages which can pit people within a country against each other or can generate strength in diversity, depending on the context. All of these cleavages constitute social identities which people may adopt strongly or may feel have little to do with them personally.

The political theorist Benedict Anderson influentially described social identity cleavages as imagined communities. Unlike an actual community, which is based on shared everyday interaction between people, such as students and teachers in a school or the neighbors who live on the same street, an imagined community is a wider group that people perceive themselves to be a part of. Imagined communities are groupings in which people believe they have an identity similar to others and feel a kinship bond with many whom they have never met.

The most common imagined community is that of nationality. Someone who lives in Alaska along the Canadian border lives in closer proximity to Canadians than they do to the rest of the United States, but they imagine themselves as Americans because Alaska is part of the U.S. This view of themselves means they are likely to feel they have more in common with someone in southern California than they do with a Canadian who lives a few miles away from them.

These imagined communities can have extraordinary power in influencing the political situation of a country or countries. They shape how people view themselves and thus maintain the power of the state. The U.S. government would have serious troubles if everyone in Alaska began to identify as Canadians socially. There might be separatist movements or pushes to make Alaska a Canadian province. There could even be violence between Alaskans who saw themselves as Canadians and those who viewed themselves as Americans. While this seems far-fetched with regard to Alaska, the power of huge numbers of people self-identifying with an imagined community creates just these sorts of tensions and problems around the world. The state has a vested interest in attempting to manage the imagined communities within its borders to keep citizens loyal to the state and keep other social cleavages under control. By looking at specific cleavages, how countries have attempted to create formal institutions to try to keep these tensions under control and how states respond to and create social divisions in the population will be examined.

Eleventh Night Protestant revelers in Newtownabbey, Northern Ireland signify their allegiance to the United Kingdom by burning a Republic of Ireland flag on a bonfire.

Ethnic

After the end of the Cold War, the idea of ethnic identification became extremely prominent. During the Cold War, the primary form of imagined community was nationality, which was underpinned by identification with either communism or capitalism. During this era, people were less concerned about identifying with cultural or ancestral groups that formed the basis of the imagined community of ethnicity and instead adopted more tangible identifications. After the end of the Cold War, the old social identifications based on political ideology began to break down, and people increasingly sought other forms of kinship bond. This led to the idea of ethnicity as an important imagined community. Ethnicity can be defined as an imagined community based on the idea of a shared past. This shared past need not be real and in many cases is essentially invented. However, adherents to the social identity of ethnicity argue that belonging to the community is inherited at birth. People claim any number of traits as the basis of ethnicity, ranging from religion to culture to tribal ancestry.

Ethnicity has recently been grounds for some violent cleavages and conflicts, even though it is an entirely human construct. Given how amorphous the concept of ethnicity is, it is often used as a catch-all term to try to establish boundaries between one's group and other social groups; it is often simply a means to attempt to inculcate religious-group identification as something one is born with. Ethnicity becomes a means to persecute groups of people based on their common religious grouping, even if an individual is not a member of that religion or feels no allegiance to it. An imagined community, such as ethnicity, can often be imposed upon people, not as a means of self-identification but as a way others can persecute a group of people who otherwise may seem to have little in common.

A Mexican Zapatista rebel leader is fighting for the rights
of indigenous peoples of Mexico in the Chiapas conflict.

Ethnicity as a means of persecution was used in Bhutan in 1990 when the government expelled Hindus from the country in an attempt to maintain Buddhism as the dominant state religion. In the former Yugoslavia, religion also transformed into ethnicity as it became a means for different groups to persecute and engage in violence against others, even if they were not religious. In many cases, such as in Bhutan and the former Yugoslavia, groups do not want to openly acknowledge that religion is at the core of their differences and the ensuing violence because they wish to maintain the idea that religion brings peace. "Ethnicity" becomes a kind of codeword which is used to mean religious groups.

Nigeria is often cited as an example of ethnic diversity and ethnic tensions. However, the majority of the tensions there are along religious lines—between the Muslims in the North and the Christians in the South. The various ethnic groups in Nigeria, which are identified based on tribal ancestry, often are not a strong source of social identity. The Yoruba, for example, form an ethnic group based on a shared language, yet they have abandoned their traditional religions in favor of a mix of Christianity and Islam. In the Nigerian context, the imagined community bond of ethnicity is not enough to unite people across religious lines; often violence between Muslims and Christians involves members of the same Yoruba ethnic group.

Russia and China have similar issues which are often framed in terms of ethnic conflict but are religious in nature. In Russia, there are many different groups with different cultural heritages and even different physical features. However, the main sources of "ethnic" tension tend to be between groups that identify based on religion. In China, the main sources of "ethnic" tension are in Tibet and Xinjiang, prominent enclaves of Buddhists and Muslims, respectively, which constitute the most conspicuous cleavages. Because "ethnicity" is a term which is used to paper over religious divisions, many political scientists view it as a problematic category for comparative purposes because it is broad and lacks defining characteristics that would apply to all members of an "ethnic" group.

Racial

Unlike ethnicity, race as an imagined community has much more specific content, in that it is related to human physical features, most prominently skin color. While race is still an imagined community because there is no scientific reason to link one's skin color to one's social attitudes, it can be a powerful identifier that can create major problems of discrimination. While countries like the United States have a long history of racial divisions dating back to the days of slavery, the United Kingdom's history of racial tensions is much more varied.

As a colonial empire, the U.K. expanded its political control across many parts of the world and brought with it first a system of slavery, as was seen in the pre-independence United States and throughout the Caribbean, and then the long-persisting colonial attitude of the racial superiority of the white Englishman in later colonization waves in India and Africa. Given these colonial possessions, most of the racial tensions were in colonized areas rather than at home in the U.K., thus allowing the U.K. to avoid many of the problems of the U.S. related to the post-slavery era.

After decolonization, however, many people in formerly colonized countries, such as India, Pakistan, and Nigeria, decided to move to the U.K. for a better life after learning English in colonial schools and becoming immersed in British culture. Racial tensions in the U.K. are a much more modern phenomenon associated with the wave of post-colonial immigration into the U.K. that created a much more racially diverse society.

In the early 1900s, the U.K. first started to restrict immigration from former colonial possessions. This resulted in an upsurge of hostility toward immigrants and led to the country's first race-based riots in 1919. The problem emerged again in the 1980s as black Britons of Caribbean and African descent faced disproportionate levels of poverty and police harassment. This led to tensions between blacks and whites, as well as between these two groups and British-Asians (predominantly Indian and Pakistani in origin). The U.K. is becoming increasingly racially segregated as housing patterns show evidence that people of the similar ancestral racial background are moving to areas dominated by their racial group. A similar situation exists in France. People of Arab origin from France's former colonial possessions in North Africa tend to live in enclaves in the suburbs of major cities and are not well integrated into the rest of French society. This perpetuates the idea that these people are outsiders and leads to discrimination.

In the last ten years, both the U.K. and France have seen major outbursts of violent riots by racialized groups who have sought to protest police discrimination. Part of the reason these protests turn into riots with non-political outcomes, such as looting and destruction of property in one's community, is that these groups lack a political voice to articulate their problems. Instead, the U.K. and France now have significant political parties which argue that all immigration should be stopped and sometimes even advocate deporting racial minorities.

Cars burned in Liverpool during the 2011 England riots, which was incited by racial tensions triggered by the police shooting of Mark Duggan, a member of the Black community.

In the case of the U.K. and France, racial identifications became a problem for the state as it caused tension and even violence among its citizens. In the U.K., researchers have noticed that parents will tend to send their children to schools in which the majority of the students are of the same race. While this racial segregation is not legally enforced as it once was in the United States, many in the U.K. advocate American-style policies to integrate schools so that students can interact with those from a variety of races on a daily basis, allowing cross-racial and cross-cultural friendships to be made among students who help tear down racial prejudices. So far, there has been no action from the U.K. government, and many argue that the state has a material interest in maintaining racial division in the U.K. as a form of economic ideology; if people blame all their problems on people of another race, then they are less likely to blame the government or the economic system. Sometimes states may seek to play up racial cleavages if they think they can benefit from them; at other times they may view the potential for violence as something that needs to be suppressed since it may make everyday life intolerable.

Its colonial past shapes the Mexican view of race. Unlike in North America, where the British sought to wipe out the indigenous people, Spanish colonists sought to convert the indigenous people to Christianity. This created a situation where instead of treating the native people as hostile nations to conquer, the Spanish colonists viewed them as colonized people to rule over and convert. Over time, there was much blending between the native Aztec and Mayan groups and the Spanish colonizers, which led to a three-level racial system with the rulers being European Spanish, the middle group being the Mestizos, people of mixed indigenous and European blood, and the indigenous people at the bottom. These three racial groups stratified into a caste system, with the white European Spanish as the wealthiest and as political elites, with the Mestizo in the middle, and the indigenous people as the poorest. Over time, the majority of Mexicans today are Mestizo, but there are still prejudices which lead many people to believe that someone with lighter skin is more socially and politically important than someone with darker skin.

Class

Class is perhaps the oldest and most prominent political cleavage. In its most basic form, economic class is the division between the rich and poor, with the poor always constituting a large majority and the rich a small minority. Political divisions in every country have some element of class division, and it is always a concern in every country whether the government is thought to be working in the interests of the poor or the rich. In ancient Greece, the philosopher Aristotle used class as a basis of classifying regimes. Since the poor were always in the majority, Aristotle said that democracy as majority rule was inherently rule by the poor. Since the rich are always a minority, rule by the few meant an oligarchy. Class has continued to be the basis of different forms of government; in the Middle Ages, feudalistic governments put landowners in direct political control over the serfs, people who worked the land that they did not own. The return to democracy in the modern era was meant to once again empower the many (therefore, the poor) with political power. The famous German political philosopher Karl Marx argued that even in modern countries with elected governments, these governments still acted on behalf of the rich and at the expense of the poor majority.

Marx believed that eventually the poor would rise and overthrow the class system, creating a society without class divisions. The idea of eliminating all class divisions is somewhat utopian, and it is a common theme in political philosophy, not just among Marxists but among liberal and conservative thinkers as well. In contemporary politics, the idea of the middle class is often used to refer to the majority of the population, with the concomitant assumption that class divisions are no longer a serious issue because divisions are not so pronounced with the majority in the middle. For the most part, when politicians today refer to "the middle class" they are referring to middle income, and the idea that very few people are poor and very few people are rich, with most falling in the middle in terms of how much money they make. However, economic class is not directly tied to income and is more properly defined regarding ownership, authority and how an individual makes money.

1891 English political cartoon is criticizing the differences
in quality of life between the working class and the middle class.

The working class is made up of people who make money by selling their labor for a wage and generally have little to no control over what they do at their job. In most countries, the vast majority of the population is working class, but in some developed countries being working class no longer means to be poor. The middle class is people who sell their labor for a wage in exchange for exercising some measure of control over the working class. This means that bosses and managers in a company are middle class, as well as those who are tasked with some measure of authority, such as the police, religious leaders, judges, and lawyers.

In many cases, people in the working class may make significantly more money than someone in the middle class, but this does not change their class status. For example, a computer programmer at Apple may make $100,000 a year but has no control over what they are told to work on; they do what their boss tells them. In contrast, a manager at a McDonald's may only make $40,000 per year, but if they have the power to manage other employees and tell them what to do, they are middle class. The ruling class is those who make their money through owning things and exercise top-level authority. For example, Sergey Brin and Larry Page, founders of Google, make their money, not through salary, but from the profit Google makes.

Measuring how divided a country is by economic class is much easier than with the other social divisions. Political economists have developed a measure called the Gini coefficient which is used to measure how economically unequal a country is by looking at how wealth is distributed through society. A Gini coefficient of 0 means that everyone has the same amount of money, and a Gini coefficient of 1 (or 100%) means that one person has all the money and everyone else has nothing. Since Gini measures wealth distribution, it does not exactly line up with the class composition of society. However, it is generally considered to be a good heuristic for class inequality. A *heuristic* in social science is a measure which approximates a complex relationship. When looking at the class situation of the six countries under study, their Gini coefficient can be compared to other countries and to the United States. As of World Bank statistics from 2010, the United States had a Gini value of 41.1%. Sweden ranked as the most equal country with a Gini value of 25.0%. Seychelles, a small island country in the Indian Ocean off the coast of Africa, was rated the most unequal country with a Gini value of 65.8%.

China is an interesting country when it comes to class structure. Before the Communist revolution in 1949, China was an extremely unequal country with very rigid class boundaries in place since the feudal era. Peasants who worked on farms had no chance of moving up, and the government and the bureaucracy were largely passed down from father to son. Against this backdrop of extreme inequality, the Communists won popularity by promising equality for the peasants. While the revolution eliminated many of the rigid structures from the previous era, the Communist Party solidified into a new ruling class. The Communist Party also replaced the system of landlords and peasants with a new class divide between rural peasants, urban industrial workers, and professionals in a system which very much favored the rural peasants. During the

Cultural Revolution in the late 1960s and 1970s, the Communist Party attempted to remake the class composition again by attacking the educated urban class and sending people to live in the country. Not only did this disastrous policy harm the urban workers, but it also harmed the peasants who now had less access to doctors and schools.

After 1979 when China abandoned its Cultural Revolution policies and began to move away from communism and into capitalism gradually, the class structure changed again, this time favoring urban industrial workers. Peasants flooded into cities to work in factories assembling cheap consumer products which were mostly exported. Cities began rapidly expanding in population, and a new industrialized working class emerged. As China continued to grow into the 1990s and 2000s, wages and jobs increased, leading to an overall improvement in the life of the poorest sectors of the population. At the same time, however, the new factories that were opened were largely run by former members of the Communist Party who had traded political power for economic riches. A new class of multi-billionaires is emerging in China, and even though the poor are improving their conditions, the rich are also getting richer. Thus, inequality remains a problem. China's Gini coefficient in 2011 was 37.0%; while it is more equal than the United States, its general trend is toward greater inequality as it becomes more capitalist.

A luxury cruise ship off the coast of Hainan, China.

The United Kingdom has a long history of class structures, going back to feudalism in the Middle Ages when serfs were kept tied to the land owned by nobles. In the industrial era, a new underclass of exploited factory workers was created that informed the work of Karl Marx. In the modern era, the U.K. retains a similar class system to the United States and most other developed countries in which the majority of people are working class. The U.K. has a Gini coefficient of 38.0%, meaning it is slightly more unequal than China but not as unequal as the United States. Unlike some other countries, the U.K.'s government explicitly recognizes that society is divided by class and even has a five-level ranking system which divides people into high professional management (CEOs, senior executives), low professional management (mid-level and low-level corporate managers), a mid-level category (small business, self-employed professionals and people in technical occupations), people who work in routine or semi-routine occupations (data entry or retail sales) and finally the long-term unemployed at the bottom.

While many political economists are critical of how the U.K. makes these divisions, they generally appreciate the fact that the state keeps statistics on how many people are in each class since it makes analysis easier. Political economists also appreciate the fact that the U.K. government officially acknowledges class divisions, making policy to address inequality more likely. Governments that tend to ignore class division (or even, as in the United States, promote ideologies which insist there are no class divisions) tend to have less government action to reduce inequality. In the U.K., economic class is also strongly tied to social class, which means that people in different economic classes tend to have different common traits. The most notable of these traits is an accent, which usually corresponds to the economic class an individual was brought up in. This can create situations of discrimination. Even if someone can become educated and qualified for a professional position if he or she have a lower class accent the upper-class people doing the hiring may be less inclined to give them a job.

Iran also follows a general three-level class structure with a few in the ruling class, some in the middle class and the vast majority in the working class. After the revolution in 1979, the composition of the ruling class changed on some levels. Before 1979, the ruling class was the usual group of wealthy landowners and industrialists, plus people with ties to the king. After the revolution, the wealthy maintained their position, but a new sector of the ruling class emerged—the highest level of religious clerics. Before the revolution, the religious leadership was middle class. The revolution elevated them to the position of a ruling class through the Guardian Council and the adoption of Sharia law. The working class in Iran has trouble with upward mobility because unions are controlled by the government and are largely just Islamic organizations that tell workers to accept their position in society. While in most countries unions are an important tool for workers to organize and win rights and concessions from the upper class, in Iran unions have become a tool of oppression by the upper class religious and economic authorities. In this sense, the wealthy elite in Iran had no problem switching their allegiance from a king to the Islamic clerics since both promoted policies which kept down the working class. Iran's Gini coefficient is 38.3, making it slightly more equal than the U.K. but less equal than China.

The issue of poverty dominates Mexico's class system. In 2013, the Mexican government estimated that 33% of Mexico's population lives in poverty. Despite this high level of poverty, Mexico is home to some of the richest people in the world. Carlos Slim, who owns the biggest telecom companies in Mexico and all of Latin America is thought to be as rich as Bill Gates. This is evidenced by Mexico's Gini value of 48.1%, which makes it significantly more unequal than the United States. Part of Mexico's extreme inequality stems from the neoliberal economic policies it adopted in the 1990s. They opened their borders to large global corporations who came in and set up factories to take advantage of very low Mexican wages. If workers attempted to fight for better wages and better working conditions in what were often sweatshops, these companies simply closed down their factories and relocated to China and elsewhere. This left the former factory workers worse off than before. Many of them had been small-time farmers who, although in poverty, could grow enough food to feed themselves. Lured to the city by the promise of steady wages, they sold their land in the countryside. This left them landless and homeless when the factories moved away. In the meantime, the Mexican ruling class was able to profit greatly from the lack of business regulations and expand their operations throughout Latin America.

Slums of Ramos Arizpe, Mexico

Nigeria is another country plagued with poverty and inequality, although with a Gini value of 43.0% it is not nearly as unequal as Mexico. Nigeria's economy tends to be divided into two parts: one part is related to the country's vast oil reserves, and the other part is a traditional and often informal economy based on buying and selling goods or services produced individually. As a result, there is a large amount of structural unemployment in Nigeria and few sources of steady employment outside of the oil sector. While economic class divisions remain a serious issue in Nigeria, this cleavage tends to be in the background of the other major cleavage, that of religion. The southern part of the country, predominantly Christian, is where the oil reserves are located and where the largest city, Lagos, is found. As a result, the south tends to be better off economically than the Muslim north. In many ways, the religious tensions in Nigeria are economic class tensions in another form.

One issue that comparative politics seeks to study is precisely this sort of social cleavage. Comparative political scientists will examine similar countries and try to figure out whether Nigeria's north-south divide might be fixed with economic growth. This is an important question for Nigeria. Some argue that religious tensions would die down if more of the wealth were distributed to the north. Others argue that the economic division is a result of religious discrimination and that if secularism could be introduced people in the North would have more economic opportunities. This is a classic problem of trying to determine which is the independent variable (the cause) and which is the dependent variable (the effect) in this situation.

Russia, like China, is another example of a country which has gone through some changes to its class system in the 20th century. Prior to 1917, Russia was a Tsarist feudal system where peasants had very little wealth or power and no chance of economic advancement. The Communist Revolution overthrew this system and generally greatly increased equality, with the working class as the principal beneficiaries. While Karl Marx argued that communism would result in a classless society, in Soviet Russia, the Communist Party became the new ruling class. During the Soviet era, a policy of full employment was pursued, meaning anyone capable of working was guaranteed a job. This system ensured that there were very little poverty and no real unemployment. After the fall of communism in 1991, the neoliberal shock therapy of the early 1990s destroyed the working class and caused poverty to skyrocket. It also created a new class of billionaires called the Oligarchs, who were former Communist Party officials who were simply given formerly state-owned enterprises. Beginning with the election of Vladimir Putin, the economy has stabilized somewhat, but poverty and inequality remain a serious problem.

1908 painting by Sergey Vasilyevich Ivanov depicting serf life in Russia.

Russia's Gini coefficient provides an interesting empirical example of this change in the class system. In the final years of communism in 1988, the Gini value was just 23.8% in Russia, meaning it was perhaps one of the most equal countries in the world, even better than Sweden's current 25%. After the fall of communism and the program of neoliberal economic reforms, poverty and inequality sent the Gini coefficient up to 48.4% in 1993 and made Russia one of the most unequal countries, even worse than Mexico. In just five years, Russia went from being one of the least class-divided societies to one of the most class-divided societies measured by its inequality. As of 2010, Russia's Gini value is 39.7%, making it more in line with the U.K. in terms of inequality. Despite the inherent political problems with the communist system, it did keep people out of poverty and prevented the accumulation of wealth by oligarchs.

Gender

Gender as a social cleavage can manifest itself in different ways. The division between the relative political power of men and women goes back to the earliest political communities (which explicitly excluded women). Religion became a mechanism for justifying and reinforcing the exclusion of women from politics, and it still plays a major role in promoting gender divisions in many countries around the world. As the idea of feminism, meaning equal rights between men and women, spread across the world, the social divisions between men and women have dramatically lessened in many countries.

In addition to the cleavage between men and women, gender also covers the division between heterosexual and homosexual people, which can be a major source of conflict in those countries which are still rooted in traditional religion-defined gender roles. Gender also interacts with the economic class, as the traditional exclusion of women both from positions of political power and from economic leadership helps reinforce unequal, male-dominant relations between the sexes. In countries like Saudi Arabia, where women have almost no political or economic rights, the gender division is more marked than in a country like Norway, which has a strong history of feminism and religion has little influence on society.

Before the reforms of 1979 in China which marked the official abandonment of communism and the introduction of capitalist reforms, gender equality was an explicit goal promoted by the government. In the communist era, women were, for the first time in Chinese history, granted the same full legal status as men. In 1954, equality between men and women was written into the Chinese constitution. The government of that era developed programs to help women get jobs traditionally only available to men and ensured that men and women were paid the same for doing the same job. After the move toward capitalism began in 1979, gender inequality increased as there was a return to traditional conceptions of gender roles. Despite China's backward progress, it is still one of the least unequal countries regarding the economic disparity between men and women. However, the senior political leadership of China is almost exclusively male.

1979 was also the year China adopted their "one child" policy in an attempt to limit the rapidly growing population. This policy had problematic gender implications, as many traditional-thinking families believed that only a son could pass down the family name and inherit money from the parents. This led to a situation where male babies were much preferred over female babies in many parts of the country. As a result of sex-selective abortions of female fetuses, the ratio of males to females born in the 1979 to 2016 era was skewed heavily toward males. Starting in January 2016, China has changed their policy to allow each family to have two children, in part as an attempt to try to balance out the ratio of males to females in the population and discourage families from aborting female fetuses.

Despite a history of strong feminist activism throughout the 20th century, the U.K. still faces major gender imbalances in politics and the economy. While the average woman has made considerable gains in the last hundred years, the top positions in society in the U.K. are overwhelmingly dominated by men as compared to similarly developed countries. Of the hundred biggest corporations in the U.K., only seven have female CEOs. Regarding representation in Parliament, only 22.7% of Members of Parliament are women. By comparison, the average number is 30% for a wealthy developed country. The U.S. Congress has 26% female representatives, Canada has 31%, and Norway has 47%. Despite being a wealthy developed country, women in the U.K. still face considerable challenges in getting elected compared to the situation in similar countries. As a result of the U.K.'s lagging performance on gender equality, in 2015, British Prime Minister David Cameron announced new measures which will require large corporations to disclose their pay rates for men and women to the government.

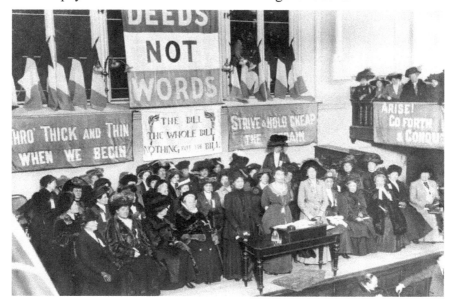

Caxton Hall in Manchester, England hosts a suffragette meeting circa 1908.

Gender inequality in Iran is a major problem, and it is linked to the theocratic legal structure based on Islamic Sharia law which does not afford women very many rights. The status of women in Iran, however, is not simply a matter of being held back by traditional religion. Under Iran's first era of democratic government in the 1950s, women strongly supported the newly elected government, which promoted women's rights issues. It promoted programs to bring Iranian women into higher education and opened up avenues for women to get high-paying jobs that were traditionally for men only. The democratic government even discouraged women from wearing the Islamic hijab headscarf in public. Into the 1960s and 1970s during the reign of the Iranian Shah, women's rights continued to flourish as women won important legal battles which ensured equality under the law. During that time, very few women wore traditional Islamic dress, and they were free to choose their clothing.

It was not until the revolution of 1979 that women's rights began to be rolled back in the name of religion. While women were active participants in overthrowing the Shah, who had become oppressive and had used a secret police force to torture and imprison dissidents, the status of women declined after the Islamists consolidated power. Secular law was replaced with religious law, which mandated that women have to wear traditional Islamic clothes, called hijab. While women in Iran are only required to wear a scarf which covers their hair and not the more restrictive Islamic coverings found in Sunni countries, this was a significant setback for women's rights considering women had previously been free to choose not to wear this covering. In recent years, women have begun to test the laws related to hair coverings by wearing their hijabs loose, letting their bangs hang over their face or wearing them high on their forehead. These acts of mini-protest have led to crackdowns from the religious authorities who ordered police to enforce dress codes more strictly. In 2007, police in Tehran arrested hundreds of women for "bad hijab," with some receiving sentences of up to two months in jail.

The gender equality situation in Mexico is fairly bad. It was ranked 84th out of 125 countries regarding gender equality by the World Economic Forum in 2012. While this is a fairly low ranking, gender divisions in Mexican society have been very slowly improving throughout the country's recent history. Women hold only 14% of the seats in the Mexican legislature, and women in positions of political leadership have been extremely rare until recently. In 2012, PAN ran Josefina Vázquez Mota as their candidate for president, which represented a major advance for women in high-level positions of political authority in Mexico. Women in Mexico make up only 29% of the workforce and also face serious problems related to violence. Mexico has one of the highest murder rates of women in the world and one of the highest rates of domestic violence. While recent governments have taken steps to support programs which help promote gender equality, they have done little to address the inherent culture of machismo, which views women as inferior to men. Unlike Iran, where the problems stem from an oppressive government, Mexico's gender inequalities are bottom up; societal norms and the traditional culture promote patriarchal ideas about how men should always be in charge of "their" women.

Mexico's lower house Chamber of Deputies

While only 14% of Mexico's legislature is made up of women, in Nigeria that number is only 6%. Throughout Nigeria's modern history after it achieved independence, there has been systematic discrimination against women and a simple lack of recognition of the role of women in society. The Nigerian government has aimed social programs almost exclusively at men, even in occupations that are dominated by women. Despite the stark gender divide, which is reinforced by strong identifications with either Christianity or Islam, women in Nigeria do make up half of the workforce. Prior to colonization, women had important economic roles in farming and as the primary shopkeepers who sold things at the market. Despite their relatively even position in the economic realm, the government has persistently ignored women in their development efforts, and the country lags behind other developing countries in gender equality. Gay rights are also a serious issue in Nigeria. Both major political parties are quite conservative, and religious leaders have the power to sway the government to adopt discriminatory policies.

Russia, like China, has gone backward on gender equality since the fall of communism. For whatever other problems communism may have had, it promoted women's rights and gender equality in the economy and led to a fairly equal society. In 1936, equal rights for men and women were written into the Russian constitution, and the Soviet government promoted programs which allowed women to rise through the ranks to the upper levels of management in state-owned enterprises. While women did well economically in the Soviet era, they were still largely excluded from the political leadership, and there were very few high-ranking women within the ruling Communist Party. After the transition to capitalism, women's pay rates dropped dramatically, and they were often the first to be fired when there is a layoff. It is estimated that women's wages had dropped as much as 30% relative to men's just five years after the transition to neoliberal capitalism.

This was also a period in which the Orthodox Church reasserted its power and reinforced traditional gender roles. A further gender divide in Russia relates to life expectancy. While women have higher life expectancies than men across the world due to biological differences, in Russia this gap is much wider. Women in Russia can expect to live eleven years longer than a man. Many social scientists point to the increase in alcoholism in the 1990s as an explanation. During this period of economic decline, many men lost their jobs and turned to alcohol abuse.

Rwandan parliament convening in December 2013.

While not one of the six countries under study, Rwanda presents a unique case for gender equality; their parliament is composed of exactly 50% women and 50% men. This is done by design. Half the seats in parliament are reserved for each gender, guaranteeing that an evenly balanced legislature is always created. This scheme has been very controversial, and some have argued that it enables undeserving people to get into parliament simply based on their gender rather than their ability to appeal to the electorate. Feminist groups have also criticized the parliament's structure, arguing that it creates a second class of female seats that are not taken as seriously as the male half of the seats. Official schemes to reserve places in the legislature for groups who are traditionally under-represented in parliament, such as women, remain highly controversial across the political spectrum. As will be shown in the next section, similar schemes that guarantee seats based on religious identity are very prominent when it comes to certain (approved) religious minorities.

Religious

Today, religious divisions are perhaps the most pronounced of all the social divisions, and religion is the most likely social cleavage to result in violence. Religious division can be an issue within a country or across the borders of countries, and it is often the primary self-identification of people. If people feel more attachment to their religious identity than to their identity as a member of the state, this can create problems for the state since these religious identities may undermine the state's control of their territory. In some cases, religious identity can lead people to join terrorist groups which have no allegiance to any state, such as al-Qaida, or ones which are trying to create new states, such as the Islamic State of Iraq and al-Sham (ISIS) which is active in Syria and parts of Iraq. Such groups have the goal of either destroying existing states or trying to create new ones based on strict Islamic principles. In some cases, religious terrorists are only interested in attacking their government because they believe it is not religious enough. Sometimes religious tension in a country is between two different sects of the same religion.

Religion as a social cleavage is both old and new. As Enlightenment ideals about rationality and personal freedom spread throughout Europe in the 1700s and 1800s, countries increasingly adopted both official and unofficial forms of secularism. *Secularism* is the separation of church and state, meaning that the government allows freedom of religious belief in exchange for religions staying out of politics. This arrangement enabled religious freedom to grow; governments no longer persecuted people for their beliefs and they could now act without fear of being condemned by religious leaders, who were expected to confine their preaching to holy matters.

Even in the Middle East, secular ideas tended to predominate in the 1950s and 1960s, with religion seen as something to be kept private and not a source of public law. This, of course, was a big change from the Middle Ages, when religion dominated all aspects of European society. By the early 1980s, religion began to make a comeback as a major source of social division. As people became less inclined to identify with a political ideology due to the winding down of the Cold War, many people went back to religion to explain the changes in the world, even though it had not had a prominent place in many societies for a hundred or more years. Today, religion continues to grow in importance as a source of personal identity, putting it into conflict with other identities and with other religious identifications.

Religion as a social cleavage in China is very complicated. The Chinese government has declared China to be officially an atheist state. At the same time, the Communist Party has declared that China has five official religions: Buddhism, Taoism, Islam, Protestantism, and Catholicism. Therefore, while China is an officially atheist state, it has five religions that are actively protected by the government. Even though China officially recognizes five religions, the vast majority of Chinese people are not religious. As of 2005, 61% are atheists; a further 29% consider themselves to be uninterested in religion and just 7% claim allegiance to one of the five official religions. Part of the reason for the high numbers of atheists and non-religious people in China is because the traditional Chinese religions were never organized into official hierarchical structures, and some of those practices have been integrated into daily life by the non-religious over the years. Superstitions about certain numbers or the color of dogs (black dogs, rather than cats, are seen as very unlucky) are parts of traditional Chinese religious beliefs. They have been stripped of their seriousness and are now viewed, not as religious edicts, but simply as superstitions that people take half-seriously.

The Sacred Heart Cathedral of Shenyang, China.

China also has a long history of resisting conversion attempts by foreign missionaries. In 1899, the Boxer Rebellion was an outbreak of war in which Chinese nationals sought to expel Christian missionaries. China believed the missionaries were being used by Great Britain, Russia, and the U.S. to imperialistically conquer China through inculcating a foreign religion. It was called the Boxer Rebellion because the Chinese patriots who fought the foreign missionaries and their armies practiced kung fu, which to the British made them seem like "boxers." While the rebellion was put down and its leaders executed, the event discouraged the Western powers from trying to colonize China, either through military force or religious conversion. Today, the Chinese government officially protects Catholicism and Protestantism.

The protection of Islam and Buddhism as official religions relates to China's colonial expansion. Xinjiang, the most northwestern province in China, is made up of 58% Muslims and is an area that is only marginally historically associated with China. It was originally colonized and converted to Islam in the 1100s by Turkic people, who were later conquered by the Mongols. Eventually, China adopted the region as a kind of buffer area in the mid-1800s against numerous incursions from Tajik and Mongol groups. With the fall of the Qing dynasty in the early 1900s, the region's status as protected by China came into question. Muslim groups in the area joined up with Turkmen militaries to initiate a rebellion, which China put down and established their full control of the region. After the Communist revolution, another rebellion, this time initiated by the Soviets, was put down, and China recognized the area as an autonomous province in 1955. To try to quell religious separatism among the Uyghur Muslims, China officially recognized Islam as a state religion, and they reserve seats in the legislature specifically for Uyghurs. These efforts seem not to have paid off, as China is increasingly experiencing problems with Islamic terrorist attacks in Xinjiang.

China's recognition of Buddhism as a state religion stems from its control of Tibet. Historically, Tibet first rose to prominence as a major Buddhist theocratic monarchy in the 7th century. It spread out across Tibet and controlled major parts of what is now China and India. After the fall of the empire in the 842, Tibet was ruled by both Chinese and Mongol governments for most of its history while still maintaining a strong Buddhist tradition. The province came under direct Chinese control during the Qing dynasty in 1720, but by the mid-1800s their control over the territory had evaporated.

In 1904, the British sent a small military expedition to Tibet to fend off Russian influence, which was met with armed resistance by Tibetans. Due to the vast superiority of British weapons technology, 600 Tibetans were killed while only 12 British soldiers died. Fearing territory on their borders which had traditionally been under their control might fall to the British or Russians, China sent in their military, deposing the ruling Dalai Lama and installing their government. After the Qing Dynasty fell in 1912, the new Chinese government apologized for having thrown out the Dalai Lama, who then returned to rule Tibet as a king, and declared the country an independent state.

After a period of crisis in the 1940s led by uncertainties over succession to the throne, China once again brought its military into Tibet. In 1950, the Dalai Lama agreed to accept that Tibet was to be part of China if he could continue to rule it autonomously. There was an uprising in 1959 after rumors spread that the Chinese government was going to attempt to kidnap the Dalai Lama. This uprising was put down by the Chinese military, and the Dalai Lama fled to India. Tibet had been a feudal monarchy under the Dalai Lama with a system of serfdom. China had agreed to leave this in place and introduce slow reforms, but after the 1959 uprising, the Chinese government abolished feudalism in Tibet.

This piece of Chinese and Tibetan history remains controversial; supporters of the Dalai Lama rightfully claim that the Chinese military violently put down unrest and killed tens of thousands of people. At the same time, the Dalai Lama operated an extremely oppressive system in which serfs had no rights, and all wealth was concentrated in the hands of the Buddhist kings and religious leaders. Like with Xinjiang, China has attempted to integrate Tibet into the country by providing seats in the legislature for Tibetan Buddhists and officially protecting Buddhism as a state religion.

While China protects its five-state religions, any religion other than those five is dealt with harshly. One of the major underground religious movements in China is called Falun Gong. Falun Gong is a relatively new religion, beginning in the early 1990s. It incorporates elements of Buddhism and Taoism with meditation and exercise. The religion rapidly grew in popularity in the late 1990s, and the Chinese government became worried that its large number of adherents were a threat. Since Falun Gong was independent of the state, the government worried that a popular leader could emerge and counsel Falun Gong members to rebel. As a result, practitioners of the religion have been persecuted, with China criticizing the religion as a fraud and comparing it to Scientology. It is interesting that China chooses to persecute Falun Gong members while attempting to integrate Tibetan Buddhists and Uighur Muslims into wider Chinese society and reserves a significant number of seats in the legislature for them.

Chinese police arrest a Falun Gong practitioner.

The United Kingdom has an official state religion, the Church of England, which grants the leadership of the Church an official position in government. The 26 highest bishops of the Church of England are given seats in the House of Lords, the upper house of the British legislature. The U.K. has no separation of church and state, as the church is directly involved in the government, and the Queen is the official leader of the Church of England. This gives the leadership of the Church of England the ability to create laws which can then be passed in Parliament. The Church of England, or Anglicanism as it's more commonly known as is a form of Catholicism which denies the supremacy of the Pope. The religion was created, or rather broke away from regular Catholicism, in the 1530s when King Henry VIII was denied a divorce from his wife by the Pope. King Henry simply started his church where he could do what he wanted, and the Church of England was born. The influence of the Church of England has been declining dramatically, and church attendance has been in a continual downward trend since 1950.

Despite the establishment of an official state religion, British citizens are rapidly turning away from religion altogether. A 2015 survey found that 49% of U.K. citizens said they were not religious at all, with the Church of England only having 20% of the population as believers. Although half the population professes membership in a religion, the same study found that only 10% of the population regularly attended religious services.

Despite the declining influence and importance of Christianity in the U.K., Islam is trending upward in numbers of adherents due to immigration. Immigrant Muslims also tend to be much poorer than average and are more likely to be arrested and jailed. This has led to tensions between not just Christians and Muslims, but between atheists and

Muslims as well. Many people see the increased adherence to Islam as a threat to the growing trend in the U.K. of setting religion aside. The U.K. Independence Party often uses anti-Muslim rhetoric in its campaigning, which has won them a significant amount of support. More left-wing groups argue that because the U.K. is not a secular country, Muslims can get privileges from the state that are unfair. Even though the Church of England is the official religion, the U.K. government has been moving toward granting increasing amounts of government recognition to other religions as well. While many Muslim groups believe this is only fair, the growing contingent of atheists points out that separating religion from the government altogether would be the best method.

As a theocratic democracy, Iran's official state religion is Islam. It is estimated that 90% to 95% of Iranians are Shia Muslim, while another 5-10% are Sunni Muslim. As an Islamic state, the laws of Iran are based on religion and provide very little freedom from religion. Despite being an Islamic state, Iran recognizes Zoroastrianism, Christianity, and Judaism as protected minority religions. People are free to practice these religions and are not persecuted by the government for doing so. Like China, Iran even reserves seats in its legislature, the Majlis, for representatives of these minority religious groups. There is a seat reserved for a Jew and a Zoroastrian after every election, as well as two seats each for traditionally Christian Armenians and Christian Assyrians. Given that these minority religions make up a tiny percentage of the overall population, these reserved seats provide religious minorities with a significant amount of representation in the Majlis.

Zoroastrian fire temple in Yazd.

Despite these recognitions, there are still significant problems created by religious divisions. The Baha'i faith, which is Iran's largest minority religion, does not get any seats in the Majlis and tends to be actively persecuted by the government. Because Baha'i began in Iran in 1840 as an offshoot of Shia Islam, the authorities consider it a heresy and not a separate religion; as a result, members of the Baha'i faith are denied basic civil rights and are actively discriminated against in employment. In many ways, Baha'i is like Mormonism in the United States. The biggest targets of persecution, however, tend to be atheists.

Apostasy (renouncing Islam or converting to another religion) is a crime punishable by death in Iran, and it is most often aimed at atheists who have rejected Islam. Given that the state's official laws and government are based on Islam, the religious authorities often use the charge of apostasy against any citizens critical of the government. After the student protests in 2009, two of the leaders were sentenced to death for apostasy after they made comments critical of the influence and power of Islamic clerics. There was no evidence either had renounced Islam or had converted to another religion, but since criticism of the government amounts to criticism of religion in a theocracy, both were convicted of apostasy.

The Mexican constitution of 1917 set out a strict separation of church and state. The Roman Catholic Church had been extremely politically powerful before this time, and it unofficially controlled government policy. The new constitution set out to limit the power of the church in political matters. The government limited the number of priests in the country, and religious leaders were not allowed to vote or hold office to ensure that religious teachings remained politically neutral. In 1992, amendments to the constitution were made which eroded the separation between church and state. Official recognition was provided for Roman Catholicism, and restrictions on priests were lifted. Against this backdrop, religion is not a notable social cleavage in Mexico. 82% of the population claim allegiance to Roman Catholicism and even those who consider themselves to be non-religious or atheist still report a cultural attachment to Roman Catholicism.

Part of the reason why someone who never attends church and does not believe in God might still identify as a Roman Catholic is because the religion has long been tied to Mexican national identity. In particular, Our Lady of Guadalupe, a painting in a prominent Mexican church, is linked to Mexican national identity. For many non-religious Mexicans, statues and replicas of Our Lady of Guadalupe serve as symbols of national pride. Before international soccer games, supporters often touch a statue of Our Lady of Guadalupe on the way into the stadium to bring good luck to their country's soccer team—not as a religious ritual, but more an expression of national pride.

Russia has a rich religious history, with the Russian Orthodox Church historically being the primary religion. Prior to the Communist Revolution in 1917, the Orthodox Church was the state religion of Russia and was deeply ingrained in the ruling Tsarist autocracy. As a result of its association with the authoritarian and feudal Tsarist regime, the new Communist government made it an explicit aim to eliminate the influence of the Orthodox Church since they saw it as aligned with principles that were incompatible with Communism. This was a somewhat difficult task as the overwhelming majority of Russians were Orthodox Christians. The Soviet government tolerated religious belief so long as it was kept private and did not interfere with politics. As a result, most of the more highly educated people associated with high-level positions in politics and the economy abandoned religion, though many ordinary people continued to practice it in private.

The Mandylion 12th century Russian icon

The official hostility of the Russian government toward the Orthodox Church changed when the Soviet leader Josef Stalin enlisted the Orthodox Church to rally regular Russians to the patriotic cause of fighting the Nazis during World War II. The Orthodox Church was permitted to make political statements once again, causing membership to grow significantly.

After the fall of the USSR, there was another significant growth in membership in the Orthodox Church; the chaos of economic decline and political change had left people seeking spiritual answers. Today, it is estimated that about 41% of Russians adhere to Orthodox Christianity, 38% are not religious, and 6.5% are Muslims. Under the leadership of Vladimir Putin, the Orthodox Church is once again becoming increasingly aligned with the government. Putin has even passed laws against blasphemy and banned certain minor religions at the urging of the Church. This had caused tensions recently when the Russian punk band Pussy Riot was arrested and jailed for blasphemy after playing songs mocking Orthodox Christianity in front of a major church. In the Caucasian mountains in Russia's south, the majority religion is Islam which has also created much social tension. Many of these Muslim republics within Russia have sought to become independent countries, and Chechnya's attempt to break away led to war. Russia has also been plagued with terrorist attacks carried out by Islamic radicals. Russia's social cleavage on religion is split three ways between Orthodox Christianity, non-religious people who are opposed to the alliance between church and state and the Muslims in the South.

Regional

Regional cleavages are another significant problem in many countries, but in many instances, they are simply the result of one of the above-imagined communities happening to congregate in the same area. In Nigeria and Russia for example, the regional tensions are entirely a result of certain regions being dominated by a different religious group. It would be unlikely, for example, for Nigeria to experience tensions between the north and the south if everyone in those regions followed the same religion. Regional tensions are usually a dependent variable, meaning they are not the cause of divisions. One notable exception is in the U.K., where regional tensions between Scotland, Northern Ireland, Wales, and England can be reduced to the region.

Since all of these regions of the U.K. share the same language, race, religion, and similar class composition, their traditional status as independent countries is a source of major tension. Scotland had been an independent country with its unique history until 1707 when its king agreed to a treaty to subordinate it to England. As a result of this history of independence dating back to ancient Roman times, many in Scotland continue to resent being part of the United Kingdom and long for independence, as evidenced by a recent referendum which almost led to the separation of Scotland from the U.K. In an attempt to appease demands for independence, in 1999 the U.K. "devolved" authority from the central government to the regional parliaments in order to give them more autonomy. While this was not the creation of a federation, as the national Parliament still has the final say on all matters, it did allow Scotland, Wales and Northern Ireland some power to make their own decisions on certain issues. The goal of devolution was to make these regions more content with being part of the United Kingdom, but it led to demands for full independence in Scotland.

MP Jim Murphy campaign urges constituents to vote to remain part of the United Kingdom during Scotland's independence referendum in 2014.

Regional autonomy in China and Russia has been a tricky issue as well. Sometimes it can lead to people accepting being part of a wider country, and sometimes it fuels demands for full independence. What to do with regional cleavages is one of the most important topics within comparative politics, and scholars compare federal, central and "devolved" systems to try to figure out which would work best in each country.

Civil Society and Social Capital

Civil society and social capital are generally considered to be any non-state political actor. While the term civil society is unusually broad and can refer to anything from a neighborhood watch group to a corporate lobbyist, it was a key idea promoted by dissidents in Eastern Europe during the Cold War. In totalitarian states, the government controls all aspect of political life, and there is no civil society because people were not permitted to engage politically outside of the state. Dissidents in Poland, Czechoslovakia, and Hungary, all countries part of the Soviet Eastern Bloc, focused on building the capacity to engage in political activities not controlled by the state as a means of undermining totalitarian control. Even if they were not directly opposing the government, their goal was simply to open up space where civil society could flourish and slowly chip away at the total control of society by the state.

Today, we see transnational networks of human rights advocates and environmental groups attempting to build something resembling a global civil society. Groups such as Amnesty International and Greenpeace operate independently of states and seek to build social capital, which is a form of bottom-up political pressure, to force governments to respond to issues such as climate change and human rights abuses. In many cases, states resist the idea of global civil society, even if they accept the existence of internal civil society. For example, when Greenpeace and Amnesty International seek to pressure the Russian or Iranian governments, the leaders of these countries often claim that these are foreign entities which have no business commenting on domestic Russian or Iranian politics. Given that the issues of climate change and human rights are inherently global issues, these attempts to create a global civil society are another example of how globalization is continuing to challenge the authority of state sovereignty.

Media Roles

The media can have an immense influence on what people think about the government and what sort of opinions they share. Until recently, people were usually only exposed to media originating from their own country. With globalization, people can increasingly consume media from around the world. This has made it harder for governments to control media within a country, but it has also made it easier for governments and corporations to influence the opinions of people in another country. There are three models of media ownership which can determine who has the most control over a country.

Reporters converge on U.S. Secretary of Defense William S. Cohen.

The first model is when there is no state involvement, and corporations entirely control the media. Where this is the case, as in Mexico, corporations can use their control of the media to shape public opinion. In Mexico, the Televisia Corporation dominated Mexican television throughout much of the 20th century and was openly in favor of the PRI political party. PRI's continued dominance of the country was propped up through a media situation where the corporations controlling the media promoted pro-PRI point of view, which led to favorable policies for Televisa. Corporate-dominated media enables corporations to shape the opinion of voters and create certain political outcomes. Voters need to be vigilant and alert to this sort of manipulation when going to the polls, but this is rarely the case.

The second model is to allow free corporate media but also to balance it with state-owned media corporations which operate at arm's length from the government. In the U.K., the BBC is a public broadcaster whose mandate involves producing programming in the public interest. It is funded by fees paid by every British citizen with television and is established by Parliament, but the government has no control over it. As a result, the BBC tends to be less inclined to favor a specific political party and tends to be less biased than the corporate networks. By having the BBC balance out the corporate networks, media consumers in the U.K. are more aware of how corporate-owned media can promote specific agendas, as they can always compare news and reporting to that of the BBC.

The third model is when the state or subject directly control the media to direct censorship. Iran allows corporate media independent of the government, but what they publish is strictly controlled by the state. In China, the main media outlet, CCTV, is directly owned and controlled by the state and serves to promote the government's interests. With the rapid spread of the internet in China, social networking sites are undermining the government's control of the media, leading to new forms of censorship by the Chinese state. They have implemented the Great Firewall of China, a set of legislation designed to block any websites and content critical of the Chinese government. The government also directly monitors social media, leading activists to develop a set of commonly known code words for referring to the government. Some Chinese activists have taken to using the term "grass mud horse," which in Mandarin is the name for a type of alpaca that sounds similar to an obscenity. By calling the government "grass mud horses" on social media, activists can insult and criticize the government while also claiming they are just talking about alpacas and mean no harm. Given the continued prevalence of the internet and the increasing difficulties of censorship, the Chinese government faces serious obstacles if they wish to continue to censor the media.

Political Participation

Political participation by citizens can take a number of forms. Voting is the most obvious, but in most countries, the voter turnout rate has been in decline for the past 50 years. In advanced democracies such as the U.K., voter turnout peaked in the 1940s and 1950s and had been declining ever since. Part of this decline is explained by the fact that people increasingly view parliamentary democracy as a bad form of government but the best one available. This leads to a defeatist attitude in which people believe there is nothing better to replace representative democracy with, though overall they believe that representative elections do not result in good government. The outcome of such growing attitudes is to not vote at all, especially in the context of political parties in the U.K., which all seemingly have similar ideologies.

If voting does not work to bring change, there are many unofficial means to engage in serious political action, ranging from strikes and protests to full out revolutions. The U.K., in particular, has a history of labor activism in which unions engaged in massive strikes. There are two types of strikes: one focuses on improving conditions within a given workplace, and the other seeks to improve the conditions of all workers. The second type of strike is political in nature, and one such occurred in 1926 in the U.K. A general strike was called to get the government to change its mind on legislation that would reduce wages and force the government to deal with the poor working conditions of workers across the country. A general strike is a call which asks all workers to stay home from work, regardless of what their job is. In 1926, One million seven hundred thousand British workers across some industries went on strike for better wages and workplace conditions.

Protestors at the G-20 London summit.

While general strikes are often seen as the most threatening form of protest, public rallies of dissent against the government are important political actions as well. In 1989, protesters in China flooded into the Tiananmen Square in Beijing to demand freedom of speech, freedom of the press and an end to corruption in the Communist Party. The government responded by sending in the military, including tanks, to suppress the protest. Hundreds and possibly even thousands of protesters were killed, and even today talk of the protests is heavily censored in China. Such demonstrations, even if they start small, have the potential to topple regimes or bring sweeping changes if allowed to grow. This is why regimes often react with violence and harsh crackdowns as a means of maintaining control in the face of a loss of public support. After questionable elections in 2009 in Iran, mass street protests by reformers wanting to loosen Islamic laws led to the state executing and jailing hundreds of protesters and banning the Reformist movement from running candidates in elections.

An *uprising* is considered halfway between a protest and a revolution, and it often involves armed resistance. In 1994 in the Mexican state of Chiapas, an uprising by the Zapatista Army of National Liberation (EZLN), largely organized by indigenous Mayans, occurred in response to military activities by the Mexican state that were meant to put an end to self-organized political units in Chiapas. The uprising and creation of a militia, originally formed in self-defense, resulted in the EZLN declaring war on the Mexican government. The Mexican military crushed the actual military uprising after two weeks, and both sides signed peace accords.

The Mexican government did not uphold their side of the bargain, and in 1997 they sent para-military (groups trained by the military but not officially associated with them) forces into Chiapas to murder prominent community leaders, killing 45 people. This harsh reprisal won the Zapatistas international sympathy, in part because they were very adept at communicating using the internet and telling the world about the repression they faced. While the Zapatista uprising was successfully quashed, the ensuing murder of 45 civilians was a scandal for the ruling PRI political party who had been in power since 1917. Many scholars argue that the Zapatista uprising was a significant factor that led to the downfall of the dominance of PRI in Mexican politics and enabled PAN to win the 2000 election on a promise to solve the issues in Chiapas peacefully.

A full-scale *revolution* is when the people can overthrow the existing regime. In the six countries studied, the most famous example is the 1979 Iranian revolution which overthrew the American-supported Shah Pahlavi. The Shah had become increasingly authoritarian and was notorious for his secret police force, called SAVAK, which would kidnap and torture anyone suspected of opposing the Shah. These human rights violations led to civil resistance by student groups who wanted Iran to be a free society. The Shah's economic mismanagement had caused a severe recession, at the same time he was displaying his extravagant wealth, which led to resentment from the working class organized by left-wing groups. Concurrently, the Shah's program of promoting secularism and undermining traditional Islamic values led to resistance from Iran's Shia Muslim clerics who supported joining protests. Eventually, these three groups came together in street protests, and the Shah was overthrown.

Street protestors of the Iranian Revolution confront armed regime soldiers.

The goal of the revolution was not explicitly to create an Islamic state. The more liberal student groups wanted a return to the pre-Shah constitution, and the left-wing working-class groups opposed the influence of Shia clerics. However, the clerics, led by the popular religious leader Ruhollah Khomeini, were the most organized and were able to impose the new framework of the Islamic Republic on Iran. The Islamic movement for suppression immediately targeted many of the student groups and left-wing working class groups. This eliminated the two major competing factions who had helped bring about the revolution and allowed the clerics to consolidate their control over the country. Many Iranians who had opposed both the Shah and the clerics fled the country out of fear of political repression. It is important to remember that the Iranian Revolution was not an Islamic revolution, but that it was popularly supported by many groups across society. The Islamic Clerics were simply the most organized and most willing to engage in violence against their fellow revolutionaries to secure control of the country after the revolution.

Social Movements

As mentioned above, social movements are increasingly becoming global in nature. The alter-globalization movement, for example, does not oppose globalization as some of its critics wrongly claim but aims to create a new kind of globalization based on democracy rather than corporate rule. This movement has been critical of the global financial institutions which have promoted treaties that enshrine corporate rights into international law and can overrule the democratic sovereignty of elected governments. The alter-globalization movement has also brought to global attention the policies promoted by the IMF and the World Bank, which force developing countries to change their economic policies in exchange for loans. Many of these same policies, called neoliberal economic reform, were responsible for the 2008 global financial crisis and the ongoing financial crisis in Greece. Even though the alter-globalization movement's predictions about the outcome of these economic policies seemed to have come true in 2008, their protests have been met with harsh state repression across the world.

While the alter-globalization movement deals with global problems and positions itself as a global solution, comparative politics also studies the internal social movements of countries. Given the level of dominance by the Chinese Communist Party, social movements in China are very constrained regarding the space they can operate in. One of the focal points for activism in China is the level of corruption in the government since many former high-ranking Communist Party members ended up as owners of huge corporations because of their connections to the government. One such Chinese dissident is the artist Ai Weiwei, who uses art and the social network site Sino Weibo to criticize corruption and human rights violations in China. Given his international reputation, China did not want to jail him directly for his political comments and instead arrested him for tax evasion charges. After three months in jail, he was released, and he continues to be a thorn in the side of the Chinese government by inspiring others in China to follow his example and criticize corruption in the government.

Despite the harsh religious climate in Iran, the country is filled with vibrant social movements which are a serious threat to clerical authority. The 2009 Green Movement was spurred by claims that the 2009 presidential election was rigged, and they were the biggest street protests since the 1979 revolution. The movement was led by the Reformist presidential candidate, Mir Hossein Mousavi, who supported liberal and democratic reforms to reduce the power of the clerics in Iran. Protesters who demanded fair elections free of fraud were met with mass arrests from the government. Women's groups are also well organized in Iran and tend to focus their attention on the restrictive Islamic dress codes. In an attempt to subvert the religious authorities without getting arrested, many Iranian women engage in small-scale protests by taking selfies without hijab in public places and posting these pictures on social media to connect women activists and subtly undermine the harsh religious laws.

Mexico has a vibrant tradition of political movements challenging the state as well. After the 2006 Presidential elections, massive street protests were demanding a recount and alleging fraud. The results were extremely close, and the protesters were mindful of Mexico's history of rigged elections. Eventually, the protests died down after the government refused to budge, but reforms were put in place for the next election. More recently, a movement has arisen around the issue of 43 students who went missing in 2014. The protesters believe the drug cartels murdered the students and that the government is covering this up because of the connection between the governing PRI and the drug cartels. Thousands of people continue to organize protests and hunger strikes demanding the government at least investigate the disappearance of the students, but so far the government remains unresponsive, leading many to fear a return of the days of repression and corruption at the hands of PRI.

Mexican political graffiti reads, "They took them alive.
We want them back alive. Solidarity with the 43 disappeared students."

While religious tensions are most prominent in Nigeria, in 2012 the Occupy Movement had a significant impact in Nigeria. Demonstrators linked the wider issue of corporate greed, which Occupy was opposing, with the government's policies that were increasing the price of gasoline despite Nigeria being one of the world's largest producers of oil. The Occupy Nigeria protesters complained that oil revenues were being given to large corporations and ordinary Nigerians saw no benefit from their country's immense oil reserves. Many activists focused on occupying gas stations to prevent people from filling up their vehicles to bring attention to the skyrocketing cost of gasoline. The protests were met with extreme violence from the federal police, who shot and killed 23 protesters. The government eventually agreed to subsidize public transit to quiet the protests. However, repression continued. Nigerian filmmaker Ishaya Bako filmed a documentary about the protests which was banned by the government. It won an African Academy Award for best documentary and was praised by international human rights groups. Many scholars believe that it was these protests that spurred the working class in Nigeria to turn against President Goodluck Jonathan and led to his defeat in the 2015 presidential elections.

Russia is increasingly seeing political movements arise, despite its long history of preventing civil society activism. After the 2011 legislative elections were condemned as being improperly held, in such a manner as to benefit Vladimir Putin's United Russia party, street protests occurred on and off for the next two years. The primary aim of this movement was to ensure that there were transparent and fair elections in Russia. The actual protesters came from a wide range of groups, including students, middle-class professionals, anarchists, socialists and even far right-wing nationalists. The protests eventually led to reforms which will be in place for the 2016 legislative elections. In March 2014, there was another mass street protest led by a philosophy professor and a Russian rock star that opposed the Russian military intervention into Ukraine. Over 30,000 people protested in Moscow, and the movement was supported by most of the liberal and left-wing Russian opposition political parties as well as some prominent scientists and philosophers (some of whom lost their jobs for their public opposition to the government).

Citizenship and Representation

Some of the political movements mentioned here are purely civil society groups, and some have ties to political parties. In the case of the recent protests in Iran and Russia, these protests were directly led by political parties opposed to the government. Some movements, such as environmentalist groups in the U.K., are not tied to any political party whatsoever. One of the issues comparative politics looks at is the relative effectiveness of these two models of social change. Do mass movements get more results when they form a political party and try to get elected, or are they better at pushing for change by remaining outside of the party system, regardless of which party is in power? There are many arguments for and against each method, and the effectiveness of each technique depends on the country.

Anti-war protest in London against military intervention in Syria.

In the case of social movements linking up with political parties, it enables a second path toward reform if protests do not change the government's mind. If the movement can form a political party and get elected, then it can directly bring change itself. Those who argue in favor of mass movements keeping their distance from political parties argue that this ensures that activists focus on issues and do not get caught up in partisan games or focusing on getting elected, instead of pressuring the government for change right now.

In addition to the debate surrounding representation and social movements, comparative politics also analyzes the connection between representation and citizenship. While it has become standard that citizenship is a legal construct which grants certain rights, such as the right to vote, there are challenges to the modern regime of citizenship in relation to representation. With economic globalization came an increase of migrant workers who sought to move to places where there were jobs after their local economies were devastated by free trade policies. This is especially problematic in Mexico after many former farmers sold their land to work in garment factories which then moved to China. Left with no opportunities, many of these people illegally crossed the border into the United States looking for jobs. Due to their status as illegal immigrants, they are not granted any political or legal rights and often face exploitation by employers who know the workers have no legal recourse and no political representation.

A second issue is the refugees, who are people who flee their home country due to violence or persecution. With the civil war in Syria starting in 2014, there has been a major wave of refugees fleeing that country and heading to Europe through Turkey. How to settle refugees is a difficult political problem. Having fled their home country, they cannot be sent back to face certain death, yet they have no legal or political rights outside of their home country. The refugee issue also puts the entire idea of human rights into question. If people only have rights in the states where they were citizens, does the concept of human rights mean anything? Refugees need rights as humans since they are rendered stateless, but it is only the rights that come with belonging to a state that is recognized.

In reaction to the recent great increase in refugees and immigrants, many countries are seeing a rise in racist attitudes which are linked to the fascist attitude toward citizenship. In fascist ideology, citizenship, and thus political rights, are not a legal-political construct but a racial or religious one. According to fascist ideology, citizen rights should only be granted to those who share the country's most common racial and/or religious traits. Minority groups are considered not to be citizens and can have their basic rights taken away, as was the case with Jews in Nazi Germany. The present wave of post-fascist political parties in Europe are not genocidal authoritarians, but they still promote the fascist idea that citizenship rights should not be permitted to immigrants or refugees whose race or religion differs from that of the majority in the country.

Chapter 5

Political and Economic Change

Much of the cross-case coverage contained in this chapter centers on processes of change. These processes of change are introduced through an exploration of political and economic trends. The countries studied provide illustrative examples of this interaction, which can take the form of political and economic reform, revolutions and even coups d'états. Contrasts are provided to enable distinguishing between types of political and economic change.

Since the end of the Cold War, a wave of democratization has occurred throughout much of the developing world and in the former Communist bloc. To highlight contrasts in development, comparisons between Russia, Mexico, and Nigeria democratic transitions are offered. This analysis includes an examination of the preconditions, processes, and outcomes. Successful, preliminary and foundered democratization transitions across the studied countries are made. Further explanation is given to why democratic consolidation often requires new elite pacts, constitutional arrangements to minimize conflict and acceptance of democracy by key social groups. The included featuring of the economic preconditions and effects of stable democracies provides a useful counterpoint to studies of countries facing upheavals of political change. Commonly-occurring conditions and paths that lead to breakdowns of authoritarianism are provided. Other relevant factors are contributing to regime change, such as cleavages within a regime, breakdowns in state capacity, international pressure and a substantial degree of mobilization by opponents, are discussed in detail.

In addressing the significant economic policy shifts undergone over the past 25 years for the six studied countries, investigations are made into the intended and inadvertent consequences of economic reform packages. Through this, a framework for understanding not only the basic economic policies but also the interaction between domestic economic reforms and their political effects are highlighted. For instance, countries such as China and Mexico have revised fundamental national "bargains," changing the relationship between capital and labor that dates back more than half a century. Further, outcomes of income gaps, rising standards of living and differential access to social services and education to economic policies and their impact are comparatively explored. Issues concerning corruption and economic inequality within the context of economic change are also investigated.

Given that political and economic interdependence among countries has become increasingly important, a variety of approaches to development (e.g., dependency, import-substitution industrialization, export-led growth, globalization) are defined to establish familiarization. To explain how global and domestic forces interact in such a context, discussions are made concerning how certain previously domestic economic policy responsibilities have been pooled by participating states in supranational organizations (e.g., the World Trade Organization, the European Union). Additionally, attention is given to the dynamics of globalization along with an evaluation of how these dynamics bear on themes such as sovereignty and the ideal of the nation-state. Some resulting responses to globalization reaffirm state sovereignty, while others reject it by taking their religious, cultural or ethnic identities as a reference point. Thus, examinations of the cultural aspects of globalization are undertaken. Fragmentation and the interplay between worldwide consumer culture and class, gender, ethnic and religious identities are presented as critical aspects contained in these discussions.

Revolution, Coups, and War

There are many different theories of change which can be employed to attempt to explain political and economic changes ranging from moderate reforms to revolutions. While in reality, economic and political changes are often strongly tied together, there has been a tendency in political theory to try to explain the change as being primarily driven either by economic or political conditions. Theorists influenced by the German philosopher Georg Hegel's theory of change argue that political conditions drive major societal changes. In this theory of change, the primary reason people would take part in a revolution or protest movement is that they are being denied political rights or their political freedoms are being restricted in some way. On the flip side, Marxist-influenced theories of change argue that economic conditions drive change; they argue that people join movements for change because they are economically exploited in some way. Today, many theorists of change are less one-sided and more willing to argue that societal changes are driven by a range of complex factors, including economic and political conditions.

For example, the Arab Spring movement in Egypt from 2011 to 2013, which overthrew dictator Hosni Mubarak, had some factors that led to it. The people were sick of the lack of political freedom due to the control of the state, but they were also upset about the lack of employment prospects among the youth of the country. Both factors worked together to spur a push for change. Despite these two influencing factors, many analysts claimed that technological modernization was the determining factor for change. This theory of change is called technological determinism, and, like the other two theories mentioned above, it is equally one-sided. Technological determinism theory believes that the spread of the internet and social media to Egypt led to the fall of its dictatorship because it believes that the new technology is invariably linked to democracy. This theory is wrong as well, as it indicates that China should have had a revolution due to technology and ignores the fact that the Mubarak government promoted and encouraged internet use in Egypt.

Egyptian police prevent protestors from advancing further during the
Day of Anger protest on January 25, 2011.

Political and economic changes are usually linked, and revolutions cannot be explained by pointing to a single idea as the cause. The complexity of political change can be demonstrated by looking at radical changes that have occurred in some countries through revolutions and coup d'états. A revolution is always a risky affair, where the outcome is unknown. While a revolution requires massive popular support to overthrow the old regime, the issue of what comes after the revolution is a matter of intense conflict as well.

In popular accounts of revolutions in Russia, China or Iran, it is often simply assumed that the revolutionaries in Russia and China wanted a communist dictatorship and the Iranians wanted an Islamic theocracy, so they overthrew the existing system and put in place their preferred form of government. In reality, this is far from the truth. In the case of Russia, the 1917 revolution was supported by broad sectors of the population who opposed the tyrannical rule of the Tsar. Many of the revolutionaries sought to give full political control to the Soviets, which were workplace councils organized by democratic means. One of the slogans of the revolution was "all power to the Soviets." These revolutionaries wanted the Soviet Union that was radically decentralized, where workplace and neighborhood councils ("soviets") would hold political power, and the central government would deal merely with external affairs.

After the successful overthrow of the Tsar, Russia fell into civil war as foreign powers intervened, which the Communist Party used as an excuse for centralizing power. In 1921, there was a major rebellion in the city of Kronstadt on the part of people who had supported the revolution but opposed the centralizing tendency of the Communist Party. The Kronstadt rebellion led to a series of left-wing groups revolting against the Communist Party, demanding local democracy and less centralized control. The Communist Party and the Red Army eventually crushed these rebellions through force, allowing them to stabilize their control of the country.

The same situation happened in Iran after the 1979 revolution. The revolution itself was not motivated by a demand for Islamic theocracy but instead by opposition to the oppression of the Shah. Many people who participated in the revolution were opposed to Islamic principles but put up with the participation of the Islamic Clerics since they had a common enemy in the Shah. At one point during the revolutionary protests, a demonstration of 100,000 members of the Iranian Communist Party marched through the streets of Tehran, including women protesters who did not wear the traditional Islamic head coverings. After the Shah was overthrown, the various factions who united in opposing the Shah each tried to fill the power vacuum. The Islamic Clerics were the most organized and most willing to use violent force against the liberal and left-wing groups, and they ended up taking control of the Iranian state.

There is a tendency for revolutions, even ones which are committed to freedom and democracy, to lead to authoritarian governments. This is precisely because, once the old government is overthrown, it opens up space for a new regime to capture the state. This new regime is often authoritarian itself, not because the revolutionaries wanted it, but because authoritarians are more willing to use violence to achieve their aims. In this sense, revolutions are often literal revolutions, being "a complete turn in a circle" that ends up more or less back where it began. Freedom and equality are often what motivate a revolution, but violence is what creates a new regime. At the same time, a revolution which does not result in a violent power struggle is usually not a proper revolution. If the transition to a new regime is smooth, it is usually because the regime has not changed, only the people who are running it. Revolutions are dangerous and risky, and yet at the same time they are the only way to successfully get rid of old regimes that the people no longer support.

A *coup d'état* is different from a revolution in that a coup d'état is not popularly supported. Mass participation in protests drive revolutions and organizing alternative forms of government. A coup d'état is when one sector of the elite decides that the current regime has become intolerable and moved against it. Coup d'états are almost always initiated by the military of a country against the government, as was the case in the 1966 Nigerian coup. This coup d'état plunged Nigeria into a civil war after the region of Biafra later attempted to secede from Nigeria and become its own country.

A defiant Boris Yeltsin stands on top of a tank used in the attempted August Coup.

There are generally two types of military coup d'état, those led by generals and those led by colonels. Generals tend to be close to the senior leadership of a country, and a general's coup tends to be reactive and conservative in nature. Senior military ranks usually initiate Generals' coups who see their government as being "too progressive." For example, General Augusto Pinochet led a coup d'état in Chile in 1973 against an elected socialist government. By contrast, Colonels' coups tend to be directed against governments which have become corrupt or stagnant. Colonels, being middle-rank officers, are not as close to the government and are more willing to move against it. While generals' coups and colonels' coups are not always along these lines, there is a strong correlation.

Trends and Types of Political Change

One of the major trends in political change since 1991 has been a sweeping wave of democratization. Many of former Soviet bloc countries have transitioned from single-party dictatorships to elected governments with varying degrees of democracy. In North Africa and the Middle East, the Arab Spring movements of 2011-2013 toppled dictators in Tunisia, Egypt, Libya, and Yemen, with some of these countries adopting electoral democracy. Much of sub-Saharan Africa has also seen a wave of democratization, as military and colonial dictatorships were overthrown in countries such as Nigeria and South Africa. In 1990, only three countries in Africa could be considered electoral democracies; today the number is over 20.

This wave of democratization has led political theorists such as Francis Fukuyama to propose that liberal democracy is the perfect form of government and the end goal of all of political history. Despite the fact that since 1990, people increasingly agree that electoral democracy is the best form of government, the same polls also show that people since that time increasingly view electoral democracy as a bad form of government. What this means is that global polling indicates that while people believe there is no better system of government than electoral democracy, they don't necessarily think it is a great system. This trend toward seeing electoral democracy as a bad form of government without any better alternative is demonstrated by the fact that voter turnout numbers have consistently dropped across the mature democracies in the last 40-50 years. Many people today would seem to agree with former British Prime Minister Winston Churchill's quip that "democracy is the worst form of government, except all those other forms that have been tried from time to time."

Such attitudes raise the question in comparative politics of how to evaluate political change. Is the transition from a dictatorship to an elected government necessarily a sign of progress which will improve the condition of a country? Many scholars who agree with Fukuyama's assessment that electoral democracy is the end point of history, and the best system, rank countries based on whether or not they are full electoral democracies and assume that electoral democracy is always better than a dictatorship or semi-democratic elections.

Other scholars of comparative politics argue that this approach is too simple and the actual conditions in a country need to be analyzed. If switching from a dictatorship to an elected democracy keeps the same people in power, as it did in many of the former Soviet Republics, do elections constitute a serious improvement? Uzbekistan, for instance, became an independent country and held its first ever elections in 1991 after the collapse of the Soviet Union. Islam Karimov was elected president, which essentially changed nothing because he had been the leader of the region appointed by the Soviet Communist Party before independence. Karimov has won every election since 1991 and is still in power today. Therefore, Uzbekistan is ruled by the same person who ruled it when it was under a dictatorship; as a democracy, it simply continually re-elects the same person. To those scholars who see elections invariably as "progress" and a sign of good government, Uzbekistan is a success story for its democratization. Scholars who look at the actual material conditions of a country argue that Uzbekistan has not improved at all despite having elections, as Karimov is still in power, still functioning as a dictator, albeit an elected one.

A second complication with the wave of democratization relates to how competitive these elections are. As with the case of Uzbekistan, elections are mere charades which reconfirm Karimov's hold over the country. Even in some countries where elections are considered legitimately free and fair, they are still dominated by a single party. Botswana and South Africa are considered to have relatively fair elections, yet a single party has dominated both these countries' elections since they became democracies. Is a country democratic if a single party always wins, even if these elections are not rigged in their favor? Again, it depends on what method of comparative analysis is being used. Some scholars like to point to Botswana and South Africa as great examples of democratization, but others argue that they have simply become elected dictatorships where a single party still dominates all of political life.

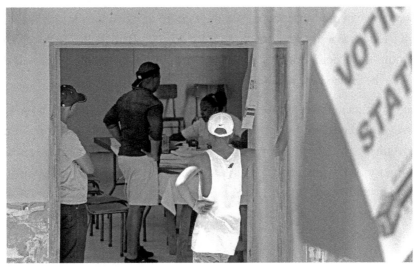

First-time South African voters register for the 2014 election, a multi-party contest which saw 249 of 400 National Assembly seats go to one party, the African National Congress.

A third complication with the wave of democratization is the problem of what happens when democracy backfires, and the people elect a government that seeks to do away with democracy. In 1991, Algeria held its first multi-party elections since it became an independent country in 1962. An Islamic political party which promised to rule Algeria as an Islamic theocracy and cancels future elections won the election. To defend democracy, the military stepped in and overthrew the democratically elected Islamic government in a coup d'état. This was highly ironic, as the military was overthrowing the democratically elected government in the name of defending democracy. The result was a civil war which lasted for eleven years.

A similar event happened in 2013 in Egypt. After the Arab Spring protesters overthrew the dictator, elections were held and won by the Islamists, whom the Arab Spring protesters opposed. Feeling that the new elected Islamic government was a betrayal of the revolution, the protesters overthrew the democratically elected government as well, arguing that such a government would impede the political freedom that they were seeking for Egyptian society. This raises many questions about political change and elections as a goal. If elected governments threaten democracy, is it legitimate for the people or the military to overthrow these governments? Some comparative political scientists say yes, some say no.

Components

The key factor in this wave of democratization was the collapse of the Soviet Union as a major power and alternative to the United States. With the notable exception of China (who had their sphere of influence), when the Soviet Union fell, the vast majority of its allied dictatorships were overthrown by the people of those countries as well. Some of these revolutions were peaceful, some were violent, and some kept the same people in power, only now they could claim legitimacy because they were elected. In addition to the collapse of the Soviet Union as a rival super-power, dissident groups in many of these countries had been operating under the radar, organizing people to support the cause of political freedom against dictatorship. While economic determinists often argue that these countries simply collapsed because of the failures of communism as an economic system, the slogans of most of the protesters related to demands for political freedom and dignity, not a desire for capitalism. Many scholars argue that the real problem that people had with the governments of the former Soviet satellite countries was the authoritarian and sometimes totalitarian forms of government in place.

Promoting or Inhibiting Factors

One of the interesting components of the wave of democratization across the former communist countries and the military regimes of Africa is how certain countries have managed to avoid this trend. Despite a history of great political changes and protests, China has remained relatively unfazed by these movements for democracy. Despite major protests and scandals inside of China, such as the Tiananmen Square protests of 1989 which demanded more freedom and protests in 2014 and 2015 against corruption in the Chinese Communist Party, there seems to be an acceptance within the country that electing a government would not make much of a change. The Communist Party argues that it must remain in control of the country to continue to grow China's economy. As long as the party can deliver on this promise, it seems able to fend off demands for multi-party elections.

Countries such as North Korea and Saudi Arabia have managed to fend off calls for democracy through the use of ideological propaganda and violent coercion. Unlike China's dictatorship, which is based on a kind of social contract promising economic prosperity, North Korea and Saudi Arabia focus on maintaining ideological and religious homogeneity enforced by violence. Speaking out against the government in either of those countries leads to being executed for blasphemy, as criticizing the government is seen as attacking the religious and ideological grounding of the nation.

The fear of violent reprisal from the government can inhibit waves of democratization, while a sense that everyone is on one's side against the government can result in overthrowing dictators. The method of how a dictator is overthrown can vary, as some revolutions that brought democratization were non-violent, such as in East Germany in 1989, in Portugal in 1974 and Czechoslovakia in 1989. Sometimes protesters can have a non-violent intent but be attacked by the state, as was the case in Romania in 1989 and Egypt in 2011, where protesters were met with violence from the state but eventually were able to resist attacks by the police and win the support of the military. While armed insurrections have tended to be relatively unsuccessful, they did set the stage for democratization in South Korea. After students protesting the military government were murdered in 1980, residents took up arms to fight back against the government in the Gwangju Uprising, demanding the government resign and hold elections. Hundreds of people were killed and many more jailed. Today, the Gwangju Uprising is commemorated in South Korea as the beginning of the movement for democracy and human rights that was eventually able to overthrow the military dictatorship in 1987.

A mural in Portugal commemorating the military-led, civilian supported Carnation Revolution.

Consequences

The consequences of the wave of democratization beginning in 1990 have been varied. Some of the former Soviet Bloc dictatorships such as Poland and the Czech Republic have turned into fully democratic multi-party democracies, some have become democracies dominated by a single party, as with Russia, and some have become elected dictatorships, such as Uzbekistan. Electoral democracy itself is not a cure-all solution, as the wave of democratization has had mixed results. The main consequence has been the reorientation of international relations after the end of the Cold War. The United States emerged as the world's only superpower, no longer kept in check by the power of the Soviet Union. With the failures of the American interventions in Iraq and Afghanistan and the inability to democratize those countries, many international relations experts are arguing that the world is now becoming a multi-polar one, where there can no longer be dominant superpowers, just strong regional powers.

While electoral democracy has produced mixed results, it is still generally seen as preferable to unelected dictatorships. The few remaining unelected dictatorships face global pressures to hold elections. Against this context, a new wave of democratization may be emerging which demands more substantive democracy, rather than simply just holding elections. The protests in Iran in 2009 and Mexico in 2006 demonstrate that even in countries with electoral democracies there will be strong movements of people demanding more democracy and for elections to be fair, free and competitive. In the United Kingdom, there have been efforts to change the electoral system and replace the first-past-the-post method with a fairer and more democratic proportional system. In Canada, there have been pushes to abolish the unelected Senate to make the legislature fully democratic. Across the world, the Occupy movement (first seen in Occupy Wall Street, then widely emulated) sought to bring more democracy into the economic realm; the movement demanded that governments represent the people and not corporations.

Trends and Types of Economic Change

The period starting in the late 1990s saw a wave of democratization on the political front and a wave of privatizations on the economic front. These economic changes were driven by top-down pressure from corporations, while bottom-up pressure from citizens drove most of the waves of political democratization. As with political change, economic change can have some different sources, but it has tended to be more elite-driven lately, as opposed to the citizen-driven pushes for political change. Economic change in the past has come through popular revolutions, such as Russia in 1917 and China in 1949, which sought not only to oust corrupt and authoritarian dictatorships but also to bring sweeping economic changes through adopting elements of communism.

To understand the context of major economic changes such as communist revolutions or the spread of neoliberal globalization, a brief history of the international political economy is necessary. From 1870 to the outbreak of World War I in 1914, the international economy was dominated by competing for imperial interests, with the United Kingdom the most powerful economic actor. During this period, most countries used the gold standard, which meant that currency value was directly tied to the price of gold. As an era of competing for imperial projects and overseas colonies, the international economy was highly integrated. Countries competed with each other to exploit and extract value from their colonies to send back home and to sell the products of their industries to other countries. There was very little regulation in this era, and many scholars see it in retrospect as the first wave of economic globalization.

The competing imperial economic projects soon spilled out of the confines of mere economic competition and turned into military conflict with the outbreak of World War I. During World War I; industrial production shifted to focus on domestic production to support the war effort. Many countries in World War I ran short of gold reserves and as a result had to suspend the convertibility of currency to gold; most countries abandoned the gold standard altogether by the end of the war. Many countries had economic problems financing the war, and hyperinflation became an issue in some countries without currencies pegged in value to gold. At this time, the U.K. became heavily indebted to the United States, and the U.S. emerged as the major economic power of the world. After the end of the war, many countries went back to the gold standard.

This was problematic because their currencies could not fluctuate relative to those of other countries. These governments were unable to devalue their currencies to make their exports cheaper to stimulate their economy, and they could not engage in policies to increase the money supply. So while the abandonment of the gold standard during World War I resulted in hyperinflation (especially in Germany), the subsequent return to it caused deflation, which shrinks economies.

While Europe was suffering through the 1920s, the United States boomed since its export industries were not destroyed during the war. This was also an era of next to no financial regulation, and American banks engaged in major speculative activities. Meanwhile, France had forced Germany to pay punitive reparations which were bankrupting the German economy. By the end of the 1920s, the unregulated financial markets in the United States had caused an incredible stock market bubble which burst in October 1929. Even though the international economy was not very integrated at this time, the collapse of the American stock market sent shockwaves around the globe because the U.S. had now emerged as the biggest economy in the world. People in the United States and Europe lost confidence in the financial system; banks began to collapse, industries went out of business and unemployment skyrocketed. In response, most countries cut back on government spending, which only made the crisis worse. The United States refused to forgive European war debts and also refused to act as a lender of last resort to bail out the collapsing European countries. The widespread popular sentiment drove these American policies in favor of isolationism, but they ended up transforming an economic crisis into a global Great Depression.

The economic crisis in Europe led to a loss of confidence in political leadership. In Germany, the fascist Nazi party led by Adolf Hitler rose to power. Italy shifted to fascism in the 1920s, and Spain did so in the 1930s. During World War I, the Russian Tsar had been overthrown and replaced with a communist government. The outbreak of World War II amidst the Great Depression was economically beneficial. It caused governments to discard their policy of cutting spending and engage in massive spending projects to build up machinery for the war. After the war, countries realized that the British political economist John Maynard Keynes was right, and the way to get out of a recession is for the government to spend more money, not less.

A disabled German World War I veteran begs on the streets of 1923 Berlin.

After the war, the countries of Western Europe got together to create a new regulated international financial regime which was meant to prevent the conditions that had led to the outbreak of World War II. Countries adopted Keynes's economic ideas, which were based on the concept of counter-cyclical economics. When the economy was doing well, the government should cut spending to prevent a bubble from forming, and when the economy was doing poorly, the government should increase spending to stimulate the economy. Keynes realized that when the economy was in a recession, companies would lay off many workers and cut back on expansion to save money to stay afloat. If all the companies are cutting back and firing workers, this creates a vicious spiral of economic decline. Keynes realized that the only economic actor who could break this spiral of decline was the government.

At the same time, the Soviet Union had emerged as a major power, and communism had become a competing economic system in Eastern Europe and China. The Soviet Union had rapidly industrialized, moving from a largely rural-based economy before 1917 to a competitive economic superpower with the United States by the early 1950s. In the wake of the defeat of fascism and the beginning of the Cold War, Keynesian economics was a form of capitalism that had appeal for the working class of Western Europe and kept them from joining communist movements. The U.K., the U.S., and other Western European countries, under the influence of Keynesian economic theory, increased minimum wages, put in place major social programs to help the poor and regulated the financial markets to prevent major crashes.

Despite the success of both the Soviet communist system and the American-led Keynesian system at rapidly growing the economy from the period of the 1940s to 1970s with almost no major economic crises, problems occurred in the 1970s as a result of the world's dependence on oil. In 1973, Egypt and Syria launched a surprise attack on Israel in an attempt to win back territories Israel had taken from those countries in the 1967 Six-Day War. The U.S. and its allies supported Israel by sending them military arms, and the Organization of the Petroleum Exporting Countries (OPEC) responded by placing an oil embargo on the United States, Canada, the U.K., and other U.S. allies. The price of oil skyrocketed, and the U.S. abandoned the gold standard, leading other countries to adopt floating relative currency values. In 1979, a second oil crisis occurred after Iran dramatically decreased oil exports to the U.S. There were gas shortages in the U.S., and the economy suffered.

A small-town American gas station abandoned during the 1973-1974 winter fuel crisis.

In the wake of these oil crises, the cost of oil went up very fast, which caused not only the price of gasoline to skyrocket but also the price of shipping food and anything else that relied on long-distance transportation. The result was a dramatic increase in inflation which also slowed the economy. Until this point in time, inflation had been driven by rapid expansions of the money supply, which meant that the economy was growing very quickly. Keynesian economic policy was designed precisely to prevent inflation due to bubbles and deflation due to the economic slowdown. However, in this period in the 1970s, there was what came to be called "stagflation," which was economic slowdown accompanied by inflation. Keynesian economic policy was unprepared to handle this because such a situation had never happened before. The Soviet economy also ran into problems during the 1970s, although it benefitted from the higher oil prices as a major oil producer. The Soviets were lagging in adopting computer technology, and the ill-advised invasion of Afghanistan in 1979 hurt the economy.

Into the late 1970s, there was a feeling that the international economy was becoming increasingly unstable. Some radical right-wing economists backed by large corporations proposed a return to the deregulated era of liberal economics before World War I. This movement in favor of financial deregulation, cutting social spending, privatization of government-owned industries and global integration of the economy came to be known as neoliberal economics. This movement managed to win favor in many countries by attaching itself to conservative religious movements. In the United States, neoliberal economists and business elites joined with conservative Christian groups to remake the Republican Party into a socially conservative, economically neoliberal party. In Mexico, the PRI began to undertake neoliberal reforms in the 1980s, but it was not until the PAN party came to power in 2000, backed by conservative Catholics, that the country's economy was fully transformed along neoliberal lines.

In the Soviet Union, the impossibility of its invasion of Afghanistan succeeding played a major role in bringing about not only a general decline in economic efficiency in the 1980s but also a loss of confidence in the political leadership. The USSR was also hit hard by a major drop in the price of oil in the mid-1980s, which hurt its export income. Also, continued corruption and stagnation in state-run industries due to an inability to adapt to new computer technologies and a growing informal black-market economy contributed to the country's economic decline.

After the popularization of neoliberal economics in the 1980s and 1990s, this doctrine spread around the world. Sometimes it was established through a combination of domestic alliances with religious groups (such as in the United States, India, and Turkey), sometimes it was imposed top-down in a coup d'état (such as in Chile) and sometimes it was a result of structural adjustment programs forced on countries by the International Monetary Fund and the World Bank. This economic system did not globalize because of an international agreement, as had been the case with the Keynesian system, but through the strength of corporations who saw that this economic theory would enable them to operate at a transnational, global level, unchecked by regulatory interference from individual states. The Keynesian era of 1949 to 1980 had been characterized by national economies where corporations lived inside a country and trade and finance were heavily regulated by states. In the neoliberal era, corporations could float from state to state with no allegiance to any one country, and through corporate rights treaties such as the World Trade Organization or the Trans-Pacific Partnership, they were able to use their power to control states, rather than the other way around.

In the neoliberal era, which began in the 1980s, governments were able to get the inflation problems of the 1970s under control. The return to deregulated financial markets, however, ushered in a return of the boom-bust cycle that had been prominent before World War II and was responsible for the Great Depression. Since the early 1990s, neoliberal economics has led to a series of major economic crises which have threatened the viability of the global economic system. The global economic crisis of 2008 led to a major shift in thinking, and many prominent political economists began to question the viability of neoliberal economic theory and called for a new international agreement to set forth regulations on how the global economy would operate. Such a meeting never occurred, and the global economy continues to be mired in structural problems due to a lack of political will to negotiate a new framework that would create global economic stability.

Components

The components of economic change are usually some form of economic crisis. There is very little motivation to change the economic system when it seems to be doing relatively well. As Chinese Communist leader Mao Zedong said, "everything under the heaven is in crisis, the situation is perfect," meaning that a crisis is also a great opportunity for change. Interestingly enough, Mao's death in China created a political crisis and instability, eventually allowing Deng Xiaoping to outmaneuver Mao's chosen successor. Deng encouraged criticism of Mao's Great Leap Forward policies, which resulted in mass deaths due to starvation, inhumane working conditions and the barbaric treatment and violence the rural population was subjected to in the drive to meet unrealistic production quotas. This resulted in widespread economic stagnation. After observing Singapore's rapid economic development through focusing on export-led growth, Deng initiated a serious of reforms to transform China's economy to a version of state-controlled capitalism and away from Mao's communist system.

Agriculture commune workers, using lamps,
toil the fields at night during the Great Leap Forward.

Deng's gradual reforms and slow privatization process have led to China emerging as a major economic powerhouse. Meanwhile, Russia's transition from state communism straight to neoliberal economics was an unmitigated disaster, as Russia rapidly de-industrialized and went from the world's second-biggest economy to a state of underdevelopment. The contrasting examples of Russia and China regarding their economic change from communism to capitalism are very interesting from a comparative politics point of view. One thing that political economists encourage is to compare economic systems not just in terms of simple ideas like communism as opposed to capitalism, but also in terms of what form of capitalism. Russia's unquestioning acceptance of neoliberal capitalism collapsed its economy, while China's more cautious approach of state-managed capitalism led to an explosion of growth. In this sense, the form of the economic system matters more than the general ideology. Russia might have been better off had it stuck with communism, while China definitely would have been worse off. Such comparisons are the basis of major points of study and debate within comparative political economics.

Promoting or Inhibiting Factors

The main promoting factor in the wave of privatizations after 1990 was the strength of neoliberal economics as an ideology. With both communism and Keynesianism having suffered serious problems, neoliberalism seemed like the only alternative. British Prime Minister Margaret Thatcher was famous for her TINA doctrine, which stood for There Is No Alternative, meaning that neoliberal economic reforms had to be accepted because they were simply the only economic policy left. In countries such as the U.K. that had been dominated by Keynesian economic thinking, certain industries were owned by the state because it was believed that handing this industry to the free market would result in a monopoly. Telecom and railways for example, where it makes no sense to have rival companies laying their phone lines or railroad tracks, were owned by the state to avoid corporate monopolies that would create price gouging. Neoliberal economics encouraged the privatization of these industries, which helped create more giant private monopolies.

In Mexico, the government nationalized the oil industry in 1938, creating Pemex as the national oil company. As a valuable natural resource, the Mexican government argued that the Mexican people were best served by owning this resource directly so that the people could profit from it, rather than corporations. After the election of Vicente Fox's neoliberal PAN in 2000, there were calls to privatize Pemex, which by then had grown into one of the largest state-owned enterprises in the world. The Mexican people were overwhelmingly opposed to such direct privatization schemes, and as a result, successive Mexican governments have used Pemex as a corrupt means to funnel money to sympathetic corporate backers. By turning a blind eye to fraud inside Pemex, the Mexican government is blatantly allowing contractors who do business with Pemex to defraud it of hundreds of millions of dollars. In part, the government does this to win support from corporate backers. It is also trying to discredit Pemex as corrupt to once again try to privatize it. The issue of Pemex privatization remains an extremely sensitive topic in Mexico, and a massive anti-privatization rally occurred in Mexico City in 2013.

Nigeria faces similar issues, as its government is planning massive privatization of parts of the state-owned oil industry in 2015 and 2016. The beginning of these privatizations in 2015 led to a dramatic increase in fuel prices inside Nigeria, which spawned the Occupy Nigeria movement. Protesters were angry that Nigerians had to pay more for gasoline after the government was no longer making money from selling oil and eliminated fuel subsidies. Natural resource privatization is an especially problematic issue. When these resources are privatized, the wealth generated from them generally goes into the pockets of foreign corporations, and the people of the country get no benefit from the resources of their country. The case of Nigeria is especially illustrative. At the same time, the government partially privatized the oil industry, it could no longer afford the fuel subsidies that Nigerians argued they deserved since it was their oil. Today, Nigerian oil profits are increasingly going to foreign corporations while Nigerians see no benefit. The government argues that privatization will create more jobs, but workers in the oil industry have protested, saying that private companies will employ fewer Nigerians and bring in foreigners to do their jobs.

Consequences

The consequences of the wave of privatizations have been somewhat mixed but mostly negative for the average citizen. Privatizations in developed countries such as the United Kingdom have led to the formation of private monopolies, allowing corporate elites to acquire huge sums of wealth while the average customer has to pay more for the same service due to a lack of competition. Neoliberal economics has brought about a huge increase in wealth inequality across the world. Privatizations are one of the main causes for this because they directly increase costs to consumers, decrease government revenues, cause the government to reduce spending on social programs and increase the profits of the ultra-wealthy.

A homeless New York City resident sleeps on Broadway in affluent Manhattan.

In the case of Russia, privatization created a class of oligarchs with immense wealth while poverty dramatically increased. Chinese privatization has been more beneficial. Jobs have been created, but China's wealth inequality is also dramatically increasing, with a new class of billionaires emerging who can exploit extremely cheap labor and sell cheap and highly profitable products to the United States. In Nigeria and Mexico, privatization of natural resources is controversial and largely problematic. Mexican billionaire Carlos Slim benefited from taking over the previously public Mexican telecom system. Governments like to privatize industries because it gives them a one-time infusion of cash which they can spend extravagantly to shore up their short-term prospects for re-election. In the long term, the decline of government revenues tends to be severely problematic.

Relationship between Political and Economic Change

One of the most intense debates in all of political science relates to the relationship between political and economic change. As mentioned earlier, a major debate in political theory has been between Hegelians (who believe political change causes economic change) and Marxists (who believe the opposite), with many other theorists arguing that neither causes the other, but the two are interrelated. Another major theorist of political and economic change was Max Weber, who argued that the economic change from feudalism to capitalism was driven by Protestant religious values and not by anything specifically political or economic. Hegelians argued that capitalism was a result of the fall of the monarchy, and thus political change brought economic change, while Marxists argued that feudalism was unsustainable and the shift to capitalism caused the feudalist political structure to fall with it.

In the branch of comparative political studies which focuses on developing countries, a major point of debate is the link between capitalism and democracy. Many scholars had argued that these two were linked, and thus if a country were able to adopt one of these traits, it would soon adopt the other. This was a popular idea during the Cold War when most communist countries were one-party dictatorships. The idea was that if either democracy or capitalism could be introduced into a country under a communist dictatorship, then it would soon transform into a capitalist democracy. The fall of the Soviet Union seemed to confirm this idea of a link between capitalism and democracy, but since 1991 this connection has come under sharp criticism.

Many of the post-Soviet states which became capitalist failed to become democratic in the American sense of having competitive multi-party elections. China adopted capitalism while maintaining a strong single-party system of dictatorship, as did Vietnam and countries such as Uzbekistan. Scholars of economic development also questioned the idea that democracy plus capitalism was the best way for a country to move from being poor to being rich. China and South Korea rapidly developed under dictatorships, while many of the new democracies in Africa have failed to improve their economic situation. Many development theorists are now arguing that democracy is not the best system to allow capitalism to flourish and that capitalism works better under an authoritarian government where workers have few rights. These theorists point out that when countries like the U.K., the United States and France first industrialized in the 18th century, the political situation in each of these countries was hardly democratic and was instead characterized by the oppression of workers, both economically and politically.

So, while economic and political change is often closely linked, it remains difficult to argue that either side is dominant or causes the other. Ideas about certain economic systems being inherently linked to certain political systems have also come undone. Capitalism is no longer viewed as working best in a democracy, and socialism is no longer seen as needing a dictatorship since elected governments in South America in the 2000s have brought about socialism through elections.

Globalization and Fragmentation

One of the most significant changes in the recent history of the world is the onset of globalization in a variety of areas. The primary driver of globalization is technology. While previous periods of world history have seen aspects of globalization — such as the open trading period before World War I, the cultural exchanges among the cities of ancient Greece and the political cohesion of the far-flung Roman Empire — all these periods lacked the technology which has today made the Earth seem a lot smaller. Modern airplanes allow traveling anywhere in the world in less than a day; modern telecommunications allow not only communication with someone on the phone across the world but also the ability to log on to the internet and meet new people at random who live on the other side of the globe. This technological integration is what made possible the political, social, cultural and economic globalization that took off in the late 1990s.

At the same time that this technology allowed people to connect and integrate, it has also enabled fragmentation. Immigrants from Pakistan and the Middle East who move to the U.K., for example, can continue to watch satellite TV from home and spend their time on websites dedicated to people from their home country. They may not interact with or even share a common culture with the people they live next door to, creating a new form of urban ghettoization. Opposition to foreign cultural products has led to the rise of nationalism and religious fundamentalism in many countries, often facilitated by the spread of these very same foreign products. While capital can now flow freely across borders, migrant workers cannot readily follow the jobs created by capital, causing issues of illegal immigrants. Wars started by the increase in religious fundamentalism have led to refugee crises. Below, the economic, cultural, political and regional reactions to globalization will be examined.

The Bengali community protests against the National Front and their racist supporters in East London in 1978.

Interlinked Economies

The interlinking of economies began to occur with the fall of the Soviet Union. Now that the world was not divided into rival ideological camps, corporations began looking for new markets. In combination with the now all-pervasive economic theory of neoliberalism, countries began opening their borders to foreign investment and foreign corporations. In countries such as China, they began by setting up special economic zones where products were produced to be exported without tariffs or controls by the government. In other countries, international treaties such as the WTO empowered corporations with the right to challenge any laws and practices of member states they found restrictive, creating a new global economic order in which corporations were free to float from country to country. Since there was no global political order, corporations now existed on a transnational level and could no longer be regulated by individual states. This new era of transnational capital is one of the main aspects of economic globalization.

With corporations now able to freely move from country to country, they can offer to set up factories in countries in exchange for meeting their demands. These demands ranged from lowering the minimum wage, exemption from the workplace and environmental safety regulations and being granted tax shelter status. States generally agree to these demands since there is little they can do to prevent a company from simply moving to another country. As a result, the economy has become globally integrated, and individual states have much less control over economic matters than they did prior to the adoption of neoliberal globalization.

With the global financial system integrated, the 2008 economic crisis affected the entire world, even though it began in the U.S. residential housing market. The same risky collateralized debt obligations which collapsed major American investment banks were also being bought by banks in Iceland and Ireland, causing collapses in the banking system in those countries as well. Economic problems can no longer be isolated to a specific country and can easily become a contagion that spreads panic throughout the global system. Due to the lack of global regulation, this system remains in place, and the eight years of stagnant economic activity from 2008 to 2016 is now being called the Global Great Recession by many political economists.

One of the major aspects of neoliberal globalization is the ease with which corporations can move large sums of money around. This became a major issue in Argentina in 2001, as an economic crisis brought on by neoliberal economic reforms caused a loss of corporate confidence in the country. Overnight, corporations and billionaires filled armored cars and trucks with money as they withdrew all their holdings in Argentinian banks and shipped the money out of the country. This example of extreme capital flight caused a run on the banks, meaning that the banks did not have enough cash on hand to allow all their depositors to go to an ATM and take money out. When the government realized what was happening, it did not place limits on the large sums of corporate money fleeing the country but placed limits on how much money people could withdraw from their bank accounts. Eventually, some banks collapsed entirely, and many Argentinians lost their life's savings. After this, Argentinians took to the streets and overthrew six consecutive governments in street protests before finally Nestor Kirchner was elected and restored confidence in the financial system.

Handing immense power over to corporations at the expense of governments was supposed to bring a new era of global prosperity, in which a globally integrated economic system would provide advantages for everyone. A small developing country would now have the entire world to sell its products to, rather than just a few million people. The idea was that economic globalization was supposed to bring development and prosperity to all. The reality has been that a tiny, elite share of the global population has captured almost all of these gains from economic globalization.

Mounted Argentinian police in Buenos Aires charge protesters.

In January 2016, a new study found that just 62 billionaires control half of the entire world's wealth. In addition, the poorest 50% of the world's population have gotten poorer since the advent of neoliberal globalization. Inequality is now recognized to be one of the biggest economic problems of the globalization era. Even in developed countries such as the U.S. and the U.K., the working class has not seen their real wages (which are adjusted for inflation) increase in twenty years, while the top 0.1% of both of those countries have massively increased their wealth.

Critics of economic globalization are often misunderstood in their criticisms. They tend to critique the lack of any global regime of economic regulation, rather than the idea of globally integrating the economy. Technology means that the economy will continue to be inherently globally integrated, and the focus of these critics is often on building the political capacity to regulate the financial and economic system across national borders. Unfortunately, states do not often agree with each other, and getting every country on board for a new regulatory regime for global finance has proven impossible.

Many international relations theorists call this a situation of global anarchy, as at the global level there is no overall global government and states remain unwilling to cooperate on regulations. In many cases, smaller countries can simply be bought off to win the votes to stop such agreements. At the International Whaling Commission, Japan was able to win a vote removing restrictions on killing whales by simply paying off member countries to vote their way. People became suspicious when land-locked countries such as Congo voted with Japan, even though such a country would have no material interest in whaling. If bribery could so easily block an international agreement on an issue such as this, it is easy to imagine how difficult creating a new regulatory regime for global finance would be.

Global Culture

Cultural globalization is another contested and controversial aspect of globalization. Given that the first wave of globalization was dominated by the agenda of major corporations based in America, people worried that cultural globalization would turn everyone in the world into an American. There was a real fear that everyone would eat at McDonald's, listen to American pop music and wear American blue jeans. Many believed that cultural globalization was going to be cultural imperialism, with a single Americanized global culture eliminating all the cultural differences of the world. (This was the subject of Billy Wilder's 1961 satire *One, Two, Three*, with James Cagney as a dynamic Coca-Cola executive actively promoting the "Coca-Colonization" of West Germany.) In reality, corporations had already moved away from having loyalty to any country, and those corporations that people feared would spread American cultural imperialism, such as McDonald's, were quick to adapt their menus to local cultures. McDonald's has even opened vegetarian restaurants in parts of India where most of the population do not eat meat. It turned out that corporations realized that adapting to local tastes was much more profitable than attempting to impose foreign tastes.

A McDonald's restaurant in Buenos Aires offers kosher meals.

Corporations are now properly global, and they have often won support for their neoliberal economic agenda of deregulation and open markets by aligning with the most conservative cultural traditions in a country. Looking at the example of India, proponents of neoliberal economic globalization joined forces with conservative Hindu fundamentalists and nationalists. When the Bharatiya Janata Party (BJP) was elected in

1998 and 2014, it pursued policies of opening India's borders to foreign corporations at the same time that it promoted conservative Hindu religious values. The same thing occurred in Turkey, where Islamists promoted neoliberal economics, and in the United States, where evangelical Christians joined up with the neoliberal corporate elite to remake the Republican Party from the late 1970s on. Economic globalization, in finding allies with local religious fundamentalist and conservative cultural groups, has promoted a process of cultural fragmentation. Corporations have been able to make more money catering to local niche markets and being supportive of local cultural traditions, while in exchange the cultural and religious conservatives support neoliberal economic policies.

The flip side of this cultural fragmentation is the increasing trend toward cosmopolitanism. Cosmopolitan culture is the idea that an individual can freely adopt elements from different cultures around the world that he or she enjoys. The cosmopolitan might listen to Colombian music, such as Shakira, do yoga associated with Hinduism, read African literature and eat Japanese sushi every day. Cosmopolitan culture is about mixing all the best aspects of different cultures from around the world, and it is an actualized form of cultural globalization. Cosmopolitans do not reactively claim their own culture is superior, as do the fundamentalists mentioned above, nor do they believe that culture must be limited to the region from which it originates. Cosmopolitans know that sushi tastes good, regardless of whether you are Japanese or not, and they know that you do not have to be Colombian to like Shakira's music.

On the other hand, cultural fundamentalists who endorse cultural fragmentation would argue that people should not engage with other cultures and should stick to their own. Some cultural fundamentalists even argue that enjoying foreign culture is offensive. A cultural fundamentalist in Iran, for example, would argue that a woman wearing western-style clothing and not covered up with the Islamic hijab is insulting her culture. Other cultural fundamentalists claim that enjoying aspects of other cultures is a form of cultural appropriation, which is offensive to the culture one is enjoying. These fundamentalists would argue that someone from the U.K. who does yoga every day is appropriating traditional Hindu culture and is being offensive to all Hindus by "stealing" their sacred practices. This is an example of how globalization complicates culture, especially through technology, as the idea of music, food or exercises from a faraway country was simply not something most people ever knew about before technology connected the world. Even in the 1960s and 1970s, a lot of Americans considered Chinese or Italian food to be foreign and strange. In the U.K., because of the relatively bland nature of traditional British cooking, the most popular food is now curry.

Reactions against Globalization

While globalization has prompted major changes in the fields of economics, culture, and technology, politics has been left behind. States have either had their power forcibly reduced by globalization without the ability to regulate at the global level, or they have willingly enabled transferring authority to corporations. Although there are a global economic system and global culture, a framework of global politics is still lacking. The United Nations remains an international political organization, which means that it still presumes that states are the highest level of political authority. The UN has no authority to compel a member state or a corporation to do anything and does not have any authority at the global level. Problems which are truly global in nature, such as the environment, are difficult to deal with at an international level, and many scholars argue that the international state system which places state sovereignty as the highest level of political authority is obsolete (or should be) for an era of global integration and global problems.

As a result of the lack of political capacity to respond to problems with globalization, as well as the inability to create a globalized political framework, a major protest movement started in the late 1990s called the Alter-Globalization Movement. This movement was a loose coalition of a variety of different activists who endorsed different causes. The movement combined environmentalists, people from the labor movement, peace activists, human rights campaigners, and various indigenous activists. The goal of the movement was to globalize democracy by giving regular people a say in all the new issues created by globalization. One of the main points of contention that the movement opposed was the undemocratic nature of how the new globalized neoliberal economy was operating. States were negotiating treaties in secret to give corporations more power, and once in place, these treaties enabled corporations to sue governments to make them change environmental and labor laws. The Alter-Globalization Movement demanded democratic accountability on a global scale to match the global scale of corporations.

Alter-Globalization Movement slogans in Le Havre, France protesting the 37th G8 summit.

The movement engaged in some high-profile protests which brought public attention to previously obscure and even secretive organizations, such as the WTO, the IMF and Free Trade Area of the Americas. The movement established a yearly meeting called the World Social Forum, meant to promote democratic globalization. Eventually, the movement fragmented, and protests and activism dropped off into the early 2000s. In 2011-2012 a new movement with similar concerns sprung up called Occupy Wall Street. These activists were angry that the United States government had bailed out banks and corporations after the 2008 economic crisis but had not bailed out the American people. These activists sought to draw attention to how governments were acting in the best interests of global corporations instead of the best interests of their people. This movement began in the U.S., but rapidly globalized and eventually there were Occupy protests in 82 different countries. These protests all concentrated on how 99% of the population were not receiving fair treatment from their governments, who were more oriented to enabling and enriching the billionaire class. While in the U.S. this was aimed at government collusion with banks and financial capital, in Nigeria the Occupy movement focused on the role of the government in privatizing parts of the oil industry and raising gasoline prices for average Nigerians.

These movements have sometimes been labeled as anti-globalization by the corporate media, but this is a misnomer. The goal of these movements is to globalize democratic politics, not to reassert the power of states. While the Alter-Globalization and Occupy Movements were on the left of the political spectrum and promoted a different form of globalization, in much of the world a new movement on the right also began at this time which focused on opposing foreign culture and opposing immigration.

In Europe, far-right political parties sprung up who claimed that large-scale immigration and the spread of foreign culture were destroying their country's national identity. In the United Kingdom, the British National Party (BNP) was created, which opposed cultural globalization and the political globalization of the left-wing Alter-Globalization Movement. The BNP argued that immigrants were destroying English culture and soon the country would be taken over by foreigners. They advocated deporting immigrants, especially Poles and Muslims, and withdrawing the U.K. from the European Union. At the same time, far right-wing religious fundamentalists began to oppose cultural globalization during this period as well, seeing the availability of foreign culture as a threat to their traditional authority.

Regionalism

Regionalism has emerged as a halfway position between the international state system and globalization. Regionalism has taken on two forms, attempts to create political unions and attempts to create economic unions. The most common regional groupings are economic blocs, which can range from free trade areas to groups of countries which use a common currency. Since being a small country in a globalized world can pose difficulties, there is often a strong motivation for states to join up with their neighbors to create regional economic unions. Examples of such economic unions are the European Union, MERCOSUR in South America, NAFTA in North America and the Association of Southeastern Asian Nations (ASEAN). Some of these groupings have political aspirations, such as MERCOSUR and the European Union, but the political aspects tend to be overshadowed by economic concerns.

An interesting counterexample is the African Union, which is political in nature but has economic aspirations. Given a large number of countries and the diverse economic and political structures in Africa, the AU has so far been unable to become more than just an international political organization. Unlike the EU, however, the AU has taken an explicit military role by sending African Union troops into member countries, such as Sudan and Somalia, in an attempt to end conflicts and enforce peace treaties. The AU also authorized military forces to act under the AU banner in the 2008 invasion of the island of Anjouan by Comoros.

Anjouan was an autonomous island that was part of the country of Comoros, which had been taken over by a military dictator. Being a small country of a series of islands, Comoros appealed to the AU to help it to invade the island to restore democracy. The invasion was successful at removing the military dictator, and elections were held later that year. Part of the mandate of the AU is to develop its regional authority in dealing with military conflicts to keep American and European soldiers from getting involved. This is a major aim given the long-remembered legacy of colonialism in Africa. However, even in the case of the successful invasion of Anjouan, the AU and the Comoros government still relied heavily on military support from France.

Kenyan soldiers deployed in the African Union Mission in Somalia (AMISOM).

The EU is an interesting case of regionalism as well, as it is one of the few regional blocs to use a common currency. There are benefits and drawbacks to a currency union, which people have learned over the past two decades. One of the major advantages is that individual currencies do not fluctuate against each other, and the price of trading goods with other countries within Europe will be relatively stable. It also makes it easier for people traveling from country to country inside of Europe, since their money is always worth the same everywhere. A disadvantage of this system is that the European Central Bank makes all monetary decisions for all countries. This can cause trouble since the ECB raising the interest rate because Germany's economy is strong could cause a major recession in Greece, whose economy is weak. If they lower the interest rate to stimulate Greece's economy, they could cause a bubble to form in Germany, which would lead to a collapse in the German economy. The inability of member states to control their monetary policy has proven problematic, especially for countries like Greece. There have been threats from Greece to pull out of the Eurozone currency, but overall the Greek government feels that they are better off inside the euro currency zone than outside of it, even if it severely limits the ability of the Greek government to control its economic situation.

The in-between status of regional blocs has created something of an identity crisis for many of them. In the case of the EU, the corporate elite in Europe want the EU to function solely as an economic union, and they have worked to undermine the power of the European Parliament. At the same time, both the Alter-Globalization left and the nationalist right have opposed the EU in many countries. In 2005, the EU developed a new constitution, and many member countries allowed the people to vote on whether or not they should ratify it. The largest of these votes were in France, which is one of the most powerful European Union countries, both politically and economically. The citizens of France ended up voting to reject ratifying the EU constitution as a result of a strange alliance between the left and the far right.

The corporate elite and the conservative government both urged the French to vote in favor of the treaty for economic reasons. Left-wing groups argued that they supported the EU, but that this treaty undermined the EU as a political and democratic institution; they urged supporters to vote against the EU constitution since it was primarily about enshrining corporate power. The far right joined the left in opposing the constitution. The far right argued that France's involvement with a greater European project would undermine French culture and nationality. Even though the left and the far right disagreed with the other's arguments as to why they should oppose ratifying the constitution, their combined opposition was enough to defeat the pro-ratification side.

Competing French posters urging voters to support or reject the drafted EU constitution.

After a similar No vote in the Netherlands, the new EU constitution was scrapped and later rewritten. What this occurrence demonstrates is the shaky position of regionalism. Some see it as a potential avenue for the creation of higher levels of democracy that are above states, some see it as merely enshrining corporate power, and some see it as an attack on nationality and national culture. Many see it as a combination of these elements.

Approaches to Development

While the issues mentioned so far tend to be the primary topics of the comparative politics of the global north, the issue of how to economically develop a country dominates the comparative politics of the global south. Poverty and underdevelopment is the biggest problem in many poorer "southern" countries, and comparisons of how different countries have developed dominate the discussion of the comparative politics of development. There are five main theories of economic development which are influential enough to have been tried in various countries. These are modernization theory, dependency theory, import-substitution industrialization (ISI), export-led development and neoliberalism. These different theories have had different levels of successes depending on where they have been used, and which approach to development works best remains hotly contested.

Modernization theory, developed by the American liberal economist Walt Rostow in the 1960s argues that all countries develop along the same trajectory that moves them from a traditional society toward one which emulates American and European society. Modernization theory argues that the cultural traditions of a country tend to be an obstacle to growth and that American-style liberal democratic capitalism is the highest stage of growth. Modernization theory counsels countries to adopt American-style institutions, which will automatically cause the country to begin to follow the path of America's rapid economic growth in the late 1800s and early 1900s.

The major criticism of Rostow's modernization theory is that it assumes all countries will develop the same way and follow a linear model, with countries always becoming more and more developed. In reality, countries can become less developed, even if they follow American development patterns. In the case of Russia, abandoning communism and adopting American-style economics caused the country to de-industrialize and become significantly worse off. Similarly, many Latin American countries (including Mexico) strongly emulated American institutions and yet failed to develop in the same way as America.

In the 1960s and 1970s, *dependency theory* was developed, in particular, the form advocated by Andre Gunder Frank, a German-American who later lived in Chile. Frank argued that the developed countries caused underdevelopment. Developed countries were core states that extracted wealth from poor peripheral states, which held them locked into a dependent relationship. Core states would exploit the cheap labor and natural resources in the periphery, which would prevent the peripheral states from developing on their own. Frank's goal was to criticize modernization theory, and he argued that underdevelopment was not a temporary stage to growth but a permanent, imposed situation which prevented growth. Dependency theory rejected the linear model of modernization theory and argued that unless developing countries rejected their exploitation by the rich countries, they would be locked into a cycle of underdevelopment.

Sweatshops, such as this one in Indonesia, exploit cheap laborers.

Both dependency theory and modernization theory led to two practical implementations adopted beginning in the late 1970s. Those who saw the truth in dependency theory undertook import-substitution-industrialization (ISI), and those who accepted modernization theory adopted export-oriented growth strategies. The basic idea of *import-substitution-industrialization* (ISI) is that for a country to develop, it needed to break its dependency on importing finished products from the core countries and exporting its raw materials to them. To do this, ISI advocated replacing imports with domestic industries which were protected from external competition and subsidized by the state. Realizing that these internal industries were too new to be competitive with foreign industries, governments would help foster the growth of domestic industries by putting high tariffs on imports and by subsidizing local corporations. The goal was to build up the domestic industry to the point where it was big enough to compete with imports, and eventually, tariffs and subsidies could be eliminated after the mature domestic industries could globally compete and provide high paying jobs.

The Korean political economist Ha-Joon Chang argues that ISI was how every developed country got to the position it is today. He argues that 19th century America could not compete with developed European industry and engaged in ISI policies of protecting American industry. He also argues that this system was used in early industrial Europe, allowing countries like the U.K. and Germany to develop their internal industries free of foreign competition before finally opening up to competition. ISI was popular in Latin America from the 1950s and 1980s, in part because Frank's dependency theory was considered to have explained Latin American underdevelopment. ISI enabled countries such as Brazil and Argentina to make significant advances in this period, as these were countries with large populations capable of sustaining new domestic industries. On the other hand, in smaller countries such as Bolivia and Ecuador, ISI was not successful because the population was too small to support newly created industries selling consumer products. While adoption of ISI policies was positively correlated with democracy, heavy state involvement in the economy increased the potential for corruption.

Export-led development was based on modernization theory and argued that developing countries have a comparative advantage because their labor is cheap, meaning they can produce goods which can be exported and sold at a competitive price on the world market. The idea behind export-led development is that by focusing on producing cheap consumer products, a state will be able to bring in enough hard currency to buy raw materials (commodities) and, with time, move up the development ladder.

Export-led development is based on the theory of comparative advantage, which states that countries can get rich by exporting those products that they have a unique advantage in. Developing countries should be able to get rich by producing cheap products made by cheap and unskilled labor, which are then sold in rich countries. Once a country can acquire enough wealth in this way, it can then open universities and train its workforce so it can start producing high-technology products with even higher profit margins, eventually allowing a country to move through the stages of growth. This method is being used by China, which is taking advantage of the fact that labor is very cheap to produce cheap consumer products which are then exported to America to be sold at stores like Wal-Mart for low prices. Consumers like the low prices and buy Chinese products, giving China a comparative advantage.

The problem with export-led development, however, is that countries which produce natural resources tend to get stuck at the bottom level of development. Countries such as Nigeria with much oil, for example, will focus their entire economy on exporting oil. Because oil is a commodity whose price fluctuates on the global markets, this can create boom-or-bust cycles for countries. When the price of oil is high, the Nigerian economy seems strong, but a sudden drop in the price of oil can destroy their economic position. Playing to their comparative advantage has led to a non-diversified economy at the mercy of fluctuating commodity prices. Furthermore, even when things are going great due to high oil prices, Nigeria will not be able to use the incoming wealth to build factories to produce cheap Chinese-style goods because it does not have a comparative advantage in manufacturing. For this reason, critics of export-led development argue that it only works in certain countries who happen to have a favorable comparative advantage. In countries whose comparative advantage is in specific commodities, they tend to get stuck in a cycle of perpetual underdevelopment, just as dependency theory predicts. So while export-led development may work for China, whose authoritarian government and billion people mean a continuous supply of cheap labor, it does not work for Nigeria, whose economy booms or busts with the price of oil.

A Floating Production, Storage and Offloading (FPSO) vessel off the coast of Nigeria.

With the problems with modernization theory, neoliberalism has taken over as the primary right-wing theory of development. Unlike modernization theory, *neoliberalism* argues that countries do not need to emulate American institutions, and local cultural and religious traditions could provide an advantage. Neoliberalism seeks only to push a set of economic conditions, and it is less worried about states adopting democracy, ending corruption or promoting a professional bureaucracy. Neoliberal development theory also differs from modernization theory in that it promotes open borders and open trade.

Export-led development is still promoted within neoliberalism, the difference being that the exporters should be transnational corporations floating around the globe and looking for the cheapest labor and least regulation. China's model of export-led development, which is controlled by the state, is opposed by neoliberal development theorists, who argue that China would grow faster if they had global corporations running the factories rather than Chinese ones. Neoliberal economic development, however, has not always been successful, especially in Africa and South America. Argentina and Mexico went through major economic crises in the 1990s after adopting neoliberalism, and sub-Saharan Africa is becoming less and less developed. In the 1950s and 1960s, many people thought countries such as Kenya and Ghana would emerge as regional economic superpowers, but their adoption of neoliberal development ideas made these countries go backward.

While economic development is often the primary concern of comparative politics, political and social development is often just as important. Advocates of human rights argue that economic development is only one aspect of the development puzzle, and states need to accept and protect human rights to be considered developed and advanced countries. Such advocates would argue that China's rapid economic development is not being accompanied by political development and is only half successful. Others point to social development as an important measure. A country such as Cuba may lack economic development and political rights, but its social development is extremely high. The Cuban medical system rivals that of any wealthy country, and its education system is the envy of Latin America.

The country of Bhutan in the Himalayas has taken a completely different approach to development. It has declared that development should not be measured in gross domestic product, meaning the number of goods an economy produces, but instead on gross national happiness. Bhutan conducts studies to determine the happiness of its citizens, and if overall happiness goes up, this is considered a successful form of development, even if overall economic activity goes down. Bhutan argues that people do not need to be rich to be happy, and as long as people are not in extreme poverty, the only thing that truly matters is happiness. Many international observers have applauded Bhutan's approach, as it incorporates social measures of development into its index. Critics, however, observe that happiness is a very subjective thing to measure and do not trust the Bhutan government to assess it accurately. Others have pointed out that their "happiness" may be a measure of how brainwashed Bhutanese are into accepting their lot in life. Such critics would argue that applying the idea of gross national happiness would rank North Korea near the top due to the effectiveness of its state propaganda, even though North Korea often suffers from food shortages, starvation and an extreme form of totalitarian government.

Finally, another approach to development has emerged which rejects the idea of development altogether. Generally called *post-development theory*, this idea argues that classifying countries into rich and poor and asserting that developing countries need to develop into rich ones is a Eurocentric imposition of European and American categories in the world. Post-development theorists are interested in searching for alternatives to development, such as Bhutan's gross national happiness, as a way of promoting political and economic activity that arises within a country. Essentially post-development opposes the "comparative" focus of development economics, and it argues that each country has to find its way without worrying about comparing itself to external standards of development or progress. Critics of post-development theory argue that it is not simply an external narrative imposed on countries by the West, but that people in these countries genuinely want a materially more prosperous life. Critics also argue that political development and human rights are universal and not alien concepts being imposed from outside. Such critics argue that everyone yearns to be free, regardless of where he or she live, and post-development amounts to a conservative defense of underdevelopment.

Chapter 6

Public Policy

In this chapter, each of the six studied are analyzed for comparison on their public policy. The approach taken considers public policy issues as both domestic and global matters since there are broad and enduring policy areas common to most countries. Included in these common areas are considerations on how to ensure successful economic performance where poverty is widespread, how to provide for social welfare needs for citizens and how to extend and protect individual liberties and freedoms. Given that these recurring puzzles demand the attention of states' policymakers, special attention is given to how the studied countries approach these problems differently.

In recognition that a broad range of factors influences policymaking, consideration is first given to formal and informal institutional influences. Secondly, the analysis is undertaken regarding the participation of interest groups, political parties and the executive, judicial and legislative branches all have in the creation of policy. For many of the systems studied, changes in the economic substructure are revealed to have been the result of policy changes as well as causal factors in policy development.

For example, the effects of privatization in Mexico have resulted in changing policy needs. Often, adopting conservative economic policies that move away from the traditional social welfare state and its benefits also has an impact on liberal/left party politics, as has occurred in the Labour Party of the United Kingdom. How interest groups make different demands on government, with different consequences for public policy, is demonstrated.

Development strategies, another important factor addressed, have changed over time and resulted in numerous shifts and alterations in policy requirements. For example, as the Chinese economy has transformed into a socialist market system, policymakers have been confronted with unintended consequences in noneconomic areas such as population and education. Likewise, Russian economic structural changes since 1990 have caused a wide range of policy challenges in the areas of civil rights, environmental concerns and so on.

Global pressures, another topic of focus, are exerted on policymakers in both developed and developing systems. International agreements and organizations, such as the World Trade Organization (WTO), the World Bank, the EU, the North American Free Trade Agreement (NAFTA) and the International Monetary Fund (IMF) push for policy changes in all six of the countries studied. Many of the featured countries have witnessed considerable policy debates over such issues as sovereignty and the conflicting interests of global and domestic policy needs such as environmental policy, income distribution, taxation policy and the like. Very often, global consideration produces a divergence among the different interest groups within the countries themselves.

The policy concerns exampled in this chapter are often broad and may differ from country to country. Issues range from social welfare policy (including education, pension policy, and poverty issues), civil liberties (rights and freedoms), the environment, control and management of natural resources, economic performance (including employment, inflation, monetary policy in general and income distribution) and population and migration policies. Gender and ethnicity are also addressed as critical concerns to policymakers. Cumulatively, the information provided should enable discussion and analysis of policy differences in a comparative context as well as an understanding of how different systems of government create different solutions to domestic and global problems. Likewise, the content should foster the ability to move back and forth between conceptualizing political problems and the practice of politics in the countries of focus.

Common Policy Issues

The comparative approach to public policy at one time treated countries as isolated and unique, and it assumed that all public policy issues were internal to any given country. With the onset of globalization in the early 1990s, comparative public policy has shifted to study how different countries react to global issues. This shift in focus requires a global perspective, as an economic problem facing Russia in a globalized era is usually a problem that faces Nigeria and Great Britain as well. While problems which public policy seeks to address tend to be global in nature, individual states still have idiosyncratic responses to these issues. Globalization has also introduced new issues that states are often unequipped to deal with, causing comparative politics to study how transnational and supranational organizations (such as global corporations or the United Nations) now play a significant role in public policy.

Economic Performance

Economic policy in most states has been driven in the recent era by two major events. The collapse of the Soviet Union led to the globalization of neoliberal economics as the dominant theoretical approach to analyzing economic policy problems. The second event was the 2008 global economic crisis, which caused an ensuing decline in global economic performance that many political economists are now calling The Great Recession. While neoliberal approaches to economic policy (which favor privatization, reduced social spending and financial deregulation as some of the main points) were already dominant throughout the 1980s in countries such as the United Kingdom, the United States and Chile, the collapse of the state communist model provided a catalyst for this singular approach to economic development to take hold in nearly every country in the world.

The 2008 global economic crisis continues to cause problems because policymakers are still applying the same neoliberal economic policies that political economists blame for causing the 2008 crisis in the first place. Policymakers in the government are driven by a combination of pressure from transnational corporations do not change the status quo and inertia since they are not experts in economic theory and cannot develop new theoretical policy methods.

Police guarding the Charging Bull statue on the first day of the Occupy Wall Street, a protest movement critical of neoliberalism.

These two major events have shaped the economic policy of all countries in the world, and they demonstrate why a global approach to comparative public policy is necessary. Without understanding these global events, it would be impossible to analyze why countries adopted the policies they ended up pursuing. This section will look at each of the six core countries studied and how their economic policies changed and adapted in response to these two major global economic events.

The United Kingdom was one of the first countries to change the basis of their economic policymaking from a Keynesian approach to a neoliberal approach. *Keynesian economics* argues that public economic policy should be primarily focused on using government resources to prevent boom and bust cycles. Keynesian public policy is often called "counter-cyclical," since the role of the government is to slow down the economy when it threatens to develop into a bubble and speed it up when it threatens to lapse into recession. Keynesianism is somewhat counter-intuitive, requiring the government to cut back on spending when things are going well and increase spending when things are going poorly. By having the government act oppositely to the private sector, it ensures that the economy will continue to grow slowly and steadily.

Neoliberalism, on the other hand, argues that governments should operate like businesses by cutting back spending when the private economy is doing poorly and increasing spending only when the economy is booming. Neoliberal theorists believe that government debt is problematic and see public policy's primary job as avoiding accumulating more public debt. To do this, neoliberals advocate reducing social spending, raising taxes on the poor while lowering them on the rich and privatizing and deregulating industry so corporations can grow unimpeded by government policies meant to slow growth in boom times.

Neoliberalism was once considered a radical idea that was unsuitable for mainstream government economic policy, but with the election of Margaret Thatcher as Prime Minister in the United Kingdom in 1979, a steady conversion to neoliberal policies occurred throughout her tenure in the 1980s. Thatcher privatized many industries which were previously owned by the government, causing unemployment to skyrocket and the number of people in the U.K. investing in the stock market to increase. Thatcher's policies were pronounced a huge success by the wealthy, while the poor saw her economic policy as an attack on their wellbeing. As globalization picked up steam in 1989 and into the early 1990s, the U.K. went through a period of de-industrialization. Its newly-privatized major industries moved their operations to countries with cheaper labor, causing a second major recession after the initial boom period created by privatization.

The 2008 economic crisis was a major challenge for British policymakers who still believed in neoliberal economic theory. Due to the U.K.'s early adoption of neoliberalism, the financial sector was not well regulated, and British banks were participating in risky financial investments. One bank, Northern Rock, had bought so many risky mortgages both in the U.K. and around the world that the bank faced a liquidity crisis. A *liquidity crisis* is when a bank does not have enough money on hand to cover withdrawals. When the public got word of this, there were long lines of people trying to withdraw all the money out of their accounts for fear the bank would go under, and they would lose their savings. This was the first bank run in 150 years in the U.K. To prevent millions of regular customers from losing their life savings, the British government did something that was completely unacceptable to neoliberal policymakers: they nationalized the bank. There was much speculation that neoliberal economic policy was now dead and that the U.K. might be leading a shift to a new model in light of the failures of neoliberalism during the 2008 crisis. Many other countries nationalized industries to try to save them from collapse during the crisis, but by 2012, the U.K. government once again privatized Northern Rock Bank, as they returned to the neoliberal policy idea that government-owned industries are problematic.

Customers line up outside a Northern Rock bank branch during their liquidity crisis.

The second aspect of public economic policy that came to light during the 2008 economic crisis was the failure of monetary policy to solve a crisis. In Keynesian economic policy, the focus is on governments increasing or decreasing spending in response to how the economy is faring, which is thought of as sound fiscal policy. In neoliberal economic policy, the focus is on changing the bank interest rate. Ideally, these two policy measures would work in tandem to produce the desired result, but as the British Central Bank reduced interest rates to a record low 0.5%, the government also cut back on spending, causing the two policies to work against each other.

According to neoliberal economic theory, reducing the interest rate to such a low level should cause the economy to go into hyper-drive because it becomes extremely cheap to borrow money and people with lots of money have less incentive to hold on to it. This was not the case in the U.K., and the government adopted a policy of quantitative easing to try to get around the failures of monetary policy and their unwillingness to engage in serious fiscal spending. *Quantitative easing* is when the government purposely buys up large amounts of its debt in the form of privately-held bonds. Since the short-term debt was 0.5%, the British Central Bank started buying up longer-term debt, driving down the interest rate on longer-term British bonds. The goal was to push all forms of government debt to very low levels to make borrowing extremely cheap. The hope was that people would borrow money and spend it, thus restarting the economy. The policy was moderately successful, and the U.K. finally began to recover six years after the initial crisis. However, structural problems in the economy and the unwillingness of British policymakers to admit that their theory of the economy has proven to be problematic continue to hinder the U.K.'s economic performance.

China is in many ways a global outlier in terms of economic policy. While most of the world adopted neoliberal economic policy after 1990, China charted its course. As with the rest of the world, the collapse of communism was a major event in China. Unlike with Russia, however, China had begun to slowly transition to a form of state-led capitalism beginning in the late 1970s. The fall of the Soviet Union did not bring down the Chinese economy because China had already begun taking steps to open up its economy to global capitalism. This cautious approach to economic reform enabled China to avoid the economic catastrophe that Russia faced after communism collapsed.

As a result of the slow pace of reforms that were closely monitored by the state, China was much less affected by the 2008 economic crisis. China's financial system was heavily regulated by the government and was not involved in risky foreign investments like the British banks were. As an export-led economy, however, the global slowdown from the 2008 crisis did cause China's GDP growth rate to drop since their export markets could not afford to buy as many Chinese products. To help bolster the domestic economy and counter a rise in unemployment, China was one of the first countries to announce a massive stimulus package. The stimulus package was a huge increase in government spending on social programs and infrastructure to stimulate the economy. Since China had no allegiance to neoliberal policy principles, they were able to engage in counter-cyclical policies like stimulus spending faster and more effectively than other countries.

Unlike China's gradual and cautious transition to capitalism, in Russia, the collapse of the Soviet government led to a sudden and radical change. Russia's economy not only switched from communism to capitalism but also adopted the extreme form of capitalism that is neoliberalism at the advice of American economists. American policymakers who began to advise the new post-communist government in Russia advocated what they called neoliberal shock therapy to radically transform the economy overnight in the hope that this would spur a huge increase in economic growth.

In reality, Russia went into an economic depression as a result of neoliberal shock therapy, making their economy worse off than it was under communism. The failure of neoliberal economic policy led to the rise of Vladimir Putin, who realized that Russia should have adopted a more cautious approach to economic transition, as China had done. Putin advocated for a nationalist economic policy that promoted Russian corporations and small businesses. Putin's was much more pro-capitalist than the Chinese approach, but like China and in contrast to the U.K. or the U.S., Putin saw a strong role for the government both in terms of directly owning certain strategic industries and actively promoting the development of Russian companies.

Putin meets with Avtovaz automotive workers who were hard hit by the global recession.

Putin's economic reforms dramatically reversed the course of post-Soviet Russian decline. His popularity stems almost entirely from his success at drastically improving the situation of the Russian economy. These reforms, however, did not insulate Russia from the 2008 crisis. Russia lacked the regulatory framework of China, and its banks suffered from the global credit crunch when they lacked cash reserves to cover withdrawals, much like what had happened in the U.K. At the same time, there was growing concern about corporate corruption, which caused the Russian stock market to collapse. Banks faced severe problems, with one major bank going bankrupt in September 2008, and by October the chairman of the Russian central bank announced that 50 to 70 Russian banks were at risk of bankruptcy.

The Russian government had to bail out the three largest banks to try to prevent a bank run, while at the same time its revenues had declined significantly as the price of oil dropped. Since so much of Russia's economy relied on exporting oil and natural gas, the global slowdown, which sent oil prices plummeting, hurt Russia's material sector at the same time the financial sector was being hit. Despite Putin adopting a more middle-of-the-road approach between neoliberalism and China's cautious state capitalism, his economic reforms had been primarily aimed at major natural resources and production industries, leaving the financial sector largely unregulated. The Russian economy is still struggling to recover, and Putin has increasingly moved away from promoting his economic policy as a basis of legitimacy, instead touting Russia's military might and increasing presence in international affairs as the reason why Russians should continue to support him.

Iran, like China, is another outlier regarding economic policy. The 1979 revolution brought a mix of economic policies that were largely based on opposition to the policies of the previous American-backed government of the Shah. The new Islamic government initially moved toward a semi-centrally planned economy, in part to appease the large communist element which made the revolution possible. While not being communist in the sense of the Soviet Union, the Iranian government divided the economy into three sectors: state, cooperative and private. Whereas the U.K. under neoliberalism was predominantly private and Russia under communism was predominantly state, Iran sought to support all three of these elements under the guise of an Islamic economic ideology. Prices were largely set by the government rather than by markets, and the state owned most major industries. At the same time, private property, which generated income and small business, was encouraged and not outlawed as it was in communist states. The cooperative sector was largely based around Islamic charities which were responsible for providing social assistance. They received direct funding from the government and donations from wealthy Iranians. With social assistance in the hands of religious authorities and not the state, the social safety net of Iran was somewhat precarious, especially as these cooperative charities remain extremely corrupt.

Eventually, this three-part model for the Iranian economy led to major problems. The Iran-Iraq War, which lasted from 1980 to 1988, severely harmed the economy as hundreds of thousands of people died and the economy focused on fighting the war. As globalization became a global norm, Iran's inward-looking economy was still suffering from the after-effects of the war. The government sought to stimulate the economy through oil exports and the development of nuclear power technology. The suspicion that Iran was developing nuclear weapons led to international sanctions that further harmed Iran's economy in the 1990s, as they could no longer import anything other than medicine.

After President Ahmadinejad was elected in 2005, he tried to push Iran toward neoliberalism by promoting massive privatizations of state-owned enterprises. Ahmadinejad used the privatization to pay down state debt. Many economists were critical of this method of hasty privatizations promoted by Ahmadinejad, arguing that he would be emulating the Russian disaster of the early 1990s and would cause misery for the population while creating a new ultra-rich class of oligarchs.

An Iranian soldier guards against Iraqi use of chemical weapons during the Iran-Iraq War, an eight-year conflict which claimed more than a million lives and cost an estimated $1.18 trillion

As a major oil-exporting country, Iran has a major source of wealth. However, it was unable to sell their oil to the world due to sanctions and hostile actions toward other nations by President Ahmadinejad. Many economists argued that the sluggish state of the Iranian economy was a political problem rather than an economic one because they were unable to sell their huge oil reserves due to sanctions resulting from the hostile, threatening rhetoric of previous governments. The current President Rouhani seems to have agreed with these critics. His cooperation with the U.S. and the international community on the nuclear weapons issue has led to sanctions being lifted. Iranian oil can once again flood onto the international markets, which raises significant revenues for the Iranian government.

The wave of post-communist globalization in the early 1990s put considerable pressure on many oil-producing countries to privatize their national oil companies. Mexico and Nigeria, as two major oil-producing nations, have had state-owned oil production companies throughout most of their history. Since oil is an important natural resource, government control of the resources ensured that the country's natural resource wealth was funneled back to the people in that country. Both Mexico and Nigeria came under intense pressure by transnational corporations, the ideological climate of the time and international trade organizations to privatize their state oil companies. Both countries slowly took steps to do so, but in each case, they were met with extreme public resistance. Handing over natural resources to foreign corporations extracts the profit and leaves the people with very little.

In the case of Nigeria, privatizations initiated in 2012 led to a massive increase in fuel prices and spawned national protests. Due to privatization, the government could no longer afford to keep fuel prices low for Nigerians, and the revenue they had previously gotten from oil dropped dramatically. The Mexican government's attempts to privatize the state-run PEMEX oil company have led to major public protests and introduced elements of corruption within the corporation.

Mexico's economy had traditionally been corporatist in structure, meaning that society was framed as a three-part, equal relationship between the state, corporations, and labor. With the wave of neoliberal globalization in the 1990s, the PRI government began to introduce privatizations. This broke the three-way corporatist compact, allowing corporations to operate without government regulation or protection and leaving labor rights lacking. Insiders associated with the PRI government were given control of newly privatized corporations, and a class of Russian-style oligarchs emerged. Privatization always causes a temporary boom because the sale of state enterprises raises large amounts of money which a government almost always spends immediately, prompting the boom. This happened in Mexico, but the boom then gave way to a major currency and capital flight crisis in 1994.

Neoliberal policy tends to create boom-or-bust cycles, which make these policies seem wonderful during the boom and awful during the bust. Like Mexico, Nigeria was hit hard by the 2008 economic crisis as the price of oil dropped dramatically, hurting the main export of both of these countries. Foreign investment also began to decline in both countries as they became mired in violence in the late 2000s. The continuing Mexican drug wars make foreign investment extremely risky, and the Boko Haram insurgency in Nigeria is scaring away foreign investors. If both of these countries continue their policy of orienting their economies toward foreign investment, the primary economic policy challenge for both of these countries is the political challenge of first solving their problems of violence and instability.

Social Welfare

Social welfare trends also reflect the growing ideological strength of neoliberal capitalism, which argues that states should reduce social spending and leave people to fend for themselves. In many cases, the neoliberal economic policy seeks to privatize government social services, ranging from hospitals to universities. During the Cold War, most capitalist countries saw a strong welfare state as an essential part of capitalism. They believed that capitalism worked best when the government was there to provide a social safety net for those who were left behind. Ironically, the end of the Cold War was a defeat for both communism and a humane kind of capitalist society. The global wave of neoliberal economics ushered in a harsher approach to social welfare, which will be seen by looking at the six countries.

The National Health Service (NHS) is the publically funded healthcare system for England.

Although China did not make a move to neoliberalism, preferring its state-managed approach to capitalism, it has significantly rolled back its social welfare programs. Major reforms in the 1980s ended China's "*iron rice bowl*" policy, which was a government-led approach to the economy that guaranteed workers in certain industries run by the state a job for life, along with social benefits for the young and the elderly. Under Deng Xiaoping's reforms, which sought to move to a capitalist economy, many of the iron rice bowl positions were eliminated; they had become unproductive sinecures in which workers did not produce anything, leading to economic inefficiency. Many more of these positions were eliminated in 2001 under pressure from the World Trade Organization. While China's explosive growth under its capitalist reforms has lifted many of the poorest people who were never eligible for an iron rice bowl position out of poverty, China's development is still very uneven, with most of the wealth filtering to the top. Many economists see China as now lacking a proper middle class, which was once assured by the iron rice bowl policy.

Eliminating these protected positions has meant the government has had to introduce new social policies to prevent people from falling into poverty. While the Chinese state had once lauded the rural poor, who engaged in sustenance farming as the backbone of the country, the reality was that these people lived in extreme poverty. With the urban workers being protected by the iron rice bowl, in the Maoist era, China had little need for social welfare programs. In recent years, China has created programs of unemployment insurance, worker's compensation for those injured on the job, pension accounts, and even a carbon tax. While most of the rest of the world was busy cutting back on social programs, China had to create a whole welfare system to deal with new problems introduced by the transition to capitalism. While China has become much more economically unequal under capitalism, it has significantly reduced poverty due to its new commitment to social welfare spending programs.

Like most developed countries after World War II, the U.K. ushered in new economic policy of promoting social welfare. The crowning achievement of the British welfare state was the National Health Service, which made healthcare free at the point of service. As a universal single-payer system, all citizens receive healthcare free of charge without the need to pay for private insurance. The government provides all health care costs through taxes. This system significantly improved the health indicators of the poor in Great Britain, as they had previously been unable to afford healthcare payments. This system was overwhelmingly supported by the people and by all the main political parties until recently when in 2015 the ruling Conservative Party began to introduce measures to privatize parts of the NHS under the guise of neoliberal economic policy.

In countries with similar public healthcare systems, such as Canada, there have also been pushes to introduce privatizations, with neoliberal economic ideology arguing that competition among private healthcare providers will lead to better service. In reality, however, public health care is always cheaper overall than private healthcare because private healthcare requires that a profit is made, so everyone has to pay more. Healthcare continues to be a very contentious public policy issue, and countries with private systems, such as the United States, are realizing that a purely private system is problematic.

In Iran, social welfare is covered by two components. Social security benefits such as old age pensions, unemployment insurance, health insurance, and disability benefits are covered by the Social Security Organization, which is a non-governmental agency with a legal mandate that workers can voluntarily pay part of their salary into to be covered by social security benefits. This means that Iranians who do not pay into the Social Security Organization (SSO) are not eligible for any benefits. This is problematic since it ensures that only those with a job are covered, leaving those outside of the formal economy with no protection. It is estimated that the SSO covers about 70% of the Iranian population, leaving another 30% to rely on government-funded Islamic charities called bonyads. *Bonyads* are tax-exempt charities meant to promote Islamic values and provide help for the poor. They receive revenue from the government, private donations (charity donations are mandatory in the Islamic religion, and most such donations in Iran go to the bonyads) and profit from companies that the bonyads own.

An Iranian woman begs on the streets of Tehran.

The bonyads are highly controversial because they are seen as extremely corrupt. There is a perception that religious authorities inside the bonyads use these organizations as a way to enrich themselves while doing only the bare minimum actually to help the poor. This has created a situation where poverty in Iran is increasing rapidly; once someone does not have a job, he or she have to rely on charity from the corrupt bonyads rather than the reliable protection of the SSO. While part of the problem with increasing charity in Iran relates to international sanctions crippling the economy, high-ranking officials in the bonyads are often multi-millionaires because they take government money and private donations for themselves. The social security system in Iran is extremely weak, and due to its nature, it tends to reinforce poverty rather than help people get out of it. When social protection is offered only for those with relatively stable jobs who can afford to pay into the SSO, it leaves the poor stuck at the bottom with no government assistance.

Mexico is illustrative of how social policy changes can affect the poverty level. Mexico's poverty rate declined significantly from the 1960s until the end of the 1980s, corresponding with the PRI party's corporatist economic policy. When PRI moved toward neoliberalism in the early 1990s and joined NAFTA, which precipitated the 1994 peso crisis, poverty levels started to reverse the 30-year trend and go back up. Even as the overall GDP of Mexico increased significantly into the 2000s, poverty slowly increased. During this period, the government operated on neoliberal principles and believed that the private market would magically solve poverty through economic growth. This did not happen, and it only made the rich richer without helping the poorest people. By comparison, China used a growth-led strategy to decrease poverty. However, in China, this strategy was accompanied by an expansion of social welfare programs, whereas in Mexico they were being cut.

By 1997, the Mexican government became alarmed about growing poverty and instituted a new program to fight poverty called Oportunidades, later called Prospera after 2002. This program was based on conditional cash transfers directly to low-income families if they met certain conditions, like sending their children to school and visiting clinics regularly for preventive healthcare. By providing the cash payments directly from the government to the mother of a family, the Mexican government sought to prevent the previous waves of corruption which plagued their previous social programs. This program has been somewhat successful at slowing down the increase in poverty, but on the whole, it has not had the major impacts that the Mexican government was hoping for since the country still lacks a proper social welfare infrastructure.

This program has been influential around the world, in part because it fits with the neoliberal ideology of not spending money on social welfare infrastructure and instead gives it directly to the poor. Nigeria adopted a similar program in 2007 that was accompanied by a private-lender microcredit program which allowed those receiving money to apply for small-scale, private loans to start small businesses. This program has had little effect, however, as absolute poverty rose in Nigeria from 54.7% in 2004 to 70% in 2015. The 2015 election brought to power a new government that has pledged to create a new social safety net and does a better job-fighting corruption, which it claims is the true source of poverty in Nigeria.

Russia's social welfare policies have been, as much of the rest of the country after communism, something of a roller coaster ride. Under communism, there was full employment and very little poverty, meaning expansive social spending was not required. Once Russia adopted neoliberal shock therapy, poverty skyrocketed, and there were no state protections for the poor. Once again, Vladimir Putin's reforms reversed course for Russia; he invested in healthcare and education, raised old age pensions and developed a social security infrastructure. Putin's adoption of welfare state policies, although they were not as comprehensive as those in European countries, were extremely popular and continued to be a source of Putin's popularity.

Civil Liberties, Rights and Freedoms

Civil liberties are the set of guarantees that protect individuals from the state. These guarantees can be in the form of negative rights or positive freedoms and can be guaranteed by a written constitution or evolved through a court system. Examples of civil liberties would be things such as the right not to be tortured or freedom of the press. When someone is convicted of a crime, his or her civil liberties can be taken away, such as the right to free movement if he or she are put in prison. For such infringements on someone's civil liberties to be considered, there must be a fair court and police system that allows individuals the right to due process. *Due process* means that individuals charged with a crime have a right to a fair trial which seeks to determine if they are innocent or guilty impartially.

Many argue that the detention of non-military combatants at Guantanamo Bay represents the continued erosion of human rights.

Civil liberties can generally be broken into two categories: negative rights and positive freedoms. A *negative right* is something an individual holds and requires no action by the individual. The right to personal property and bodily integrity, for example, are negative rights that each of us holds against everyone else and which are backed by the state. As negative rights, these civil liberties do not require any action on one's part but instead protect them from the actions of others. The rights to personal property and bodily integrity mean that neither other people nor the state can steal a citizen's property or harm their body in any unlawful manner. It is these negative rights which protect one's private life, as they are the basis for laws against murder, stealing, assault and other crimes that harm private lives.

Positive freedoms, on the other hand, relate to one's public life and their involvement in politics. Positive freedoms cannot simply be held, as they involve the actions of individuals. Freedom of the press is an example of positive freedom, and it is one which only exists through action. As positive freedom, freedom of the press means newspapers, websites and television programs that are critical of the government can be published. Freedom of speech, which is also positive freedom, works in the same manner; it means that individuals have the right to speak their political opinions in public. If an individual thinks of freedom of speech as a negative right, then it amounts to nothing more than talking to oneself. Positive freedoms make sense only through their public exercise, and they protect individual ability to engage in public politics.

While both are part of the broad definition of civil liberties, positive freedoms and negative rights have a variety of names. Negative rights are sometimes called personal liberties, and positive freedoms are sometimes called political rights, which can be confusing. Civil liberties as a whole are often simply called "human rights" by many scholars. Remember that negative rights or liberties protect us against others, and positive freedoms or political rights give us the ability to interact with others. When analyzing civil liberties in comparative politics, it is important to remember this distinction, as some countries may be touted as having a good civil liberties record, but only for one aspect of it.

A properly free country must allow both positive freedom and negative rights to protect its citizens' personal and public lives. Studying civil liberties is difficult because every government believes that it provides comprehensive rights for its citizens. When countries accuse each other of rights violations, it often leads to counter-accusations and denials. To avoid this problem, scholars of comparative human rights tend to rely on non-governmental organizations which monitor human rights around the world. The agenda of these organizations is less tied to any individual state, making their analysis of domestic rights situations more accurate than what states say about each other. Some of the most important global rights organizations are Amnesty International, Human Rights Watch and Doctors Without Borders.

China has had a fairly problematic record when it comes to civil liberties. Since the transition to capitalism, it has significantly increased its protection for negative rights but lags behind much of the world regarding positive freedoms. Amnesty International and Human Rights repeatedly condemn China for its lack of freedom of speech and assembly, meaning that public political dissent is extremely limited and not tolerated by the government. Human rights groups are also critical of China's use of the death penalty for a wide array of crimes, making China the world's leading executioner. In total there are 46 possible crimes which carry the death penalty, including some rarely-used offenses related to political dissent. While most of China's executions are for murder, there remains a significant minority of executions directed at political opponents.

Chinese police detain a civilian during the 2012 crackdown in Tibet.

Freedom of speech is somewhat limited in China, and public protests are illegal. Due to the Chinese government's philosophy that everyone in China must work together to further the aims of the state, any dissent is considered intolerable and often results in prison sentences. China even heavily censors the internet, using what's called the "Great Firewall of China." Web pages on the 1989 Tiananmen Square massacre are blocked, and search results related to democracy are heavily censored. Media in China is also very limited in its freedom. While the government does not directly control what is published, there are harsh penalties for reporters and editors who publish material the government deems inappropriate. This creates a climate of self-censorship where journalists tend to reflect the government's opinion, not because they are told to do so, but because they fear to lose their job or going to prison if they don't.

Freedom of religion is also highly problematic in China because there are only five recognized religions that are legally allowed to be practiced. China is particularly wary of Falun Gong, which is a religion that combines elements of traditional Chinese Buddhism and Taoism with coordinated public exercise and conservative social values. The Chinese government sees Falun Gong as an organized threat to its continued hold on the government, and it actively persecutes members of the religion. Why the Chinese government is so intent on persecuting Falun Gong while offering state protection for Buddhism, Islam, Taoism, Protestantism, and Catholicism is a matter of speculation by scholars. Many believe it is because the leadership of Falun Gong refused to work with the Chinese government like the leadership of the protected religions did. Others point to China's history of armed insurrections led by religious groups as a reason why China is so intent on cracking down on Falun Gong.

Given all the criticism China receives from international human rights groups, how does the government respond? The Chinese government argues that it has a different set of human rights than those promoted in the West, based on the idea of Chinese culture valuing the state over the individual. These ideas are derived from former leader Deng Xiaoping, who was impressed with Singapore Prime Minister Lee Kuan Yew's idea of rights based on "Asian Values." Deng argued that the state has a set of rights as the representative of the people who are much more important than the rights of any person. He also argued that the right to economic security was the most important right for an individual. China argues that it is improving the human rights situation by bringing people out of poverty and ensuring that the Chinese government remains uncontested.

This is an argument that is called *cultural relativism*, the idea that every culture has their own set of values, which do not necessarily make sense to outsiders. China often claims that other countries who criticize its human rights record are simply trying to impose foreign cultural ideas on them and destroy traditional Chinese culture. While on the surface it may seem like a convincing argument that outsiders should respect Chinese culture, the argument China makes is problematic for some reasons.

First is the fact that many inside China want basic human rights and political freedoms. According to the Chinese government's argument about cultural relativism, these Chinese rights activists would have to be either foreign agents or not truly be Chinese. Considering that these activists exist across China, there would have to be elaborate conspiracy theories to explain how everyone who wanted political rights inside China was a foreign spy. The second problem is that the concept of human rights and political freedoms is not merely an aspect of Western culture. Winning political rights in most Western countries was a hard-fought battle that required getting people to change their traditional notions of how society should be structured.

If the idea of human rights isn't Chinese, and it isn't European or American, then what is it? Most ethics philosophers and philosophers of political democracy argue that the concept of political rights is universal and transcends any specific culture. They argue that activists in every country always want the same set of political rights, demonstrating that these are expressions of being human, not being part of a specific culture.

The United Kingdom first developed a concept of civil liberties with the Magna Carta, which King John agreed to in 1215. It was a result of a conflict between the king and a group of nobles, and it established a number of negative liberties. The Magna Carta is one of the first documents setting out negative liberties, whereas the concept of positive freedoms was common in ancient Greece and Rome. Aspects of the Magna Carta, such as *habeas corpus*, which is the right not to be held indefinitely without charge or trial, still form the basis of modern interpretations of civil liberties in the United Kingdom.

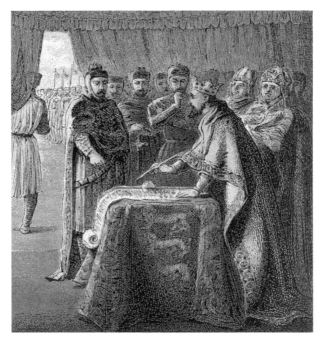

Artistic depiction of King John signing Magna Carta.

Habeas corpus, even though it is one of the oldest personal rights in the U.K., was a matter of extreme controversy in the mid to late 2000s. After the 2005 terrorist attack on the London subway system, the government passed a sweeping anti-terrorism law that allowed the government to hold those suspected of terrorism indefinitely without charging them. Many MPs in British parliament argued that this was a violation of habeas corpus, with one prominent MP resigning his seat in protest over this violation of basic civil liberties. Even in countries with a history of civil rights dating back nearly one thousand years, these issues are still a matter of contemporary controversy as governments continuously look for new ways to expand their power. The case of the U.K.'s violation of one of its oldest civil liberties demonstrates that human rights are not simply an issue for notorious violators such as China, but even in well-developed democracies such as the U.K.

While it is often thought that countries will have a progressive advance of human rights, this is rarely the case. Iran provides a good example, as they went from having some civil liberties in the 1950s to a disastrous human rights record during the era of the monarchy, to the period after the revolution where the situation has not improved much. Under the Shah of Iran, brutal secret police called SAVAK was empowered; they would round up anyone suspected of opposing the Shah, resulting in secret detentions and torture. Any citizen could be rounded up any time, and there was no respect for either negative liberties or positive freedoms. While the 1979 revolution put an end to SAVAK, the new Islamic government ushered in Sharia law, which has rolled back rights on other issues, especially women's rights.

After the 2009 Green Movement protests, which were driven by the belief that President Ahmadinejad and Ayatollah Khomeini had rigged the election to prevent a popular Reform candidate from taking power, the Iranian government arrested and tortured many activists. The Reform political party was made illegal, and many students were arrested and tortured. Human Rights Watch has declared that Iran's human rights situation had gone significantly backward under President Ahmadinejad, and the UN criticized Iran's increasing restrictions on political freedoms such as freedom of the press and freedom of assembly. Despite this turn for the worse, many Iranians are hopeful that the new President Rouhani will improve the human rights situation inside of Iran.

Like China, Iran is one of the world's foremost state executioners. The death penalty is internationally condemned as a human rights violation, and only a few countries still engage in this practice. Iran is one of the worst offenders on a per capita basis, and the death penalty is in effect in Iran for crimes that offend religious sensibilities, such as homosexuality and adultery. Iran also executes people under the age of 18. Many of Iran's harsh punishments stem from the adoption of Sharia law, under which a crime of robbery is punished with amputation of hands or feet.

Freedom for women is also restricted in Iran. Women are required to wear hijab in public, and there are various legal restrictions which treat women as less valuable than men. Unlike many Muslim-majority countries, Iran has a strong women's rights movement. This is precise because these restrictions on their freedom are relatively new; Iranian women were much more equal before the 1979 revolution. Official internet providers in Iran are also legally required to block certain sites by the government. Iranians, however, are quite tech-savvy, and the widespread use of proxies and tunneling software has made the government's attempts to control and censor the internet largely futile.

Under Iran's judicial system that enforces Sharia,
Iranian women are legally required to wear hijabs.

Faced with these criticisms, Iran also backs a cultural relativist interpretation of human rights. Iran argues that because its laws are based on Islamic Sharia, they are the most moral laws in the world (even though laws based on religion tend to be the least moral and most restrictive of civil liberties). Iran also argues that it has the best human rights record in the Muslim world and that it is the most democratic country in the Muslim world. Iran has repeatedly condemned the concept of human rights as "American imperialism," and treats any Iranian opposition, including mass movements supported by the majority of the population like the 2009 Green Movement, as the work of enemy spies. According to the Iranian government, all those involved with the Green Movement were foreigners trying to destroy Iran, which is, of course, far-fetched given there were street protests with hundreds of thousands of Iranians marching for political freedom and against the rigging of the election.

Mexico's civil liberties and human rights situation had improved greatly since the end of the one-party domination by PRI in 2000. During that era, the PRI controlled many aspects of society, and freedom of speech and freedom of the press were limited. With the emergence of a multi-party system and competitive elections in 2000, the Mexican human rights situation dramatically improved until 2006 when Mexican drug cartels began to engage in massacres, prompting the government to activate the military against them. As the drug cartels increased their influence, they began targeting journalists, police, and politicians with assassinations, causing a major chill on free speech. In the PRI era, dissent against the government was limited, and now journalists and activists have their freedom of speech limited by cartels who are more than capable of murdering almost anyone at will.

In 2014, 43 teachers and college students went missing on their way to commemorate the 1968 massacre of student protesters by the Mexican government. These students, who were on a bus, were allegedly intercepted by local police and then handed over to a regional drug cartel, presumably to be murdered. Federal police in Mexico believe that the abduction was organized by the mayor of Iguala, where the kidnapping took place. This event has become a central focus of human rights in Mexico. It demonstrates both how the drug cartels can engage in mass murder with impunity and the level of corruption involved, as local police and politicians often seem to be working for the drug cartels rather than the people who elected them. The Mexican federal government has also been criticized for its inability to investigate this incident and bring those responsible to justice properly. President Enrique Peña Nieto has faced national protests over his mishandling of the incident, and there are renewed concerns that Mexico might be moving backward on human rights issues. The drug wars, which began in 2006, are now believed to have resulted in a total of 60,000 to 150,000 deaths, making it the biggest human rights issue in Mexico today.

Civil liberties and human rights in Nigeria have constantly been under threat. Despite numerous attempts to instill rights into the constitution since independence, Nigeria has been plagued by a series of coup d'états and military governments with an authoritarian character. With the restoration of democracy in 1999, Nigeria signed some international human rights treaties and enshrined protection for civil liberties in the new constitution. While many human rights organizations hailed these developments as a significant improvement, new issues have emerged in Nigeria related to the upsurge in partisan religious identification and power struggles which have worked as a counter-force to the new acceptance of civil liberties. On the issue of freedom of the press, Nigeria has moved from direct military control of the press to allow a wider range of views to be expressed, which is a noticeable improvement. Nigerians are now more willing to exercise their freedom of speech and assembly to protest the government, as evidenced by the 2012 Occupy Nigeria movement. Under the previous military governments, public protests were illegal and met with violent force.

Nigerians assemble in support of the Occupy Nigeria movement.

Today, Nigeria's biggest problems are corruption and the growing influence of religion. As a developing country, civil servants are easily corrupted with bribes since their pay tends to be very low. The police in Nigeria is notoriously corrupt, allowing people to get away with almost anything if they can come up with a sufficiently large bribe. Corruption within the government is a serious problem, as it is consistently ranked as one of the most corrupt governments in the world, even after the transition to democracy. Politicians often take money from the public purse and siphon it off into foreign bank accounts, leading some experts to estimate that corruption has cost the Nigerian government approximately $8 billion since it became a democracy. For a developing country, this is a staggering amount that could have been spent on improving the lives of the poor. In the north, which faces an Islamist insurgency led by Boko Haram, the police tend to murder any suspects they believe to be involved with the group, seriously undermining due process and basic civil liberties.

Boko Haram themselves have significantly contributed to human rights abuses as they carry out massacres and kidnappings. In 2014, the group drew international attention when they kidnapped 230 school girls and sold them to be wives of leaders of Boko Haram. Most regional governments in the North have also adopted Sharia law, with disastrous consequences for women's rights. Combined with the corrupt police response, the north of Nigeria faces the constant threat of unlawful violence, making it an extremely dangerous place to live.

In addition to the Islamist insurgency in the North, the Christian-dominated government of Goodluck Jonathan has pursued fundamentalist Christian policies which have been extremely detrimental to human rights. In 2013, President Jonathan passed anti-gay legislation which not only criminalized being gay but also included 5-year prison sentences for any non-gay person who expressed sympathy for the plight of LGBT people. International human rights groups have condemned this legislation as directly homophobic, pointing out that Nigeria has one of the worst records in the world for human rights for gay, lesbian, bisexual and transgender people. In the Christian south, women are also routinely persecuted as witches, with Christian pastors calling for public lynchings of women accused of witchcraft.

At the constitutional level, Russia has similar protections for civil rights to the United Kingdom. Russia is a signatory to various international human rights treaties which, by law, take precedence over any law enacted by the Duma in Russia. The Russian constitution also guarantees some civil liberties, which demonstrate how constitutional and legal protections for civil rights have improved dramatically since the communist era. Despite the strong legal protection for rights in Russia, these rights are often overlooked by the state or simply not enforced.

As a member of the European Court of Human Rights, Russian citizens can appeal to this European body when they feel states are not following their legal obligations. Cases by Russians arguing that the Russian government is not respecting their rights have overwhelmed the Court in recent years, and the Russian government has criticized rulings that went against Russia in favor of their citizens. Part of the problem is that the judicial system in Russia is not independent of the political system. The judicial system should uphold rights objectively regardless of what the government may believe, but the court system is heavily connected to the government, leading to inadequate enforcement of rights.

While the Russian constitution explicitly outlaws torture and abuse by police, groups such as Amnesty International have shown that police in Russia regularly torture and abuse suspects in violation of the law. In the immediate period after communism fell, the police became incredibly corrupt, and the Russian Mafia moved in and began to control many police forces. This period from 1991 to 1998 saw the homicide rate increase dramatically, but President Putin has been able to crack down on crime. Many Russians, however, remain deeply suspicious of the police. The Russian spy service has also been implicated in some assassinations of prominent figures, both within Russia and around the world. Alexander Litvinenko was poisoned in London by Russian spies after he published a series of works pointing to the Russian spy agency's involvement in mass murders and assassinations of journalists.

Russian spies are also accused of the poisoning of Ukrainian former Presidential candidate Viktor Yushchenko during the 2004 election campaign when he argued that Ukraine should align itself with Western Europe rather than with Russia.

Viktor Yushchenko, displaying visible signs of dioxin poisoning

Russia was also accused of some serious human rights violations during its 1999 war with Chechen Islamic rebels in the south of the country. International rights groups have accused Russia of mass executions, disappearances, and assassinations of journalists covering the conflict with Chechnya. Russia remains near the bottom in rankings of press freedom, with journalists who speak critically of the government routinely targeted. Freedom of assembly and speech is also limited, as jail and arrests are common for prominent activists. While human rights improved after the fall of communism, President Putin has been keen to ignore legal protections for rights, leaving Russians with formal rights that they are unable to practice. One bright spot for Russia's civil liberties record has been its willingness to grant asylum to Edward Snowden, who revealed the extent to which the American government was spying on its citizens.

Environment

Given that the environment and issues such as climate change affect the whole planet, the emergence of climate change as a global problem is an aspect of globalization. What one country does with respect to the environment can affect the whole world. The environment cannot be treated as a series of national problems and must be treated as one big global issue. The ability to get every country to agree to take action on an issue such as climate change has proven problematic. The Kyoto Accord was supposed to be a comprehensive global treaty which committed countries to specific targets to reduce their greenhouse gas emissions. Countries such as Canada eventually pulled out of the Kyoto treaty, and the United States did not ratify the treaty. This left many enthusiastic European countries to cut their greenhouse gasses dramatically, but since those countries are relatively small, the impact was minimal without the participation of large countries.

There has also been tension between China and developed countries like the U.S. and U.K., as China argues that they need the chance to develop their economy in the same way that other countries have. China argues that they are trying to develop in as clean a way possible but should not have to meet the same targets as countries like the U.S. and U.K., whose economies developed using dirty industry. The U.S. and U.K. say that China should not get a pass and that everyone needs to reduce their emissions. This sets up a conflict between the environment and the economy since it is widely believed that helping one will hurt the other. Environmentalists have heavily criticized the World Trade Organization because of its tendency to resolve the conflict between the environment and the economy in favor of the economy. The WTO considers many environmental regulations to be just trade barriers; many corporations have sued countries at the WTO and have been able to have the environmental laws in some countries repealed.

Heavy steel industrial pollution in Benxi, China.

A notorious example of corporations forcing governments to remove environmental protections is the North American Free Trade Agreement (NAFTA) case of *Ethyl Corporation vs. Canada*. Ethyl Corporation was an American company who made a gasoline additive called MMT. This additive was found to be environmentally harmful and was banned in the United States by the Environmental Protection Agency. A few years later, Canada decided to ban Ethyl Corporation's MMT additive as well, but Ethyl Corporation sued it under NAFTA's Chapter 11, which allows corporations to sue governments for potential lost profit as a result of enacting new laws. Fearing that they would be forced to pay a large sum of money to Ethyl Corporation, the Canadian government agreed to overturn their ban on Ethyl's MMT and issued a public apology to the corporation.

Based on examples like this and Mexico's use of the WTO to overturn U.S. laws protecting dolphins, many environmentalists argue that international trade agreements are more like corporate rights treaties that prevent governments from enacting proper environmental protections. Domestic policymakers know they have to be wary of how such environmental policies will play out concerning the international economy. As long as corporations can force governments to overturn environmental protection, treaties such as Kyoto have no power to force governments to protect the environment, making for a one-sided situation.

Population and Migration

Another global issue that transcends boundaries is the issue of migration and refugees. Under the globalization of neoliberal economics, corporations are free to jump from country to country, but the movement of people is extremely limited. When companies move their factories to another country, the workers cannot follow them, and this becomes a mechanism to keep wages low. In the case of Mexico, after its initial bubble brought about by corporations setting up garment factories burst when those corporations left Mexico for Indonesia, the Philippines and China, many Mexicans sought work in the United States, often by crossing the border illegally. While many Americans call for stronger border controls and deportations, those measures do not address the root cause of illegal immigration, which is the ability of corporations to move freely across borders. Before globalization, corporations were more tightly regulated, and the capital flight was controlled by governments. This ensured that corporations could not simply jump across borders when things didn't go their way and made for a steadier employment situation.

A second major issue is refugees, which is a particular issue in Europe and the United Kingdom. With the ongoing civil war in Syria, many Syrians have been forced out of their homes and are fleeing the country. Left without a state, they must rely on other countries to take them in and help them get back on their feet. In the case of the U.K., there is growing opposition to the government's position of accepting refugees. The U.K. Independence Party, which received 12% of the popular vote in the 2015 election, argues that Syrian Muslims are incompatible with British culture and are a drain on society. Refugees are a problem because no country wants to take in an influx of people who have fled their home country, often with nothing more than the clothes on their back; yet at the same time, if every country said no, these people would likely end up killed in Syria's internal war. As with the environment issue, there is no global agreement on how many refugees each country should take, leading to many problems.

Economic Development

Economic development refers to efforts to raise the overall level of prosperity in a country. What exactly development consists of is often contested, but generally underdeveloped countries aim to become like the countries of Europe and North America, where poverty rates are low, and the average person can lead a reasonably comfortable lifestyle. While there are many different theories of economic development, with neoliberalism becoming dominant in recent decades, policy approaches can differ in various countries.

Since the capitalist reforms of 1978, China's growth has been remarkable. In terms of their economic policy planning, every five years the government develops a new plan for the next five years with some economic development goals it aims to work towards and ultimately accomplish. These plans provide economic stability and direction, as the economy is aimed at meeting these goals. In the 11th five-year plan, from 2011 to 2015, the goal was to grow the country's GDP at a rate of 8% per year. With this goal in mind, when the GDP growth rate dropped, the government would engage in stimulus policies to try to get the growth rate back up to their target. This happened in 2014 and again in 2016, leading many experts to question whether such a high GDP growth rate will be sustainable for such long periods of time. China's government is currently focused on building infrastructure to modernize the country and make it easier to do business. These major infrastructure projects include developing a major transportation network along the Yangtze River in the hope of developing this area industrially.

Completed in 2005, Donghai Bridge connects Shanghai
with the offshore Yangshan deep-water port.

Chinese policymakers operate on the assumption that if the government builds a modern transportation and telecommunications infrastructure, it will lead to the creation of modern high-technology corporations. Currently, most of China's production is aimed at assembling and making computer hardware, consumer goods and clothing. The goal for Chinese policymakers is to provide a modern infrastructure that will encourage domestic corporations to move from simply manufacturing the products designed and created in the rest of the world to designing and creating their products. Instead of merely assembling Apple products, the Chinese government hopes that the Chinese equivalent of Apple will emerge as a result of their infrastructure developments. This is called moving up the development ladder.

This model of economic development policy where the government seeks to modernize infrastructure itself to create the conditions for local companies to emerge and compete globally is almost the exact reverse of the development policy of Nigeria. The Nigerian government has been wholly uninterested in developing the infrastructure of the economy and instead relies on foreign corporations to develop it for them. Nigeria believes that infrastructure development would be hugely profitable, and by opening up its borders, it hopes to attract foreign corporations who will build modern telecom, energy and transportation infrastructure from the ground up. The Nigerian government has offered some legal protections and incentives to attract foreign corporations to develop the Nigerian economy, but so far with little success. Given the levels of violence due to the Boko Haram insurgency and the massive corruption problem, foreign corporations see Nigeria as much too risky to invest in. This has led to a situation where the Nigerian government's development policy is wholly dependent on solving other, bigger problems first.

Nigeria's development policy is somewhat problematic, as it requires the government to stabilize the country before it has any reasonable chance of attracting foreign investment. However, to stabilize the country means that it would have to invest in developing the basic infrastructure significantly. Corruption stems from poor government services due to a lack of government investment, and much of the problems with religious tensions are reflective of a lack of government effectiveness. Ironically, for Nigeria to be successful in its opposite-of-China development approach, it must first become more like China. The Nigerian government does not wish to do this, and the prevailing ideology of policy elites around the world asserts that the Nigerian model of development should work better than the Chinese model. The reality, however, is that the Nigerian model of waiting around for foreign investment has been a dismal failure, while China is on pace to become the world's biggest economy by 2025.

Mexico's development policy approach is somewhat unique to its history. After somewhat steady gains promoting domestic industry without much investment in infrastructure, Mexico decided to open up to foreign investment in the 1990s. This brought jobs for a short period, but little infrastructure development as the foreign corporations were using Mexico for its cheap labor. Developing the infrastructure was left to domestic corporations, many of whom were previously owned by the state but had been privatized.

Telmex and America Movil are two of the biggest telecom corporations in the world. The Mexican government previously owned them, and now they are under the control of Mexican billionaire Carlos Slim. He used his private monopoly to develop the telecom infrastructure of Mexico, eventually expanding to many Latin American countries. While this was initially a huge boon to Mexico, with cell phones outnumbering land lines five to one, the monopoly situation has since led to stagnation. The Mexican government realized this problem only in 2013 when they created a federal regulator to promote mobile phone and internet infrastructure development. In 2013, the Mexican government sued Telmex, claiming it was using its market dominance to gouge customers with unnecessarily high fees.

Mexico provides a somewhat paradoxical case of development. A domestic corporation was able to develop infrastructure and then go global, something which is the goal of many economic development policies. Despite the huge wealth of Telmex and America Movil, Mexico still has high poverty rates and suffers from underdeveloped infrastructure in much of the country. Part of the problem stems from the fact that all the wealth from these companies was funneled to the top, with Carlos Slim becoming the richest person in the world from 2010 to 2013. Due to the monopoly situation of Telmex, high prices have funneled wealth from the bottom to the top; regular people are overcharged for their phones so that the richest person in the world can make more money. While some argue that Telmex would never have had this sort of success if it hadn't been privatized, others point out that the Mexican economy has not benefitted from the creation of a hugely successful company.

Telmex cell phone tower in Mexico City.

Factors Influencing Public Policymaking and Implementation

Policymaking today cannot simply be confined to domestic factors. In a globalized world, policymaking is driven by a multitude of conflicting factors and levels. Policy can be driven by citizens, governments, governments of other countries, transnational corporations or international treaties. These multiple levels of influence have serious consequences for state sovereignty. One of the main questions in comparative politics today is the relation between sovereignty and democracy. If a state now makes decisions based on factors other than its citizens' wishes, has it lost its sovereignty and is it acting undemocratically? When the U.K. enacts a policy at the urging of the European Union that goes against the wishes of most English people, is this a violation of democracy and sovereignty? On the other hand, when states engage in human rights abuses and other countries intervene, this is also a violation of their state sovereignty, albeit one that often helps alleviate the internal democratic situation.

Domestic

Domestic policy concerns stem from citizens and the unique situation of a country. Mexico, Nigeria, Russia, and Iran all have a set of serious issues related to their possession of vast oil reserves, while China and the U.K. do not have these issues at all. At the same time, the oil-producing countries are at the whims of the global market, which determines the price of oil. If China and the U.K. were to develop workable, widely adopted green technologies that made them much less reliant on fossil fuels, they could drive the price of oil down (and inadvertently cause major policy issues in the oil producing countries). At the same time, when the oil-producing countries cut back on production and send the price of oil higher, oil-importing countries have to adjust their policy to deal with this sort of price inflation.

Domestic issues, such as oil, also face external ideological pressures. Mexico and Nigeria are constantly being pressured to privatize their oil companies, which is considered good neoliberal policy regardless of the unique situation of these countries. When Venezuela began to regulate their oil industry in the 2000s to distribute its profits to the poor instead of to foreign oil companies, there was immense ideological pressure against them. The Venezuelan government argued it was their oil, and they had a right to use it to help Venezuelans, but the international media and other countries demanded they allow foreign oil companies full control. Eventually, the U.S. attempted to overthrow the

Venezuelan government for not bowing to international pressure. Venezuela treated this as an attack on both its own democratically elected government and its state sovereignty. The U.S. position was that Venezuela was a "rogue state" going against the proactive capitalist norms of the global community.

Anti-American mural in Caracas, Venezuela.

International

China's economic policy is unique and runs against the global ideological current as well, causing the Chinese government to face international pressure continuously. Until 2005, the Chinese currency was pegged at a fixed rate to the U.S. dollar, while virtually every other currency in the world floats, meaning it can change in value relative to other currencies. China enacted this policy to ensure that Chinese products would always be cheap when priced in American dollars, as the U.S. is the primary export market for Chinese manufacturing. China faced considerable international pressure on this issue, as the U.S. and other countries were angry that their domestic manufacturing industry could no longer compete since the Chinese currency kept Chinese prices lower. China argued that this policy was best for its development, and complained that the U.S., the IMF, and the WTO had no right to dictate China's economic policy.

Eventually, in 2005, China gave in and agreed to let their currency change value within a narrow band. Thus, the Chinese Yuan might go up or down 0.5% relative to the U.S. dollar, but would never go down 30 or 40%. Under continued pressure from the U.S. and the IMF, China eventually increased the floating range in 2014 to 2%, but it still resists the pressure to let the value of the currency float completely relative to the U.S. dollar. This issue is an example of how what's good for one country might be bad for others and how international pressure can undermine the ability of a country to make its own decisions. While usually such violations of state sovereignty are seen as corruptive of democracy, China is an interesting example because it is not a democracy, and international pressure on the currency issue has not made China more democratic.

If violations of state sovereignty are seen as undermining democracy, why is it the case that democratic governments have proven to be the most willing to betray their people and cave in to international pressure? Once Nigeria became a democracy, it almost instantly gave in to international pressure on every issue where the previous military dictatorship had charted its course. Only China seems to be able to resist international pressure to accept neoliberal economics, despite having a style of government that is only indirectly responsible to the people. North Korea is another example of a country that, as a dictatorship, can run contrary to international norms.

This leads to wider questions about how democratically elected governments are. Is China's one-party dictatorship more accountable to the people because it is willing to do what's best for the Chinese people regardless of what the international community thinks they should do? Alternatively, are Nigeria's or Mexico's elected governments more democratic since the people directly choose those in power, even if those who were elected to end up acting against the interests of the people by letting international pressures determine their policies? These are some of the most pressing debates in comparative public policy today.

Appendix

Glossary

A

Accommodation – an informal agreement or settlement between the government and important interest groups that is responsive to the interest groups' concerns for policy or program benefits.

Accountability – a government's responsibility to its people for its actions, decisions and policy; citizens who stay aware of their governments' decisions and policies are more likely to hold their governments accountable by voting in elections; periodic elections and a *Vote of no confidence* are examples of accountability in the government of the United Kingdom.

Administration – the organized apparatus of the state for the preparation and implementation of legislation and policies; see *Bureaucracy*.

Administration – 1) a term synonymous with the government (e.g., the Bush administration, the Schroeder administration); 2) a term synonymous with the management processes of bureaucracies (e.g., the administration of the state through bureaucratic agencies).

Affirmative action – also known as "positive discrimination"; policies designed to redress past discrimination; in this case, state bureaucracies may be required to increase recruitment of minority groups.

African – a person of African descent; South African usage refers to black Bantu language speakers, the demographic majority of South African citizens.

African National Congress – largely black organization that sought the extensions of suffrage to blacks; initially non-violent.

Afrikaner – descendants of Dutch, French, German and Scottish settlers speaking a language (Afrikaans) derived heavily from Dutch; politically mobilized as an ethnic group throughout the twentieth century.

Agenda setting – the process by which a multiplicity of political problems and issues are continuously sorted according to the changing priorities attached to them; in communication research, the theory claiming that the mass media may not exercise much influence over what people think but can influence what people think about.

Alford index – a measure of class voting in the U.K. that calculates the difference between the proportion of working-class people voting for a left party and the proportion of middle-class people doing the same; the higher the index, the greater the voting according to class.

Aligned groups – pressure groups that ally themselves with a political party (e.g., trade unions with left parties and business organizations with right parties); many groups try to maintain a non-aligned status if they can because they want to work with whichever party is in power.

Amerindian – indigenous peoples of North and South America.

Anarchic order – order resulting from mutual coordination in the absence of a higher authority.

Anarchism – a stateless society that allows total individual freedom.

Anarchy – the elimination of the state and private property as a way to achieve both freedom and equality for all; belief in a high degree of personal freedom and social equality is possible.

Ancien régime – the monarchical regime that ruled France until the Revolution of 1789 when a popular uprising toppled it; also used to describe long-established regimes in other countries ruled by undemocratic elites.

Anomic group – a spontaneously-formed interest group with concern over a specific issue.

Anticlericalism – opposition to the power of churches or clergy in politics; in some countries (e.g., France and Mexico) this opposition has focused on the role of the Catholic Church in politics.

Apartheid – in Afrikaans, "separateness"; first used in 1929 to describe *Afrikaner* nationalist proposals for strict racial separation and "to ensure the safety of the white race"; declared government policy after 1948 but dropped from the official lexicon in the 1980s; elaborated thereafter into a program of hierarchically arranged administrative and representative institutions for each racial and ethnic group in which a central state, under exclusive white control, predominated.

Aristocracy – a form of government in which a minority rules under the law.

Ascriptive Identities – those identities that are not under one's control and which one is born with (e.g., race, ethnicity, gender, sexual orientation, religion, caste, species); sociologists argue that these are the reason for stratification in any society.

Assembly of Experts – a deliberative body of 86 Mujtahids that is charged with electing the *Supreme Leader* of Iran and supervising his activities; members of the Assembly are elected from a government-screened list of candidates by direct public vote to six-year terms (almost all its members are clerics); current laws require the Assembly to meet for at least two days, twice annually.

Associational group – a formally-organized group which articulates the interests of its members over long periods of time.

Asymmetrical federalism – a federal system of government in which powers are unevenly divided between provinces (e.g., some provinces have greater responsibilities or more autonomy than others).

Auction politics – a danger in democratic politics in which state power may be "sold" to the highest bidding groups.

Auditor general – the official of Parliament whose staff audit the expenditures of government departments and which provides an annual report on instances of funds being unlawfully or unwisely spent.

Authoritarian/authoritarianism – a system of rule in which power depends not on popular legitimacy but the coercive force of the political authorities; few personal and group freedoms; authoritarian regimes are also characterized by near-absolute power in the executive branch and few if any, legislative and judicial controls.

Authoritarian attitudes – a system or syndrome of attitudes based on prejudice, dogmatism, superstition, low tolerance for ambiguity, hostility to out-groups (e.g., anti-Semitism and racism) and obedience to authority.

Authority – a form of power based on consensus regarding the right to issue commands and make decisions.

Autonomous okrug – one of originally ten territorial units of the Russian Federation defined in the 1993 constitution to be among the eighty-nine members of the federation; reduced to 4 by 2008 due to some of the small ethnically-based units merging with the *Oblast* or *Krai* in which they are located.

Autonomous region – in the People's Republic of China, a territorial unit equivalent to a province that contains a large concentration of ethnic minorities; these regions (e.g., Tibet) have some autonomy in the cultural sphere but in most policy matters are strictly subordinate to the central government.

Autonomy – the ability of the state to wield its power independently of the public.

Ayatollah – literally meaning, "Sign of God;" high-ranking clerics in Iran; the most senior (often no more than half a dozen) are known as "grand ayatollahs."

Ayatollah Khomeini – the Shah of Iran; following the revolution and a national referendum, Khomeini became the country's *Supreme Leader*, a position created in the constitution as the highest ranking political and religious authority of the nation, until his death.

B

Backbencher – members of Parliament on the government side who sit on the backbenches and are not in the *Cabinet*; those similarly distant from *Shadow cabinet* posts in opposition parties.

Balance of payments – a state's running account of economic transactions (exports and imports) with the rest of the world.

Balance of power – the distribution of power between states such that no one state can overwhelm others.

Bazaar – an urban marketplace where shops, workshops, small businesses, and export-importers are located.

Behavioralism – a phase in comparative politics associated with the scientific method that values neutrality and research supported by facts; uses the methods of sampling, interviewing, scoring, scaling and statistical analysis concerning political theory.

Behavioral revolution – the introduction of more empirical analysis into the study of government and politics.

Bicameralism – a system of government in which the legislature is divided into two chambers: an upper house and a lower house.

Bill – a piece of legislation under consideration by a legislative body.

Binational state – two *Nations* co-existing within one state.

Bipolar – an international system in which there are two dominant *Nation-states*.

Black economy – the "informal economy" in which goods and services are traded for cash without the bills, receipts or financial records that would enable the authorities to levy taxes on them.

Boer – meaning literally "farmer;" modern usage is a derogatory reference to *Afrikaners*.

Bourgeoisie – a Marxist term referring to those who own or manage the means of production.

Brahmin – the highest caste in the Hindu *Caste system* of India.

Bureaucracy – an organization structured hierarchically, in which lower-level officials are charged with administering regulations codified in rules that specify impersonal, objective guidelines for making decisions; in the modern world, many large organizations, especially business firms and the executive branches of states, are organized along bureaucratic lines.

C

Cabinet – the body of officials (e.g., ministers, secretaries) whom direct executive departments presided over by the chief executive (prime minister, president); in parliamentary systems, the cabinet and high-ranking subcabinet ministers (also known as the government) are considered collectively responsible to parliament.

Cabinet solidarity – a convention that all *Cabinet* ministers publicly support whatever decisions the cabinet has taken, regardless of their personal views; see *Collective responsibility*.

Cabinet government – a system of government in which the Cabinet holds most executive power and headed by a prime minister.

Cadre – a person who occupies a position of authority in a *Communist party-state*; may or may not be Communist Party members.

Capacity – the ability of the state to wield power to carry out the basic tasks of providing security and reconciling freedom and equality

Capitalism – an economic system, and the ideology behind it that is based on private property, the profit motive, competition and a free market in which the state plays a limited role; see *Laissez-faire*.

Cash transfers – a way to provide social security payments to citizens by giving them money; an alternative to cash benefits is the provision of goods and services.

Caste (system) – India's Hindu society is divided into castes; according to the Hindu religion, membership in caste is determined at birth; castes form a rough social and economic hierarchy; see *Brahmin* and *Untouchables*.

Catch-all parties – lacking a clear social orientation, catch-all parties try to attract a broad range of supporters by advocating general policies.

Caucus – a meeting of legislators of any one party to discuss parliamentary strategy and party policy.

Causal theories – an influential approach in comparative politics that involves trying to explain why "If X happens, then Y is the result" (i.e., how does X (the *Independent variable*) cause or influence Y (the *Dependent variable*)).

Cause groups – sometimes known as "promotional groups" or "attitude groups;" a type of *Pressure group* that does not represent organized occupational interests but promotes causes or ideas.

Center-periphery cleavage – the political cleavage between the social and political forces responsible for creating centralized and modern nation-states (which usually became dominant) and other interest groups (usually on the periphery of the state) which resist this process; often, but not always, geographical.

Central agency – government agencies (e.g., the PMO, the PCO, the Treasury Board, and the Finance Department) that have certain coordinating functions across the whole federal public service.

Central planning – an economic system in which the government or workers' councils manage the economy; it controls all major sectors of the economy and formulates all decisions about their use and the distribution of income; the planners decide what should be produced and direct enterprises to produce those goods; see *Command economy*.

Charismatic authority – authority based on the populace's admiration of the personal qualities of an individual.

Charter of the United Nations – founding treaty of the United Nations (UN) that defines the purposes of the UN and confers certain powers on it.

Checks and balances – a system of government in which power is divided between the executive, legislative and judicial branches of government and these powers check and balance each other; see *Separation of powers*.

Citizenship – legal membership to a particular state (*Country*); people who are born in the UK are granted natural citizenship; in China, those who are Tibetan may not be recognized as citizens of China.

Civil culture – the term used by Almond and Verba to signify the balance of subject cultures and participant political cultures that best supports democracy.

Civil service – the body of civilian officials (not members of the armed forces) employed by the state to work in government departments; in some countries, the term applies to all public officials (local government and teachers), but it mostly includes only the officials of central government.

Civil society – refers to the space occupied by voluntary associations outside the state (e.g., professional associations (lawyers, doctors, teachers), trade unions, student and women's groups, religious bodies and other voluntary association groups).

Class – a form of social stratification that is determined by economic factors; notably the occupational hierarchy that broadly groups people into working-class (manual labor), middle-class (non-manual or white-collar workers) and upper-class (wealthy property-owning) groups.

Class de-alignment – a process of decline in the class-based strength of attachment and sense of belonging to class-based political parties.

Classical liberalism – a liberal ideology entailing a minimal role for government to maximize individual freedom.

Cleavages – deep and persistent differences in a society where objective social differences (class, religion, race, language or regional) are aligned with subjective awareness of these differences (different cultures, ideologies, and orientations) and are organized or exacerbated by political parties, groups or movements; often the basis of political conflict.

Clientalism – informal policymaking relationship between patron individuals/institutions who provide goods, services, benefits to those in less strategic or powerful positions in return for their political or economic support; may provide benefits for both patron and client in the short term as well as an opportunity for corruption (e.g., the PRI in Mexico provided access to job opportunities for workers in labor unions in return for their political support in the elections).

Coalition – 1) an alliance between two or more political units in response to opposing forces. 2) a set of parties that come together to form a government; usually with each being represented in the *Cabinet*, but sometimes one party will take all the Cabinet posts with the support of a legislative coalition.

Coalition government – a parliamentary government in which the *Cabinet* is composed of members of more than one party.

Code civil – the unique system of civil law used in Quebec; the French civil code established under Napoléon I in 1804.

Code of law – a comprehensive set of interrelated legal rules.

Coercion – a form of power based on forced compliance through fear and intimidation.

Cognitive mobilization – the process by which increasing knowledge and understanding of the world help to activate people to play a part in it.

Cohabitation – the term used by the French to describe the situation in the Fifth Republic when the president and the prime minister belonged to opposing political coalitions.

Cold War – the hostile relations that prevailed between the United States and the Soviet Union from the late 1940s until the demise of the USSR in 1991; although an actual (hot) war never directly occurred between the two superpowers, they clashed indirectly by supporting rival forces in many wars occurring in the Third World.

Collectivization – a process undertaken in the Soviet Union under Stalin from 1929 into the early 1930s and in China under Mao in the 1950s by which agricultural land was removed from private ownership and organized into large state and collective farms.

Collective defense – an alliance among states against external threats.

Collective (public) goods – goods and services enjoyed in common and not divisible among individuals.

Collective identities – the groups with which people identify (e.g., gender, social class, race, region, and religion) and which are the "building blocks" for social and political action; any given individual has a variety of identities (e.g., a Muslim woman who is a member of the Kurdish ethnic group of northern Iraq); there is enormous variation regarding which collective identities are most important for particular individuals, which ones are influential within particular countries and how effectively political systems deal with conflicts among collective identities.

Collective responsibility – the principle that decisions and policies of the *Cabinet* or council are binding on all members, who must support them in public in order to maintain the government's united front; what *Cabinet* or council members say or believe in private is a different matter, but resignation from the government should follow public disagreement; see *Cabinet solidarity*.

Collective security – a commitment by some states to join in an alliance against member states that threaten peace.

Command economy – a form of socialist economy in which government decisions ("commands") rather than market mechanisms (such as supply and demand) are the major influences in determining the nation's economic direction; see *Central planning*.

Cominform –the "Communist Information Bureau;" an international communist organization after World War II.

Comintern – the "Communist International;" also known as the Third International; the international communist organization between the two World Wars.

Common law – the accumulation of judicial precedents as the basis for court decisions; see *Customary law*.

Communications (mass) media – a general term for all modern means of conveying information.

Communism – a system of social organization based on the common ownership and coordination of production; according to Marxism (the theory of German philosopher Karl Marx, 1818–1883), communism is a culminating stage of history, following capitalism and socialism; in historical practice, leaders of China, the Soviet Union and other states that have proclaimed themselves seeking to achieve communism have ruled through a single party, the Communist Party, which has controlled the state and society in an *Authoritarian* manner, and have applied *Marxism-Leninism* to justify their rule; see *Communist party-state*.

Communist party-state – a type of *Nation-state* in which the Communist Party attempts to exercise a monopoly on political power and controls all important state institutions; see *Communism*.

Comparative Methods – process to examine and classify systems of government through their similarities and differences; can be approached by systems theory, case study system or the conceptual system; facilitates our understanding of how governments are structured and develop policy and how that, in turn, affects their international relationships (e.g., comparison of privatization in Russia and China and its impact on each country's political and economic structures and political policies).

Comparative politics – the study of the domestic politics, political institutions and conflicts of countries; often involves comparisons among countries and through time within single countries, emphasizing key patterns of similarity and difference; see *Comparativist*.

Comparativist – a political scientist who studies the similarities and differences in the domestic politics of various countries; see *Comparative politics*.

Conditionality – the requirement that certain commitments be made by receiving governments in exchange for credits or other types of assistance provided by international or foreign agencies; ensures that the goals of the donor agency are respected.

Confederations – organizations whose members give some powers to a higher body while retaining their *Autonomy* and independence, including the right to leave the confederation.

Confidence – a vote of support for the government by the majority of the members of Parliament.

Conglomerates – single business organizations consisting of some different companies that operate in different economic fields.

Congress of the people – a South African political party formed in 2008 by former members of the African National Congress (ANC); headed by ex-ANC members

Mosiuoa Lekota, Mbhazima Shilowa and Mluleki George; announced following a national convention held in Sandton on 1 November 2008; met in Kliptown, a suburb of Johannesburg, in 1955 to lay out the vision of the South African people; drafted by the Congress Alliance, consisting of the African National Congress (ANC), the South African Indian Congress, the Coloured People's Congress and the Congress of Democrats; The Freedom Charter was a result of this, which became the manifesto of the *African National Congress*.

Conciliation – arbitrating between two disputing people or groups; see *Mediation*.

Consent of the governed – people's acceptance of the form of government under which they live.

Conservationism – the attempt to manage natural resources to maximize benefits over a long period.

Conservatism – a political ideology generally characterized by a belief in individualism and minimal government intervention in the economy and society; also a belief in the virtue of the status quo and general acceptance of traditional morality.

Consociationalism – a form of democracy in which harmony in segmented societies is maintained through the distinctive roles of elites and the *Autonomy* of organized interests.

Consolidated democracies – democratic political systems that have been solidly and stably established for an ample period and in which there is relatively consistent adherence to the core democratic principles.

Constitution – a set of fundamental laws that determines what the central institutions and offices of the state are to be, their powers and duties and how they are to relate to one another and their citizens.

Constitutional monarchy – a system of government in which the head of state ascends by heredity but is limited in powers and constrained by the provisions of a *Constitution*.

Constitutionalism – the belief that governments will defer to the rules and principles enshrined in a *Constitution* and uphold the rule of law.

Constituency – an electoral district with a body of electors who vote for a representative in an elected assembly.

Content regulation – regulation of the content of the media by public bodies in the public interest (e.g., to limit violence on TV or ban cigarette advertising); content regulation of news and current affairs programs usually aims at accurate, balanced and impartial political reporting and equal access for the parties to air time.

Constructive vote of no confidence – a system in which the majority in the lower house can bring down the head of a government but not until that majority approves a successor.

Contracting out – the hiring of private organizations to provide public services.

Conventions – 1) unwritten rules that impose obligations on constitutional actors that are held to be binding but not incorporated into law or reinforced by legal sanctions; 2) meetings of political groups or parties (e.g., the Republican National Convention) to select their candidates and decide their platform.

Co-optation – to assimilate into, overtake or allowed to be absorbed by a larger, more established group (e.g., the Labour Party was co-opted by the Socialist Party).

Corporatism – a way of organizing public policymaking involving the close cooperation of major economic interests within a formal government apparatus that is capable of converting the main economic groups so that they can jointly formulate and implement binding policies.

Corporatist –a way of influencing policy in which the state gives favored status to certain interest groups; illustrated by state leaders investing funds or sponsoring programs aimed at winning the support or favor of a particular group.

Corporatist state – a system in which important interests, such as unions and business associations, are formally included in government decision-making processes.

Corruption – the use of illegitimate means such as bribery, blackmail or threats to influence or control the making of public decisions; the secret use of public offices or resources for private purposes.

Corruption Perception Index – a measure developed by Transparency International that "ranks countries in terms of the degree to which corruption is perceived to exist among public officials and politicians. It is a composite index, drawing on corruption-related data in expert surveys carried out by a variety of reputable institutions. It reflects the views of businesspeople and analysts from around the world, including experts who are locals in the countries evaluated;" ranges from 10 (highly clean) to 0 (highly corrupt).

Country – a territorial unit controlled by a single state; vary in the degree to which groups within them have a common culture and ethnic affiliation; see *Nation-state*.

Coup d'état – a forceful, extra-constitutional action resulting in the removal of an existing government, usually carried out by the military.

Credit – any transaction which brings money into the country (e.g., payments for the export of goods).

Cross-cutting cleavages – *Cleavages* that lay across from one another, thereby reducing their capacity to divide; compare with *Reinforcing cleavages*.

Cross-media ownership/Multi-media conglomeration – when the same person or company has financial interests in different branches of mass communication (e.g., when they own a newspaper and a TV channel or a publishing house and TV network).

Crown corporation – in the U.K., corporations owned by the government that assume a structure similar to a private company and that operate semi-independently of the *Cabinet*.

Current accounts surplus – a state selling more to the world than it is buying.

Custom – a generally accepted practice or behavior developed over time.

Customary law – rules of conduct developed over time and enforceable in court; see also *Common law*.

D

Danwei – a name given to a place of employment in China; all Chinese citizens have a lifetime affiliation with a specific industrial, agricultural or bureaucratic unit that dictates all aspects of their lives, including housing, healthcare, and other social benefits.

Debit – any transaction which sends money out of the country (e.g., payments for the import of goods).

Decentralization – policies that aim to transfer some decision-making power from higher to lower levels of government, typically from the central government to subnational governments, such as states or provinces.

Declaration of the Rights of Man and the Citizen – the seventeen articles, describing the purpose of the state and the rights of individual citizens, proclaimed by the French National Assembly in August 1789; a similar list had been proclaimed in the USA thirteen years earlier, in 1776.

Deep ecology – a form of environmentalism holding that nature and the natural order should be valued over individual human happiness.

Deficit – occurs when the value of a state's imports is more than the value of its exports.

Delegate – a representative role in which the individual subordinates their views to those of their constituents.

Delegated legislation – laws or decrees made by ministers, not legislatures, in accordance to powers granted to them by the legislative body.

Democracy – from the Greek *demos* (the people) and *Kratos* (rule); a type of political system that features the following: selection to important public offices through free and fair elections based on universal suffrage (the right of all adults to vote); political parties that are free to organize, offer their ideas, present candidates for public office and compete in elections; an elected government that develops policy according to specified procedures that are fair and relatively open to public scrutiny; all citizens possess political rights and civil liberties; an independent judiciary (court system); civilian control of the military.

Democratic centralism – a system of political organization developed by V. I. Lenin and practiced, with modifications, by all *Communist party-states*; principles include a hierarchal party structure in which: party leaders are elected on a delegate basis from lower to higher party bodies; party leaders can be recalled by those who elected them; and freedom of discussion is permitted until a decision is taken, but strict discipline and unity should prevail in implementing a decision once it is made; in practice, in all Communist parties (in China, the Soviet Union and elsewhere) the centralizing elements tended to predominate over the democratic ones.

Democratic deficit – a term used to convey the idea that the institutions of the European Union are not fully democratic or as democratic as they should be; often used to support suggestions that the power of the European Parliament should be increased at the expense of the Commission and the Council of Ministers.

Democratization – the transition from *Authoritarian* rule to a democratic political order; in South Africa, the term usually refers to the period of negotiated political transition between 1900 and 1994; between the ending of official bans on the liberation movements and the general elections; also known as "democratic transition."

Demokratizatsiia – the policy of *Democratization* identified by former Soviet leader Mikhail Gorbachev in 1987 as an essential component of *Perestroika*; part of a gradual shift away from a *Vanguard party* approach toward an acceptance of democratic norms; initially, the policy embraced multicandidate elections and a broadening of political competition within the Communist Party itself; after 1989, it involved acceptance of a multiparty system.

Deng Xiaoping – Chinese Communist Party leader (1978-1989) who pursued modernization at the expense of communist ideology.

Department of finance – the government department that has overall responsibility for the government's finances and its role in the economy.

Dependent variable – an important part of social (and natural) scientific research; the outcome or result to be measured or explained and which is dependent on other factors (the *Independent variables*); the effect in a cause-and-effect question.

Despotism – an individual ruling through fear without regard to law and not answerable to the people.

Deputy minister – the Canadian public servant who heads each government department, manages the department and advises the minister.

Deregulation – the process of dismantling state regulations that govern social and economic life; increases the power of private actors, especially business firms.

Developmental state – a *Nation-state* in which the government carries out policies that effectively promote national economic growth.

Devolution – a system of government in which the sovereign central government devolves (delegates) power to regional governments.

Dictator – in Roman Law, an appointed individual given exceptional powers in times of crisis; in modern times, it is used to describe an absolute ruler of a state.

Dictatorship – a non-democratic form of government in which political power is highly concentrated in individuals or organizations that are not accountable to citizens through elections or other means; see *Authoritarianism* and *Totalitarianism*.

Dictatorship of the proletariat – a revolutionary seizure of power by the "vanguard" of society, the communist party, which then rules in the name of the working class.

Diplomacy – a system of formal, regularized communication that allows states to conduct their business with each other peacefully.

Direct democracy – a system of government based on public decisions made by citizens meeting in an assembly or voting by ballot.

Direct election – election by the electorate at large (by popular election) rather than by an electoral college, the legislature or another body.

Dirigisme – a French term denoting that the state plays a leading role in supervising the economy; in contrast to socialism or communism, firms remain privately owned under a system of dirigisme; at the other extreme, dirigisme differs from the situation where the state has a relatively small role in economic governance.

Disallowance – a power given to the Canadian federal government in the Constitution Act (1867), under which the *Cabinet* can nullify any provincial law, even though it has received royal assent from the lieutenant-governor of the province.

Discretion – the flexibility afforded government to decide something within the broader framework of rules.

Disproportionality/Proportionality – a measure of the ratio of seats to votes; the more proportional the system, the closer the ratio of seats to votes; in the most proportional voting system, a party getting 43 percent of the votes should get 43 percent of the seats, or close to this figure since seats are not divisible.

Distributional politics – the use of power, particularly by the state, to allocate some valued resource among competing groups.

Distributive laws – laws designed to distribute public goods and services to individuals in society.

Dominant one-party system – a party system in which one party dominates all the others; found in democratic countries with competitive parties; to be distinguished from undemocratic *One-party systems*, where only one party is allowed to operate freely.

Downsizing – a reduction of the size and scope of government.

Door-step response – the tendency of those with no opinion or information to respond to polls and surveys with the first thing that comes into their head, often something they think they are expected to say; also known as "non-opinion."

Doxa – the Greek word for an opinion that may be at least partly true but cannot be fully expounded.

Dual society – a society and an economy that are sharply divided into a traditional (usually poorer) sector and a modern (usually richer) sector.

Dual systems – a system of local government in unitary states in which local authorities have more independence than in fused systems but still operate under the General *Authority* of the central government.

E

Economic deregulation – the lifting or relaxation of government controls over the economy, including the reduction of import taxes (tariffs) and the phasing out of subsidized prices for producers and consumers.

Economic liberalization – an economic policy that limits the state's control of the economy and increases the power of the market and the private sector; global changes may cause a country to adopt policies that lead to economic liberalization.

Ejidatario – recipient of an *Ejido* land grant in Mexico.

Ejido – land granted by the Mexican government to an organized group of peasants.

Electoral College – the body which formally chooses the president of the United States.

Electoral threshold – a way of discouraging small parties by requiring them to get a certain minimum percentage of votes cast or seats to be elected.

Elite – a small group of people with a disproportionate amount of public decision-making power.

Elite and Populist politics and culture – the political behavior of *Elites* (of various kinds) is of a different kind and usually has different results when compared to the political behavior at the grassroots level; elite politics and culture in Mexico is carried out by Spanish speaking professional politicians in "smoke-filled rooms;" populist politics involves voting and public protests and the acceptance of gifts by people who may or may not speak Spanish.

The Emergency of India (1975–1977) – the 21-month period when Indian Prime Minister Indira Gandhi suspended many formal democratic rights and ruled in an *Authoritarian* manner; during this time, many of Gandhi's political opponents were jailed, and the press was censored.

Empirical – political analysis based on factual and observable data in contrast to thoughts or ideas.

Empirical political theories – theories that try to understand how the political world works and to explain why it works that way; ultimately based upon evidence and arguments that can, in principle, be tested and verified by political science.

Empirical statements – factual statements about or explanations of the world; not necessarily "true" or "false," but amenable, in principle, to disproof and falsification; see *Normative statements*.

Environmental Performance Index – a measure of how close countries come to meeting specific benchmarks for national pollution control and natural resource management.

Episodic groups – groups that are not usually politically active but become so for a time when an issue that concerns them arises.

Episteme – the Greek word for knowledge that can be demonstrated by logical argument from first principles.

Equality of opportunity – the equalization of life chances for all individuals in society, regardless of economic position.

Equality of result – the equalization of outcomes of social and economic processes.

Equality of right – the application of the law in the same way to all.

Equality rights – a section of the Canadian Charter of Rights and Freedoms (s. 15) that prohibits governments from discriminating against certain categories of people.

Essentially contestable concept – a concept that is inevitably the subject of an endless dispute about their proper use (e.g., art, democracy, politics).

Etatism – approaches to the relationships between state and society with a very strong emphasis on state power and an accompanying reduction of social and individual rights.

Ethnic group – a group whose common identity is based on racial, national origin and/or language characteristics.

Ethnicity – group identification that typically is rooted in the belief of a common biological ancestry; a *Nation-state* may be composed of multiple ethnicities such as the Ibo, Yoruba, Hausa and Fulani in Nigeria ancestry or homeland; discrimination of various ethnicities residing in the United Kingdom has been addressed by the Race Relations Act, amended in 2000, to promote racial equality.

Ethnocentrism – the privileging of western race, culture, religion, and ways of living with concomitant prejudices against the post-colonial societies.

Eurocentrism – bias towards Western institutions and processes that emanates from various sources, including the period of colonial domination and the presumed inferiority of all non-western societies.

European Union (EU) – an organization of European countries created in 1958 to promote economic integration and political cooperation among European states; at first, the EU's mandate was primarily to reduce tariff barriers among West European states; since then, more countries throughout Europe have joined the EU, and its powers have vastly expanded to include promoting common policies on immigration, technical standards, and economic and monetary regulation.

Executive – the branch of government mainly responsible for initiating government action, making and implementing *Public policy* and coordinating the activities of the state.

Executive federalism – in Canada, a federal process directed by extensive federal-provincial interaction at the level of first ministers, departmental ministers, and deputy ministers.

Expediency Council – a committee set up in Iran to resolve differences between the *Majlis* (the parliament) and the *Guardian Council.*

Externality – a cost or benefit that does not fall on those who are responsible for the decision or action that creates the externality and which they do not take into account when they take action.

Extractive laws – laws designed to collect taxes from citizens to pay for governing society.

F

Faction – an association of individuals organized to influence government actions that will favor their interests, now known as *Interest groups*; see *Pressure Groups*.

Failed states – states in which the government no longer functions effectively; a state may fail when its leaders violate the *Rule of law* and prey on the population or when the forces of discontent within the country become more powerful than the government.

False consciousness – the state of mind of most of the working class induced by the ruling class to conceal the real nature of capitalism and obscure the real self-interests of the workers.

Farsi – Persian word for the Persian language; Fars is a province in Central Iran.

Fascism – an extreme form of nationalism that played on fears of communism and rejected individual freedom, liberal individualism, democracy and limitations on the state.

Fatwa – a pronouncement issued by a high-ranking Islamic cleric.

Federalism – a system of government in which *Sovereignty* is divided between a central government and several provincial or state governments.

Federal states – states that combine a central *Authority* (federal government) with a degree of constitutionally defined *Autonomy* for sub-central territorial units of government (states, regions or provinces).

Feminism – the belief that men and women are equal and society has always been disadvantageous to women, systematically depriving them of individual choice, political power, economic opportunity, and intellectual recognition.

Fire brigade groups – groups formed to fight a specific issue and dissolved when it is over.

First International – a loose association of socialist parties and labor unions in Western Europe, organized in 1864.

Formal legal institutions – institutions which are explicitly created by a *Constitution*.

Foreign direct investment – ownership of or investment in cross-border enterprises in which the investor plays a direct managerial role.

Foundation of the Oppressed – a clerically controlled foundation set up after the revolution in Iran.

Fragment theory – a theory proposed by Louis Hartz which argues that colonial societies such as Canada originated as fragments of the larger European society and that these societies have remained marked throughout their history by the conditions of their origin.

Framing – the theory that the way news stories are set up ("framed") influences how audiences interpret them (e.g., the use of "human interest" stories to illustrate a social problem can deflect attention from government policies that help to cause the problem to the personal misfortunes of individuals chosen as the subjects of human interest).

Free-ride – to extract the benefits of other people's work without putting in any effort oneself; the free-rider problem is acute in collective action when some individuals benefit from a public good (clean air, for example, or public transport), though contributing little or nothing to it (continue to drive around in a gas-guzzling car, not buying a pass for public transportation).

Free-market environmentalism – the view that property rights and markets best solve environmental problems.

Free trade – international commerce that is relatively unregulated or unconstrained by tariffs (special payments imposed by governments on exports or imports).

Free vote – a legislative vote in which members are not required to toe the party line.

Freedom in the world rating – an annual evaluation by Freedom House of the level of freedom in countries around the world measured according to political rights and civil liberties through "a multi-layered process of analysis and evaluation by a team of regional experts and scholars;" countries are ranked in 0.5 gradations between 1.0 and 7.0, with 1.0–2.5 being "Free"; 3.0–5.0, "Partly Free"; and 5.5–7.0, "Not free."

Functions – the special activity or purpose structures serve in the political process (e.g., interest groups to articulate interests).

Fundamentalism – a term recently popularized to describe extremist religious movements throughout the world; in the U.S., it traditionally refers to religions that believe the Bible to be the Word of God and true.

Fused systems – systems of local government in unitary states in which officials appointed by central government directly supervise the work of local government and its elected officials.

Fusion of powers – a constitutional principle that merges the *Authority* of branches of government, in contrast to the principle of *Separation of powers* (e.g., in Britain, Parliament is the supreme legislative, executive and judicial authority); the fusion of legislature and executive is also expressed in the function and personnel of the *Cabinet*.

G

Gender gap – politically significant differences between men and women in their social attitudes and voting behavior.

General competence – the power of local government units to manage their affairs, provided they observe the laws of the land, with relatively few legally-defined exceptions.

Gerrymandering – a form of electoral corruption in which *Constituency* boundaries are redrawn to favor a particular party or interest.

Glasnost – Gorbachev's policy of "openness" or "publicity," which involved an easing of controls on the media, arts and public discussion, leading to an outburst of public debate and criticism covering most aspects of Soviet history, culture, and policy.

Global Gender Gap – a measure of "the extent to which women in 58 countries have achieved equality with men in five critical areas: economic participation, economic opportunity, political empowerment, educational attainment, and health and well-being."

Globalization – the intensification of worldwide interconnectedness associated with the increased speed and magnitude of cross-border flows of trade, investment and finance and processes of migration, cultural diffusion, and communication.

Governance – the act of governing (i.e., the total set of the government's activities in each phase of the policymaking process).

Government – a government executes the monopoly on the legitimate use of physical force within a state; securing the internal and external *Sovereignty* of the state are the major tasks of any government.

Government Structure – the institutions and institutional arrangements (relationships), formal and informal through which policy decisions are made and implemented; the more democratically the government structure is organized, the more complex it is likely to be (e.g., most government structures are unitary and do not include the kind of checks and balances found in the USA); however, there are usually other limitations on the power of institutions and officials.

Grandes écoles – prestigious and highly selective schools of higher education in France that train top civil servants, engineers, and business executives.

Grand coalitions – oversized coalitions that include all parties or all the largest of them.

Grands corps – elite networks of graduates of selective training schools in France.

Great Leap Forward – an economic and social plan launched by Mao Zedong and used from 1958 to 1961 which aimed to use China's vast population to rapidly transform mainland China from a primarily agrarian economy dominated by peasant farmers into a modern, agricultural and industrialized communist society; Mao Zedong based this program on the Theory of Productive Forces; the Leap ended in economic disaster in 1960, causing one of the worst famines in human history.

Great Proletarian Cultural Revolution – the political campaign launched in 1966 by Chairman Mao Zedong to stop what he saw as China's drift away from socialism and toward capitalism; the campaign led to massive purges in the Chinese Communist Party, the widespread persecution of China's intellectuals and the destruction of invaluable cultural objects; officially ended in 1976 after Mao's death and the arrest of some of his most radical followers.

Green revolution – a strategy for increasing agricultural (especially food) production, involving improved seeds, irrigation and abundant use of fertilizers.

Gross domestic product (GDP) – the total of all goods and services produced within a country that is used as a broad measure of the size of its economy; in comparing the wealth of states, the measure used is normally GDP per capita.

Gross national product (GNP) – a broad measure of the size of an economy; similar to *Gross domestic product* but also takes into account income received from foreign sources; The World Bank started using the term "gross national income" rather than "gross national product" in its reports and statistics in 2002.

Guanxi – a Chinese term that means "connections" or "relationships" and describes personal ties between individuals based on such things as a common birthplace or mutual acquaintances; Guanxi is an important factor in China's political and economic life.

Guardian Council – a committee created in the Iranian constitution to oversee the *Majlis* (the parliament).

Guerrilla warfare – a military strategy based on small bands of soldiers (guerrillas) who use hit-and-run tactics to attack a numerically superior and better-armed enemy.

H

Head of government – the person in effective charge of the executive branch of government (e.g., the prime minister in a parliamentary system).

Head of state – represents and symbolizes the people, both nationally and internationally, embodying and articulating the goals of the regime but not exercising political power.

Hegemonic power – a state that can control the pattern of alliances and terms of the international order and often influences domestic political developments in other countries throughout the world.

Hegemony – originally a Marxist term; indicates a class that is so powerful that it does not have to rely upon force or power to maintain its rule because all other classes have accepted its values and attitudes; often used now to mean "all-powerful" (e.g., since the collapse of the Soviet Union, the USA has become the "hegemonic" world power).

Hezbollah – literally meaning, "Partisans of God;" in Iran, the term is used to describe religious vigilantes; in Lebanon, it is used to describe the *Shi'i* militia.

Hojjat al-Islam – literally meaning "the proof of Islam"; in Iran, it means a medium-ranking cleric.

Homelands – areas reserved for exclusive African occupation, established through the provisions of 1913 and 1936 land legislation and later developed as semiautonomous ethnic states during the *Apartheid* era; at their fullest extent they represented 13% of South Africa's land surface, though at one stage they accommodated more than half the national population.

Household responsibility system – the system put into practice in China beginning in the early 1980s in which major decisions about agricultural production are made by individual farm families based on the profit motive rather than by a people's commune or the government.

Human Development Index (HDI) – a composite number used by the United Nations to measure and compare levels of achievement in health, knowledge, and standard of living; based on the following indicators: life expectancy, adult literacy rate, school enrollment statistics and *Gross domestic product* per capita at *Purchasing power parity*.

Human rights – the innate, inalienable and inviolable right of humans to free movement and self-determination about the state; such rights cannot be bestowed, granted, limited, bartered or sold away; inalienable rights can only be secured or violated.

Hyper-pluralism – a state of affairs in which too many powerful groups make too many demands on government, causing overload and un-governability.

I

Ideological party – a type of political party which emphasizes ideological purity over the attainment of power.

Ideal-type – an analytical construct that simplifies reality and selects its most important features to serve as a model that allows us to understand and compare the complexities of the real world; neither a standard of perfection (as in "an ideal husband") nor a statistical average, but a simplified, theoretical abstraction from the real world that helps one compare individual cases.

Idealism – in political theory, refers to the theory that ideas have a life of their own and must be understood as the products of consciousness or spiritual ideals and values that are independent of material conditions; in international relations, refers to the view of politics that emphasizes the role of ideas and morality as a determinant of the relations between states; see *Materialism*.

Ideologues – those with an informed, broad, sophisticated and more or less consistent (systematic) view of the political world.

Ideology – a more or less systematic, well-developed and comprehensive set of ideas and beliefs about how a political, economic or social system should be organized, consisting of both *Empirical statements* about what is and "prescriptive statements" about what ought to be (e.g., capitalism, communism, and socialism).

Imam jum'ehs – prayer leaders in Iran's main urban mosques; appointed by the *Supreme Leader*, they have considerable *Authority* in the provinces.

Immobilism – in a political system, the state of being unable to make decisions or implement policies.

Impeachment – to charge a public official, usually an elected politician, with improper conduct in office before a duly constituted tribunal, usually the main elected legislative body, before removing the official from office if they are found guilty; not known much outside the U.S. and not often used there.

Implementation – the process of applying policies and putting them into practice.

Imperialism – powerful, rich countries are spreading their influence around the globe (e.g., the imperialistic goals of Britain forced China to open trade and led to the Opium Wars and Hong Kong becoming a British colony).

Import-substituting industrialization (ISI) – a strategy for industrialization based on domestic manufacture of previously imported goods to satisfy domestic market demands.

Incremental model – the theory that decisions are not usually based upon a rational or fundamental review of problems and possible solutions but come about as small, marginal changes from existing policies.

Independent variable – an important part of social (and natural) scientific research; a factor that influences the outcome or result (the *Dependent variable*) to be measured or explained; the cause in a cause-and-effect question.

Indirect Democracy – when the public participates indirectly through its elected representatives (e.g., *Republicanism*); the prevalent form of democracy in the modern age.

Industrial Revolution – a period of rapid and destabilizing social, economic and political changes caused by the introduction of large-scale factory production, originating in England in the middle of the eighteenth century.

Indian Administrative Service (IAS) – India's civil service; a highly professional and talented group of administrators who run the Indian government on a day-to-day basis.

Indicative planning – describes a national plan identifying desirable priorities for economic and social development; can be distinguished from plans developed under command economies.

Indigenous groups – populations of people that originate from a certain area (e.g., the population of *Amerindian* heritage in Mexico).

Insider groups – *Pressure groups* with access to senior government officials, often recognized as the legitimate representatives of particular interests and often formally incorporated into the official consultative bodies which "regulate" them.

Influence – a form of power based on the ability to persuade others to share in the desired objective.

Influx control – a system of controls in South Africa that regulated African movement between cities and between towns and the countryside, enforcing residence in the homelands and restricting African choice of employment; administered through passed laws dating from the early nineteenth century; abolished in 1986.

Informal institutions – institutions which are an integral part of the political process but which are not established by a *Constitution*.

Informal sector (economy) – economic activities outside the formal economy that are unregulated by economic or legal institutions.

Initiative – the initiation of legislative action on a particular issue by way of a voters' petition.

Insider privatization – a term used about Russia to refer to the transformation of formerly state-owned enterprises into *Joint-stock companies* or private enterprises in which majority control of the enterprise is in the hands of employees and/or managers of that enterprise.

Institutionalism – known as the traditional approach; has the study of political institutions as its central focus.

Institutional group – groups which are closely associated with the government and act internally to influence public decisions.

Interest aggregation – the process of sorting and sifting the wide variety of political attitudes and opinions on any given political issue so that it is reduced to a set of more simple and clear-cut "packages" of opinion.

Interest articulation – the process of expressing political needs and demands to influence public policy.

Interest groups – sometimes known as "sectional groups," interest groups are a type of *Pressure group* that represents occupational interests; the primary types are business associations, professional associations and trade unions.

Interest party – a political party with a single interest or purpose (e.g., the Green Party).

International law – the body of rules governing the relationships of states with each other.

International Monetary Fund – an international organization created to prevent another collapse in the world monetary system through the stabilization of national currencies throughout the world.

International order – the combination of major actors, rules, mechanisms, and understandings to manage the stable co-existence and interdependence of states.

International regimes – the pattern of regular cooperation governed by implicit and explicit expectations between two or more states.

International relations – an area of political study concerned with the interaction of independent states.

Interpellation – a parliamentary question addressed to the government requiring a formal answer and often followed by discussion and sometimes a vote.

Intervention – in a court case, the presentation of a view on the law without representing one of the parties in the litigation.

Iron rice bowl – a feature of China's socialist economy during the Maoist era (1949–76) that provided guarantees of lifetime employment, income and basic cradle-to-grave benefits to most urban and rural workers; economic reforms beginning in the 1980s that aimed at improving efficiency and work motivation sought to smash the iron rice bowl and link employment and income more directly to individual effort.

Iron triangles – the close, three-sided working relationship developed between government departments and ministries, *Pressure groups* and politicians that make public policy in a given area.

Islamic Republic of Iran – formerly known as Persia; since the Iranian Revolution of 1979, the official name of the country has been the "Islamic Republic of Iran."

Item veto – the power of an American president or state governor to veto particular components of a bill rather than reject the entire legislation.

J

Jihad – literally meaning, "struggle;" although often used to mean an armed struggle against unbelievers, it can also mean the spiritual struggle for more self-improvement.

Joint-stock company – a business firm whose capital is divided into shares that can be held by individuals, groups of individuals or governmental units; in Russia, the formation of joint-stock companies have been the primary method for privatizing large state enterprises.

Judicial activism – involves the courts taking a broad and active view of their role as interpreters of a *Constitution* and reviewers of executive and legislative action.

Judicial Committee of the Privy Council – a British Court that functioned as Canada's final court of appeal until 1949.

Judicial review – the binding power of the courts to provide an authoritative interpretation of laws, including constitutional law, and to overturn executive or legislative actions they hold to be illegal or unconstitutional.

Judiciary – the branch of government with the power to resolve legal conflicts that arise between citizens, between citizens and governments or between levels of government and to interpret the law and its application to particular cases.

Junta – a Spanish word meaning a group of individuals forming a government, especially after a revolution or *Coup d'état*.

Jurisprudence – the philosophy and analysis of law.

Jurist's guardianship – Khomeini's concept that the Iranian clergy should rule because they are the divinely appointed guardians of both the law and the people.

Justice – the virtue of protecting individuals' possessions within the acknowledged rules of conduct.

K

Keynesianism – named after the British economist John Maynard Keynes, an approach to economic policy in which state economic policies are used to regulate the economy in an attempt to achieve stable economic growth; during a recession, state budget deficits (because of increased government spending) are used to expand demand in an effort to boost both consumption and investment and create employment; during periods of high growth when inflation threatens, cuts in government spending and a tightening of credit are used to reduce demand.

Knowledge gap – the gap between those with a good education and understanding of the world, which enables them to acquire knowledge and understanding at a faster rate, and those with less education and understanding.

Krai – one of the six territorial units in the Russian Federation that are defined by the constitution of 1993 to be among the eighty-nine members of the federation, with a status equal to that of the republics and *Oblasts*; like the *Oblasts* during the Soviet period, the krai were defined purely as territorial-administrative units within a particular republic of the Soviet Union; differed from an *Oblast* in that part of its border was on an external boundary of the USSR or it included a mixture of diverse ethnic territories (or both); generally, a krai is a geographically large unit but relatively sparsely populated.

Kremlin – the executive branch of power in Russia; power is vested in the presidency.

L

Labor productivity – the average production per laborer in a specific period (e.g., the average number of ballpoints produced per laborer in a ballpoint pen factory in one year).

Labor Theory of Value – the average number of labor hours required to produce a particular commodity is taken as an objective measure of the value of that commodity.

Laissez-faire – a term taken from the French, which means "to let be;" in other words, to allow to act freely; in political economy, the pattern in which the state management is limited to such matters as enforcing contracts and protecting property rights, with private market forces free to operate with only minimal state regulation.

Law – enforceable rules of conduct.

Legal positivism – a theory holding that law is the command of the sovereign.

Legislation – the body of laws that have been passed by the legislature; legislating is the act of initiating, debating and enacting such laws.

Legislative oversight – the role of the legislature that involves the scrutiny or supervision of other branches of government, especially the executive and the public *Bureaucracy*.

Legislature – a representative assembly responsible for making laws for society.

Legitimacy – the condition of being in accordance with the norms and values of the people (i.e., having *Consent of the governed*); the "legitimate use of power" refers to the use of power that is accepted because it is in accordance with the norms and values of the people it concerns; when governments lack legitimacy, it is difficult to stay in power (e.g., in Nigeria the government has struggled for legitimacy because it has failed to meet the basic needs of its citizens, and the people in Nigeria are reluctant to support such a government).

Legitimation – the process of making something morally acceptable, proper or right in the eyes of the general public according to accepted standards and values.

Liberal democracy – a system of government characterized by universal adult suffrage, political equality, majority rule, and constitutionalism.

Liberal feminism – the advocacy of equal rights between men and women.

Liberalism – a theory of international relations stressing the rule of law; favors a limited state role in society and economic activity; emphasizes a high degree of individual freedom over promoting social equality.

Limited government/state – a state restricted in its exercise of power by the constitution and the *Rule of law*.

List system – a form of proportional representation in which the elector votes not for individuals but for parties who provide lists of candidates running for office.

Lobby – a popular term for *Pressure groups* (based on the mistaken belief that pressure group representatives spend much time in the "lobbies" or ante-rooms of legislative chambers).

Lobbying – an activity of interest groups aimed at influencing governors and the legislature to render a favorable policy decision(s).

Logrolling – the act of vote-trading among legislators in the process of getting *Legislation* passed.

Lok Sabha – the lower house of parliament in India where all major legislation must pass before becoming law.

Low information rationality – where citizens do not have a great deal of factual political information but have a broad enough grasp of the main issues to make up their mind about them, or else they take their cues about the issues from sources they trust; also known as "gut rationality."

M

Macroeconomic policy – government policy intended to shape the overall economic system at the national level by concentrating on policy targets such as inflation and growth.

Mafia – a term borrowed from Italy and widely used in Russia to describe networks of organized criminal activity that pervade both economic and governmental securities in that country and activities such as the demanding of protection money, bribe-taking by government officials, contract killing and extortion.

Magna Carta – meaning "Great Charter," a document signed by King John in 1215, conceding that the king is subject to law; see *Rule of law*.

Maharajas – India's traditional rulers (monarchs) who retained their positions during the colonial period but were removed from power when the Indian republic was established.

Majles – the Iranian parliament; from the Arabic term for "assembly."

Majority government – a parliamentary government in which the party in power has over 50 percent of the seats in the legislature.

Maquiladora – factories that produce goods for export, often located along the U.S.-Mexican border.

Mandal Commission – a government-appointed commission in India headed by J. P. Mandal to consider seat *Reservations* and quotas to redress *Caste system* discrimination.

Market reform – a strategy of economic transformation begun by the Yeltsin government in Russia in the 1990s and the Deng Xiaoping government in China in the 1980s that involves reducing the role of the state in managing the economy and increasing the role of market forces; in Russia, market reform is part of the transition to post-communism and includes the extensive transfer of the ownership of economic assets from the state to private hands; in China, market reform has been carried out under the leadership of the Chinese Communist Party and involves less extensive privatization.

Market regulation – the regulation of the media market by public bodies, often to avoid cross-media ownership, foreign control of important channels of national communication or cases of market failure.

Marketization – the intentional re-creation of the market forces of supply and demand; the conversion of a national economy from a planned economy (see *Central Planning* and *Planning*) to a market economy.

Martial law – a period during which the normal procedures of government are suspended, and the executive branch enforces the law with military power.

Marxism-Leninism – the theoretical foundation of communism based on the ideas of the German philosopher Karl Marx (1818–1883) and the leader of the Russian Revolution, V. I. Lenin (1870–1924); Marxism is a theory of historical development that emphasizes the struggle between the exploiting and the exploited classes, particularly the struggle between the *Bourgeoisie* (capitalists) and the *Proletariat* (the industrial working class);

Leninism emphasizes the strategy and organization to be used by the communist party to overthrow capitalism and seize power as a first step on the road to communism; socialism refers to an early stage in the development of communism; socialist regimes can be organized democratically, in that those who control the state may be chosen according to democratic procedures; they may also be governed in an undemocratic manner when a single party, not chosen in free competitive elections, controls the state and society.

Maslahat – Arabic term for "expediency," "prudence" or "advisability;" now used in Iran to refer to what is best for the Islamic Republic.

Mass society – a society without a plurality of organized social groups and interests, whose mass of isolated and uprooted individuals are not integrated into the community and who are therefore vulnerable to the appeals of extremist and anti-democratic elites.

Materialism – the theory that ideas are rooted in the material or physical conditions of life, as opposed to spiritual ideals and values which are constructs of the mind which can be independent of material and physical conditions; compare with *Idealism*.

Means testing – in contrast to public benefits that are universally available, it involves investigating a person's income and means of support to ensure that they cannot afford to pay for the service themselves; often resented by welfare applicants and is politically controversial.

Media malaise – the attitudes of political cynicism, despair, apathy, distrust, and disillusionment (among others) that some social scientists claim are caused or exacerbated by the mass media, especially TV.

Median voter – the median is the middle number in any distribution of numbers; the median voter is in the middle of the distribution with equal numbers of voters to the left and right; the support of the median voter is usually necessary to win an election.

Mediation – an attempt by a third party to reach an agreement between disputing parties by suggesting terms of settlement; see *Conciliation*.

Merit recruitment – a system of hiring public servants by qualifications rather than on party preference or other considerations.

Meso-government – a middle level or tier of government between central and local authorities; often known as the state, regional, provincial or county government.

Mestizo – in Mexico, a person of mixed white, indigenous (Amerindian) and sometimes African descent.

Microcosm – the idea that a governing body should be a miniature replica of the society it represents.

Migrant labor – workers in *Apartheid* South Africa who were denied permanent residence rights in towns under the system of *Influx control* and who would be employed on annual contracts that denied them job security; more generally, refers to laborers who move to another location to take a job, often a low-paying, temporary one.

Middle-level theory – seeks to explain phenomena in a limited range of cases, in particular, a specific set of countries with particular characteristics (such as parliamentary regimes) or a particular type of political institution (such as political parties) or activity (such as public protests).

Military-industrial complex – the close and powerful alliance of government, business and military interests that is said by some to run capitalist societies.

Minimum winning coalition (MWC) – the smallest number of parties necessary for a majority of votes in parliament.

Ministerial responsibility – the principle that *Cabinet* ministers are individually responsible to the House of Commons for everything that happens in their department.

Ministry – the entire group of Members of Parliament appointed by the Prime Minister to specific ministerial responsibilities.

Minority government – a parliamentary government in which the government party has less than 50 percent of the seats in the legislature.

Mixed economy – an economy that is neither wholly privately owned (a capitalist market economy), nor wholly publicly owned (a communist command economy), but a mixture of both.

Mixed-member-proportional (MPP) – an electoral system in which voters cast two ballots, one for a local candidate running in a territorial constituency (first-past-the-post) and the other for a list of candidates put forward by a political party (list system).

Modernization – the gradual replacement of traditional authority with legal authority.

Monarchy – a form of government in which a single person, whose authority is usually hereditary, rules under the law.

Monetarism – an approach to economic policy that assumes a natural rate of unemployment determined by the labor market and rejects the instrument of government spending to run budgetary deficits for stimulating the economy and creating jobs.

Monism – exclusive emphasis on a single principle or interest.

Mosque – Muslim place of worship; equivalent to a church, temple or synagogue.

Most different case analysis – the logic of most different case analysis is that, by comparing cases that differ widely, one seeks to isolate a factor or factors (termed the *Independent variable* or variables) that both cases share, despite their differences in other respects, that might explain their outcomes (the *Dependent variable*).

Motlanthe – President of South Africa and Deputy President of the ruling African National Congress (ANC); appointed president of South Africa by the South African National Assembly on September 25, 2008 after the resignation of Thabo Mbeki.

Movement party – a type of political party which emerges from a political movement, such as a national liberation movement.

Multi-member districts – districts that elect more than one member to a legislative body. Compare with *Single-member districts*.

Multinational state – three or more nations co-existing under one sovereign government.

Multi-party systems – where several or many main parties compete, often with the result that no single party has an overall majority.

Multipolar – a system of actions involving several states acting in concert.

N

Nation – a group of people with similar cultural characteristics that creates a psychological bond and a political community; many Nigerians do not identify themselves as members of the *Nation-state* but rather as members of a nation; compare with *Nation-state*.

Nation-state – a state based on the acceptance of a common culture, a common history and common national goals, irrespective of whatever political, social and economic differences may exist between the members of the nation-state; see *Country* and *Nation*.

Nationalization – the policy by which the state assumes ownership and operation of private companies.

National interest – interests specific to a nation-state, especially including survival and maintenance of power.

Nationalism – the feeling of loyalty and attachment to one's *Nation* or *Nation-state* and strong support for its interests.

Natural authority – *Authority* based on spontaneous deference to an individual's knowledge or social position.

Natural law – rules of conduct binding on humankind by human rationality alone.

Neoconservatism – an ideological term characterizing parties or politicians who not only advocate an end to government expansion but also believe in reducing government's role via downsizing, privatization, and deregulation.

Neo-Institutionalism – a new phrase that refers to the study of institutions and their functioning as most vital for the study of politics; it differs from traditional institutionalism as it includes many other crucial determinants in its approach.

Neoliberalism – a term used to describe government policies that aim to promote private enterprise by reducing government economic regulation, tax rates, and social spending.

New international economic order – a revision of the international economic system that favors Third World countries.

New Public Management (NPM) – New Public Management (NPM) refers to the reforms of the public sector in the U.K. under Thatcher in the 1980s and 1990s, based mainly on what was thought to be the superior efficacy of private sector practices and consisting mainly of privatization, deregulation, business management techniques and *Marketization*; known also as "reinventing government," it is said to have had the effect of "hollowing out" the state.

Newly industrializing countries (NICs) – a term used to describe a group of countries that achieved rapid economic development beginning in the 1960s, largely stimulated by robust international trade (particularly exports) and guided by government policies. The core NICs are usually considered to be Taiwan, South Korea, Hong Kong, and Singapore, but other countries, including Argentina, Brazil, Malaysia, Mexico and Thailand, are often included in this category.

New Social Movements – loosely knit organizations ("networks of networks") that try to influence government policy on broad issues, including the environment, nuclear energy and nuclear weapons, economic development, peace, women's rights, and minorities.

Nomenklatura – this is a system of personnel selection used in the Soviet Union and China under which the Communist Party maintained control over the appointment of important officials in all spheres of social, economic and political life.

Nonaligned bloc – those countries that refused to ally themselves with either the United States or the USSR during the Cold War years.

Non-decision – the decision not to deal with an issue, perhaps not even to consider it.

Nonassociational (latent) group – a group which lacks formal organization but has the potential for mobilizing politically.

Non-governmental organization (NGO) – a non-governmental organization (NGO) is a non-profit, non-violent private organization that is independent of government and seeks to influence or control government policy without actually seeking government office.

Normative – political analysis based on values, commitments, and ideas.

Normative political theories – theories about how the world should be or ought to be; based upon philosophical arguments and ultimately on subjective values and judgments; also known as a prescriptive theory, political theory or political philosophy.

Normative statements – a statement that is based upon faith, or contain a value judgment or an evaluation; sometimes referred to as prescriptive, or evaluative statements; neither scientific nor unscientific, but non-scientific; see *Empirical statements*.

North American Free Trade Agreement (NAFTA) – a treaty among the United States, Mexico, and Canada implemented on January 1, 1994, that largely eliminated trade barriers among the three nations and established procedures to resolve trade disputes;

serves as a model for an eventual Free Trade Area of the Americas zone that could include most Western Hemisphere nations.

Notwithstanding clause – Section 33 of the Canadian Charter of Rights and Freedoms, which allows federal or provincial legislatures to pass laws that may violate certain sections of the Charter.

O

Oblast – one of forty-nine territorial units in the Russian Federation defined by the constitution of 1993 to be among the eighty-nine members of the federation, with a status equal to that of the republics and *Krai*; generally lacks a non-Russian national/ethnic basis; during the Soviet period, the oblasts were defined purely as territorial-administrative units located within a particular *Republic* of the Soviet Union; see *Autonomous okrug*.

Official opposition – in a parliamentary system, the largest of the opposition parties, given a special role to play in the legislative process.

Oligarchs – a small group of powerful and wealthy individuals who gained ownership and control of important sectors of Russia's economy in the context of the *Privatization* of state assets in the 1990s.

Oligarchy – a form of government in which a minority rules outside the law.

Ombudsman – a state official appointed to receive complaints and investigate claims about maladministration (improper or unjust action) and to report their findings, usually to the legislature.

One-party-dominant system – a party system in which there are political alternatives but a single political party dominates the political process as a result of the overwhelming support of the electorate.

One-party systems – government systems in which a single party forms the government.

Order-in-council – a decision by the *Cabinet* which carries legal force.

Organizational Parallelism – a political structure through which the communist party also maintains direct control over the government and the bureaucracy.

OPEC – an acronym for the "Organization of Petroleum Exporting Countries;" founded in 1960 by Iran, Venezuela and Saudi Arabia, it now includes most oil-exporting countries with the notable exceptions of Mexico and former members of the Soviet Union; tries to regulate prices by regulating production.

Opposition – those members of Parliament who are not part of the government of the day.

Other backward classes – the middle or intermediary *Castes* in India that have been accorded "reserved" slots in public education and employment since the early 1990s; see *Reservations*.

Outcomes – the impacts or effects of *Outputs*.

Outputs – the policy decisions as they are implemented.

Outsider groups – groups with no access to top government officials.

Oversized (surplus majority) coalitions – a coalition that is larger than a *Minimum winning coalition* (MWC).

P

Panchayats – in India, elected bodies at the village, district and state levels that have development and administrative responsibilities.

Paradigmatic – classification based on a paradigm (a pattern, example or model).

Para-statals – state-owned, or at least state-controlled, corporations created to undertake a broad range of activities, from control and marketing of agricultural production to provision of banking services, operating airlines and other transportation facilities and public utilities.

Parity law – a French law passed in 2000 that directs political parties to nominate an equal number of men and women for most elections.

Parliamentary democracy – a system of government in which the chief executive is answerable to the legislature and may be dismissed by it; stands in contrast to a presidential system, in which the chief executive is elected in a national ballot and is independent of the legislative branch.

Parliamentary sovereignty – a constitutional principle of government (principally in Britain) by which the legislature reserves the power to make or overturn any law without recourse by the executive, the judiciary or the monarchy; only Parliament can nullify or overturn legislation approved by Parliament; Parliament can force the *Cabinet* or the government to resign by a *Vote of no confidence*.

Party Systems – the structure and arrangement of political parties in a political system; the floating party system in Russia is usually visible only in the months before elections; the party system in Iran is mostly visible only by observing the political statements of individuals; the party system in Britain involves three parties; the party system in France involves four or five.

Parliamentary systems – parliamentary systems are characterized by a directly elected legislative body, the fusion of executive and legislative institutions, a collective and collegial executive who emerges out of the legislature and is responsible to it and a separation of *Head of state* and *Head of government*.

Participatory democracy – that form of democracy in which citizens actively participate in government and political processes.

Partisan de-alignment – a process of decline in the strength of attachment and sense of belonging to the political parties.

Partisan re-alignment – a process in which social and economic groups show signs of a long-term change in their old party identifications in favor of new ones.

Party discipline – the convention that all members of parliament within any party vote together, as predetermined in the party caucus and enforced by the party leader (in the U.K., the *Party whip*).

Party families – groups of parties in different countries that have similar ideologies and party programs.

Party identification (ID) – the stable and deep-rooted feeling of attachment to and support for a political party.

Party state – a political system in which power flows directly from the ruling political party (usually the communist party) to the state, bypassing government structures.

Party whip – an official within a *Political party* who "enforces" party policies to party members.

Pasdaran – Persian term for guards, used to refer to the army of *Revolutionary Guards* formed during Iran's Islamic Revolution.

Pass laws – laws in *Apartheid* South Africa that required Africans to carry identity books in which were stamped the permits they were required to have to travel between the countryside and the cities; the identity books also included the details of their employment; failure to carry such books was an offense, and during the 1960s, 300,000 "pass offenders" were imprisoned annually.

Patriarchy – the domination of society by men.

Patrimonial state – a system of governance in which a single ruler treats the state as personal property (patrimony); appointments to public office are made on the basis of unswerving loyalty to the ruler; in turn, state officials exercise wide authority in other domains, such as the economy, often for their benefit and that of the ruler, to the detriment of the general population.

Patronage system – a political system in which government officials appoint loyal followers to positions rather than choosing people based on their qualifications; may also involve the exchange of favors between an officeholder and a particular group, often trading something the group wants for their political support.

Peace-building – a process for working towards objectives associated with peaceful coexistence of combatants.

Peacekeeping force – the interposition of lightly armed military forces between combatants who have agreed to stop fighting.

Peak associations – in Australia, a term for an association of industries with common interests; also known as a "peak body;" see *Umbrella organizations*.

People – a group of persons living together on the territory of a state whose common consciousness and identity usually form them into a collective entity.

People of the Book – the Muslim term for recognized religious minorities, such as Christians, Jews, and Zoroastrians.

Perestroika – the policy of restructuring embarked on by Gorbachev when he became head of the Communist Party of the Soviet Union in 1985; initially, the policy

25

emphasized decentralization of economic decision making, increased enterprise *Autonomy*, expanded public discussion of policy issues and a reduction in the international isolation of the Soviet economy; over time, restructuring took on a more political tone, including a commitment to *Glasnost* and *Demokratizatsiia*.

Performance – actual activities and results; how well the government is doing or how successful it is in offering citizens what they prefer.

Permanent secretary – the British equivalent of a Canadian deputy minister.

Personal freedom – the absence of coercion in various aspects of life.

Personal party – a type of political party founded and dominated by a single, overwhelmingly influential political leader.

Philosopher–king – Plato's view of the ideal individual ruler who rules in the common interest and is directed by wisdom and virtue rather than the constraint of law.

Planning – production and allocation of resources determined by a central authority.

Plebiscite – a nonbinding vote called by a government in which the voters express an opinion for or against a proposal; see *Referendum*.

Pluralism – a situation where power is dispersed among many different groups and organizations that openly compete with one another in different political arenas.

Plurality – a voting decision based on assigning victory to the largest number of votes, not necessarily a majority.

Pluralist democracy – the theory of modern democracy arguing that political decisions are the outcome of the conflict, competition, and compromises between many different groups and organizations representing many different interests.

Politburo – the "political bureau;" the main policymaking body of a communist party.

Political economy – the study of the interaction between the state and the economy (i.e., how the state and political processes affect the organization of production and exchange (the economy) and how the organization of the economy affects political processes).

Police – the branch of government employed to maintain civil order and to investigate breaches of the law.

Policy communities – small, stable and consensual groupings of government officials and *Pressure group* representatives that form around particular issue areas; compare with *Policy networks*.

Policy networks – compared with *Policy communities*, policy networks are larger, looser and more conflicting networks that gather around a particular policy area.

Polis – Greek city-state.

Political alienation – a feeling of detachment, estrangement or critical distance from politics, often because the alienated feel there is something wrong with the political system.

Political Attitudes – the actual relationship between political and economic institutions in a particular country as well as the politics and outcomes they create; often defined as liberalism, social democracy, communism or mercantilism.

Political behavior – a term used to refer to all political activities of citizens as well as the attitudes and orientations relevant to these activities.

Political cleavage – a political division caused by the overlap of social differences (religion, race, language, class, culture, history) with ideological differences; such *Cleavages* may be especially important if they coincide with territorial divisions.

Political consultant – a professional advisor who puts their political expertise to work in the private and public sectors.

Political culture – signifies the total of the set of beliefs, orientations, and attitudes of the citizens which influence political behavior.

Political Economy – the study of the interaction of the political processes and the economy of a state.

Political elite – the relatively small number of people at the top of a political system who exercise disproportionate influence or power over political decisions; if it exercises enough power in the system, it is a *Ruling elite*.

Political Ideology – a system of beliefs concerning the proper roles and responsibilities of people and their government; the beliefs need not to be specific to any individual state and are often universal in their philosophical underpinnings; in practice, political ideologies get altered to fit the socioeconomic realities of different nations.

Post-industrialism – the shift during the last half-century from an economy based primarily on industry and manufacturing to one in which the majority of people are employed in the service sector, which produces the lion's share of profits.

Political marginality – the condition of being on the fringes of politics and, therefore, of having little influence.

Political orientation – a predisposition or propensity to view political issues in a certain way.

Political participation – citizens actively involved in their government; making views known and holding them accountable; *Authoritarian* regimes might have political participation but their actions are not free (e.g., in China people can vote but only for the allowed parties).

Political party – an organized group of politically like-minded people that make nominations and contest elections in the hope of influencing the personnel and policy of the government.

Political patronage – government appointments made as a payoff for loyal partisan activity.

Political philosophy – an area of political study based on historical, reflective and conceptual methods.

Political police – forces reporting directly to a political leader who uses them for political purposes rather than law enforcement.

Political process – the interaction of organized political structures in making and administering public decisions for society.

Political socialization – the process of how one's political beliefs and political culture are arrived at (family, education, media, experiences, church, employment, etc.) and transmitted from generation to generation; childhood socialization is most important, but socialization continues in adulthood as well (e.g., Islam is a major factor in the political socialization of the people of Iran).

Political theorists – scholars engaged in the study and theorization of political theory, one of the sub-disciplines of Political Science.

Politics – a process of conflict resolution in which support is mobilized and maintained for collective action.

Polity – a form of government characterized by *Popular sovereignty* but exercised within a constitutional framework to prevent the oppression of the minority by the majority rule.

Polyarchy – Robert Dahl's term for pluralist forms of liberal democracy, in which there is competition between and, at times, alliances between many different interests.

Portfolio – in the U.K., the administrative responsibility carried by a minister, usually some combination of departments and other agencies.

Popular sovereignty – supreme *Authority* residing in the consent of the people.

Post-materialism – the shift in values since the late 1940s from an emphasis on public order and material prosperity to an emphasis on self-fulfillment.

Post-modernism – denotes a departure from traditional lines of analysis, where the given set of universal assumptions are rejected and mocked, and subjective interpretations become the reference point.

Power sharing – constitutional arrangements to ensure that the major political parties share executive *Authority*; these can include mandatory coalitions and allocation of some senior official positions between parties.

Power – the ability to get other individuals to do as one wants them to do.

Power vertical – a term used by Russian president Vladimir Putin to describe a unified and hierarchical structure of executive power ranging from the federal level to the local level, which can be reinforced by various mechanisms such as appointments by higher-level officials and oversight of activities by higher organs over lower ones.

Pragmatic party – a type of political party concerned primarily with winning elections.

Precedent – a previous judicial case used as an example for deciding the case at hand.

Prefects – French administrators appointed by the Minister of the Interior to coordinate state agencies and programs within the one hundred French departments or localities; prefects had enormous power until decentralization reforms in the 1980s transferred some of their responsibilities to elected local governments.

Preferential (alternative) ballot – an electoral system in which voters rank the candidates.

Prerogative – the residual powers of the Crown that can be exercised at its discretion.

Presidential systems – in presidential systems a directly elected president is the executive, with a limited term of office and a general responsibility for the affairs of state, who shares governance with a separate and independently elected legislature.

Pressure groups – private and voluntary organizations that try to influence or control particular government policies but do not want to become the government or control all government policies.

Prevention – attempt to hinder or deter delinquent behavior.

Prime Minister's Office – support staff appointed by the Prime Minister to carry out political functions.

Priming – the theory that the mass media can "prime" the populace to focus on certain things and in certain ways by highlighting some issues rather than others (e.g., focusing on foreign rather than domestic policy, which would favor parties that are thought to be better at foreign policy).

Primus inter pares – Latin phrase meaning "first among equals."

Private law – laws controlling relations between individuals.

Private member's bill – public bills introduced in the U.K. Parliament by members who are not in the *Cabinet*.

Privatization – the sale of state-owned enterprises to private companies or investors; those who support the policy claim that private ownership is superior to government ownership because for-profit entities promote greater efficiency; a common central component of *Structural Adjustment* programs to curtail the losses associated with running these enterprises and generate state revenue when they are sold.

Privatization voucher – a certificate worth 10,000 rubles issued by the government to each Russian citizen in 1992 to be used to purchase shares in state enterprises undergoing the process of *Privatization*; vouchers could also be sold for cash or disposed of through newly-created investment funds.

Privy Council – a ceremonial body, made up of all present and former *Cabinet* ministers.

Privy Council Office – a governmental department that supports the prime minister, the *Cabinet* and cabinet committees in devising government policy.

Proclamation – the announcement of the official date a new law will take effect.

Productivity – the efficacy with which goods are made; see *Labor productivity*.

Progressive tax – a tax rate which increases as the amount of one's income increases.

Proletariat – the "working class;" a Marxist term referring to those who sell their labor to the *Bourgeoisie*.

Property franchise (suffrage) – the requirement that citizens own a stipulated amount of property to receive the right to vote.

Proportionality/ Disproportionality – a measure of the ratio of seats to votes; the more proportional the system, the closer the ratio of seats to votes; in the most proportional voting system, a party getting 43 percent of the votes should get 43 percent of the seats, or close to this figure, since seats are not divisible.

Proportional representation (PR) – a system of political representation in which seats are allocated to parties within multimember constituencies, roughly in proportion to the votes each party receives; usually encourages the election to parliament of more political parties than *Single member-district* winner-take-all systems, such as in the U.S.

Protest vote – where citizens vote for a *Political party* not because they support it but because they oppose other parties and their candidates.

Provincial courts – Canadian courts created by provincial statute, staffed by judges appointed by the province to deal with matters such as small claims and minor criminal offences.

Provision of goods and services – a way to provide social security for citizens by offering them not money but specific facilities such as housing or job training; cash transfers are an alternative to goods and services.

Public authority – *Authority* based on institutional office-holding.

Public debt – the accumulated sum owed by the government to its creditors.

Public law – laws controlling the relations between the state and individuals in society.

Purchasing power parity (PPP) – a method of calculating the value of a country's money based on the actual cost of buying certain goods and services in that country rather than how many U.S. dollars they are worth; widely considered to be a more accurate indicator for comparing standards of living, particularly in countries at very different levels of economic development.

(Public) policy – some general set of ideas or plans that has been officially agreed on and which is used as a basis for making decisions; the long series of rationales, activities, decisions and actions carried out by officials of government in their attempts to solve problems that are thought to lie in the public or collective arena.

Public-private partnerships (PPPs) – formal cooperation between government and private groups to obtain specific goals.

Public sector – that part of social, economic and political life that is not private but controlled or to some degree regulated by the state or its agencies.

Public service model – the system of organizing radio and TV in which broadcasting licenses are granted to public bodies, usually supported by public funds, for use in the public interest rather than for profit.

Pyramid debt – a situation when a government or organization takes on debt obligations at progressively higher rates of interest to pay off its existing debt; in some cases, a structure of pyramid debt can result in a default on the entire debt obligation if the interest owed becomes unmanageable.

Q

Qualified majority – the raising of the simple majority requirement of "50 percent plus one" to a higher level, to protect the rights of the minority.

QUANGOs – an acronym for "quasi-nongovernmental organizations," the term used in Britain for unelected bodies that are outside traditional governmental departments or local authorities; have considerable influence over public policy in areas such as education, healthcare, and housing.

Qur'an – the Muslim holy book.

R

Race – a group of individuals differentiated through distinct physical characteristics and common ancestry.

Radical feminism – a belief that men and women constitute "sexual classes" and that women's traditional subordinate status is the result of a system which is controlled by men.

Rajya Sabha – India's upper house of parliament; considerably less significant politically than the *Lok Sabha*.

Readings – first, second and third readings mark the introduction of and subsequent debate on proposed *Bills* in the legislative chambers.

Realism – in international relations, refers to the view of politics that emphasizes the role of self-interest as a determinant of state policies and hence the importance of power in these relations. In realist theory states (and other actors such as business organizations) are presumed to act more or less rationally to promote their interests.

Recall – the ability of voters in a constituency to remove their elected representative from office using a petition.

Recruitment of Elites – the process by which newcomers become members of the political elite; in China, the recruitment of elites occurs through *Guanxi*.

Red Guard – a mass movement of civilians, mostly students and other young people in the People's Republic of China, who were mobilized by Mao Zedong between 1966 and 1968 during the Cultural Revolution.

Red Tory – a conservative with collectivist leanings.

Redistribution – the process of reallocating wealth and income to achieve an economic or social objective.

Referendum – the submission of a public matter to direct popular vote; see *Plebiscite*.

Reform liberalism – a liberal ideology which advocates a larger role for the state in providing equality of opportunity.

Regressive tax – a tax that weights more heavily on low incomes.

Regulations – the rules that explain the implementation of laws; when Congress passes a law, it sets broad principles for implementation, but how the law is actually implemented in practice is determined by regulations written by executive branch agencies; the regulation-writing process allows interested parties to influence the eventual enforcement of the law, whether it will be strict or less so.

Regulatory agency – government agencies established to administer regulatory laws in certain fields (e.g., the Canadian Human Rights Commission).

Regulative laws – laws that control individual and organizational behavior.

Reinforcement theory – also known as the "minimal effects theory;" the theory that the mass media can only reflect and reinforce public opinion, not create or mold it.

Reinforcing cleavages – *Cleavages* that lay one on top of the other, intensifying them; compare with *Cross-cutting cleavages*.

Rentier state – a country that obtains much of its revenue from the export of oil or other natural resources.

Report stage – the stage in the legislative process after the second reading when the House debates the committee's report on a proposed *Bill*.

Representative democracy – a system of government based on the election of decision-makers by the people.

Republic – in contemporary usage, a political regime in which leaders are not chosen on the basis of their inherited background (as in a monarchy); may, but need not be, democratic; for Russia, a republic is one of twenty-one territorial units in the Russian Federation that are defined by the constitution of 1993 to be among the eighty-nine members of the federation and named after the indigenous non-Russian population group that inhabits the republic; generally a republic was originally formed in recognition of the presence of a non-Russian national or ethnic group residing in the territory; in the Soviet period, most of these units were called "autonomous republics."

Republicanism – emphasizes the *Separation of powers* within a state and representation of the public through elected officials.

Representative democracy – a form of democracy in which citizens elect leaders who govern in their name.

Reservations – jobs or admissions to colleges reserved by the government of India for specific social groups, particularly underprivileged groups.

Residual powers – those powers in a federal system of government not explicitly allocated in a *Constitution*.

Responsible government – a form of government in which the political executive must retain the confidence of a majority of the elected legislature or assembly, and it must resign or call an election if and when it is defeated on a *Vote of no confidence*.

Revolution – the process by which an established political regime is replaced (usually by force and with broad popular participation) and a new regime established that introduces radical changes throughout society; different from *Coups d'état* in that there is widespread popular participation in revolutions, whereas coups d'état are led by small groups of elites.

Revolutionary Guard – the Iranian Revolutionary Guard (IRG) is a combined arms force with its ground forces, navy, air force, intelligence and special forces; also controls Basij force, which has a potential strength of eleven million, although Basij is a volunteer-based force and consists of 90,000 regular soldiers and 300,000 reservists; the IRG is officially recognized as a component of the Iranian military under Article 150 of the Iranian Constitution.

Royal assent – the approval of a *Bill* by the Crown.

Rule of law – a political system that all individuals are subject to regardless of their position or power; the law has *Sovereignty*; in a country that has an *Authoritarian* system, only those who are not in positions of power are subject to the rule of law; those in power may use the law to keep themselves in power (e.g., China has not established the rule of law because the CCP may not be subject to the law).

Ruling elite – a political elite that is so powerful that it can make all the important decisions in government.

Runoff system – an electoral system in which additional rounds of balloting are held (with trailing candidates dropped) until a candidate receives a majority of the votes cast.

S

Salient – something that is important, significant or prominent in people's minds.

Sanctions – international embargoes on economic and cultural contracts with a particular country; applied selectively to South Africa by various governments and the United Nations from 1948 until 1994.

Scheduled castes – the lowest *Caste* groups in India; also known as the *Untouchables*; see *Caste system*.

Scientific socialism – the term Marx and Engels used to stress that their ideology was based on analysis of class conflict.

Second International – the reunion of Socialist and Labor parties in Europe, with the exclusion of anarchists, established in 1889.

Secularism – a doctrine that mandates maintaining a separation between church and state; requires that the state be neutral toward religious faiths and that *Public policy* not be dictated by the teaching of any particular religion; a cause of conflict in regimes committed to secularism often involves where to draw the boundary between strongly held religious beliefs and the public sphere.

Security dilemma – the spiral of preparations and tensions which emerge when the defensive actions of one state lead to countermeasures being taken by another state.

Self-government – the right of members of a group to control their collective affairs.

Semi-presidential system – a government that consists of a directly elected president who is accountable to the electorate and a prime minister who is appointed by the president from the elected legislature and accountable to it; the president and prime minister share executive power.

Separation of powers – the doctrine that political power should be divided among several bodies or officers of the state, often between bodies or officers performing different government functions, as a precaution against too much concentration of power.

Sepoy Rebellion – an armed uprising by Indian princes against the expansion of British colonialism in India in 1857; following the failure of this rebellion (also known as the Indian Mutiny of 1857), Britain assumed full control of India, which it ruled until 1947.

Settler state – colonial or former colonial administrations controlled by the descendants of immigrants who settled in the territory; settler states often feature large-scale usurpation of land from the indigenous inhabitants as well as elaborately-organized racial discrimination.

Sexenio – the six-year administration of Mexican presidents.

Shadow cabinet – in the U.K., the cohesive group of specialized critics in the official *Opposition* party.

Shari'a – Islamic law derived mostly from the *Qur'an* and the examples set by the Prophet Muhammad.

Shi'i/Shi'ism – a branch of Islam; literally means "the followers or partisans of Ali;" the other branch is known as Sunni or the followers of tradition.

Single-member districts – districts that each have one representative in parliament.

Single-member plurality district – an electoral system in which candidates run for a single seat from a specific geographic district; the winner is the person who receives the most votes, whether or not that is a majority; these systems, unlike systems of proportional representation, increase the likelihood that two national coalition parties will form.

Single-member-plurality system (SMP) – an electoral system in which the candidate with the most votes wins, even though that win may not represent 51% of the votes.

Single-party system – a party system in which there exists only one party, and no political alternatives are legally tolerated.

Single transferable vote (STV) – a form of proportional representation in which electors vote for individuals rather than party lists, but they do so by ranking the candidates in their order of choice.

Shock therapy – a variant of *Market reform* that involves the state simultaneously imposing a wide range of radical economic changes, with the purpose of "shocking" the economy into a new mode of operation; can be contrasted with a more gradual approach to market reform.

Sikhs – a minority religious community in India whose members practice Sikhism; Sikhs constitute less than 2 percent of the Indian population and 76 percent of the state of Punjab.

Siloviki – derived from the Russian word *sil*, meaning "force"; Russian politicians and government officials drawn from security and intelligence agencies (such as the Soviet KGB or its contemporary counterpart, the FSB), special forces or the military, many of whom were recruited to important political posts under Vladimir Putin.

Social capital – the features of social organizations, such as trust, social norms and social networks, that improve social and governmental efficiency by encouraging cooperation and collective action.

Social class – a group whose members share common economic status determined largely by occupation, income and wealth; members of the same social class often share similar political attitudes.

Social democrats – socialists emphasizing popular consent, peaceful change, political pluralism, and constitutional government.

Social expenditures – defined by the Organization for the Economic Co-operation and Development (OECD) to be the provision by public (and private) institutions of benefits to households and individuals to provide support during circumstances which adversely affect their welfare.

Social stratification – the hierarchical layering of society into socially unequal groups; includes peasants and landowners, castes, classes, and status groups.

Social Welfare – a set of governmental policies and programs designed to help and improve the lives of a nation's citizens (e.g., material assistance to the needy, healthcare to some or all citizens, safety provisions, labor regulations, etc.); the degree of social welfare that a nation adopts is in part a result of political ideology.

Socialism – a leftist political ideology that emphasizes the principle of equality and usually prescribes a large role for government to intervene in society and the economy via taxation, regulation, redistribution and public ownership; a socialist regime, unlike a *Communist party-state*, may allow the private sector to play an important role in the economy and be committed to political pluralism.

Socialist democracy – the term used by the Chinese Communist Party to describe the political system of the People's Republic of China (also called the "people's democratic dictatorship"; the official view is that this type of system, under the leadership of the Communist Party, provides democracy for the overwhelming majority of people and suppresses (or exercises dictatorship over) only the enemies of the people; contrasted with bourgeois (or capitalist) democracy, which puts power in the hands of the rich and oppresses the poor.

Social justice – the partial equalization of wealth and income to reach a more desirable outcome.

Social movements – large-scale grass-roots action that demands reforms of existing social practices and government policies; tend to be less formally organized than interest groups (e.g., the civil rights movement in the United States that began in the 1960s).

Social security – a national system of contributory and noncontributory benefits to assist the elderly, sick, disabled, unemployed and others similarly in need of assistance; the specific coverage of social security, a key component of the *Welfare state*, varies by country.

Society – a self-sufficient group of individuals living together under common rules of conduct.

Sociotropic voting – deciding which party to vote for by general social or economic circumstances; the opposite is "pocket-book voting," based on the private interests of the voter.

Sources of authority – various methods that governments use to acquire, gain and maintain authority; governments of all types use various sources of authority to maintain their power.

Sovereignty – a state is sovereign when it holds the highest power and, in principle, can act with complete freedom and independence; internal sovereignty means that, on its territory, the state can act as it wishes and is independent of other institutions; external sovereignty refers to the fact that the state is seen as autonomous by other states.

Special (ad hoc) committee – legislative committees appointed for special, temporary purposes, such as to investigate a problem before the government prepares legislation on the subject.

Special relationship – refers to relations between the United States and Britain (the United Kingdom) and meant to convey not only the largely positive, mutually beneficial nature of the relationship but also the common heritage and shared values of the two countries.

Spectrum scarcity – the shortage of terrestrial broadcasting frequencies for radio and TV, which meant that there could only be a limited number of channels.

Spin-doctors – public relations specialists employed to put the best possible light on the news about their clients; often used in political life to imply attempts to manipulate the news.

Spoils system – the assumption that, after successfully winning an election, the political executive is entitled to appoint large numbers of supporters to the *Bureaucracy* (often regardless of their qualifications).

Spontaneous order – the pattern of mutual coordination that emerges as individuals pursue their interests in society.

Standing committee – legislative committees that are set up permanently and parallel or oversee government functions.

Stare decisis – the legal principle that precedents are binding on similar subsequent cases; the basis of the common law system.

State – a unified, geographically defined political entity; comprises a country's most powerful political institutions, including the executive, legislative and judicial branches of government as well as the police and armed forces, which claim the right to make the laws and enforce them through the use of coercion, if necessary; see *Civil society*.

Stateless society – a society without a sovereign government.

State-centric – an approach to international relations positing the sovereign state as the focus for understanding the nature and workings of the international system.

State capitalism – a strategy of economic development in which the state guides industrial, agricultural and financial policy and aims to create the political conditions for its success; unlike socialism or communism, the state does not own major parts of the economy; rather the state works in partnership with owners of private property to promote national economic growth.

State formation – the historical development of a state, often marked by major stages, key events or turning points (critical junctures) that influence the contemporary character of the state.

Statism – the heavy intervention of the state in societal affairs, especially in the economic system.

State-led economic development – the process of promoting economic development using governmental machinery.

Status – a form of social stratification determined by social prestige rather than economic factors or occupation; it is sometimes said that class is determined by how people make their money, status by how they spend it; sometimes class and status are combined into the single measure of social and economic status.

Statute – a specific piece of legislation.

Street-level bureaucrats – the bureaucrats who regularly come into contact with and have to deal with the public.

Structural Adjustment – a program to reform the economic structure of a country often involving privatization, trade liberalization and limits on the printing of currency; a country which is in debt is often required to follow a structural adjustment program if it wants to receive assistance from the World Bank or the IMF (e.g., the structural adjustment program imposed on Russia by the IMF required the privatization of state institutions and a limitation on the printing of rubles by the Russian government).

Structuralism – a theory of international relations stressing the impact of world economic structures on the political, social, cultural and economic life of countries.

Subjective or internal competence/efficacy – the extent to which ordinary citizens feel that they can make their views and actions count in the political system; the opposites of the term are "powerlessness," "inefficacy" or "low competence."

Sub-central/sub-national government – all levels of government below national/central government; covers everything below central government from community and neighborhood government, through the local government of all kinds, to the middle or meso-level of state, regional and provincial government.

Subjects – members of a society who are not involved in the political process of that society.

Subsidiarity – the principle that decisions should be taken at the lowest possible level of government (i.e., at the level closest to the people affected by the decisions); usually used in connection with the territorial decentralization of government, but it is not limited to this form.

Suffrage – the right to vote; "suffragettes" were women who fought for the right of women to have the vote.

Suffragism – a political movement by women to obtain the right to vote in an election.

Surplus value – the value invested in any homemade good that can be used by another individual; exploitation results when one person or group extracts this from another.

Superstructure – all non-economic influences in a society (for example, religion or culture); these ideas and values derive from the base and serve to legitimize the accepted system of exploitation.

Supra-national government – organizations in which countries pool their sovereignty on certain matters to allow joint decision-making.

Superior courts – in Canada, courts organized by provincial statute, staffed by judges appointed by the federal government.

Supreme Leader – head of the Islamic Republic of Iran.

Sustainable development – an approach to promoting economic growth that seeks to minimize environmental degradation and depletion of natural resources; advocates of sustainable development believe that policies implemented in the present must take into account their impact on the ability of future generations to meet their needs and live healthy lives.

Symbolic laws – laws designed to create special meaning for society, such as the adoption of a national anthem.

Syndicalism – a variation of socialism in which the workers own or control the factory or workplace.

System or external efficacy – the extent to which ordinary citizens feel that political leaders and institutions are responsive to their wishes.

T

Technocrats – career-minded bureaucrats who administer public policy according to their technical expertise rather than any political rationale; in Mexico and Brazil, these are known as the "técnicos."

Territory – terrain or geographical area.

Terrorism – the use of violence (such as murder, torture, bombing, kidnapping, hijacking, violent resistance) to spread fear and horror for political aims; what some regard as terrorism is seen as "freedom fighting" by others.

Theocracy – a state dominated by the clergy, who rule because they are the only interpreters of God's will and law.

Third International – the political organization in which the official ideology was Marxist-Leninist, or communism, established in 1921.

Third wave (of democracy) – *Democratization* across the world is often divided into "three waves;" the first, from the mid-nineteenth to the mid-twentieth century, saw between twenty-five and thirty states achieve a degree of democratic stability, depending on how "democracy" is defined; the second, from about 1950 to 1975, was mainly the result of decolonization; the third, from about 1975 to 2000, was mainly the result of the disintegration of the Soviet Union and the spread of democracy in Latin America and Asia.

Totalitarianism – a political system in which the state attempts to exercise total domination of all aspects of public and private life, including the economy, culture, education, and social organizations, through an integrated system of ideological, economic and political control; the term has been applied to both *Communist party-states* and fascist regimes such as Nazi Germany.

Township – South African usage refers to a segregated residential area reserved for Africans during *Apartheid*; they were tightly controlled and constituted mainly by public housing.

Township and village enterprises (TVEs) – nonagricultural businesses and factories owned and run by local governments and private entrepreneurs in China's rural areas; operate largely according to market forces and outside the state plan.

Traditional authority – authority based on birthright and custom.

Transitional democracies – countries that have recently moved from an *Authoritarian* government to a democratic one; also known as "newly established democracies."

Treasury Board – a *Cabinet* committee and government department whose primary responsibility is to oversee government spending.

Tribe – a community of people, tied together by a belief in common ancestry.

Tri-partism – a looser and less centralized system of decision making than *Corporatism* involving close government consultation (often with business and trade union organizations).

Trustee – a representative who acts independently in deciding what is in the best interests of his or her constituents.

Two-party system – a party system in which there are two credible contenders for power and either is capable of winning any election; party systems in which two large parties dominate all the others.

Two-party-plus system – a party system in which there are two major contenders for the power of approximately equal strength plus one or more minor parties able to win seats but not to control the government.

Typology – a method of classifying by using criteria that divide a group of cases into smaller numbers; can be used in the classification of governmental systems.

Tyranny – a form of government in which one person or a small group rules arbitrarily.

U

Ultra vires – Latin for *"beyond the power*;" used to describe an action which exceeds the conferred constitutional powers of the actor.

Umbrella organizations – associations that coordinate the activity of their member organizations.

Umkhonto we Sizwe – Zulu and Xhosa for "Spear of the Nation," the armed wing of the African National Congress, established in 1961 and integrated into the South African National Defense Force in 1994.

Unitary state/system – in contrast to the federal systems of Mexico, India, Canada or the United States, where power is shared between the central government and state or regional governments, in a unitary state (such as Britain or China) no powers are reserved constitutionally for subnational units of government.

Untouchables – the lowest caste in India's *Caste system*, whose members are among the poorest and most disadvantaged Indians.

Unwritten constitution – an un-codified constitution established through traditional practice.

Utopian socialism – early-nineteenth century socialism based on a universal appeal to reason. (A real-life Massachusetts Utopian community was thinly fictionalized in Nathaniel Hawthorne's novel *A Blithedale Romance*.)

V

Values – basic ethical priorities that constrain and give shape to individual attitudes and beliefs.

Vanguard party – a political party that claims to operate in the "true" interests of the group or *Social class* it purports to represent, even if this understanding doesn't necessarily correspond to the expressed interests of the group itself (e.g., the Communist parties of the Soviet Union and China).

Veto – the authorized power of a president to reject legislation passed by Congress; the veto may be overridden by a two-thirds majority of both houses of Congress.

Violence – the utilization of physical force or power as a means of achieving ends.

Volatility – the opposite of stability, volatility involves a usually unanticipated change in voting patterns from one election to another; some voting studies refer to it as "churning."

Voortrekkers – pastoralist descendants of Dutch-speaking settlers in South Africa who moved northwards from the British controlled Cape in 1836 to establish independent republics; later regarded as the founders of the *Afrikaner* nation.

Vote of censure – a motion of no confidence requiring the prime minister and the *Cabinet* to resign.

Vote of (no) confidence – a vote of confidence (or no confidence), to test whether the government of the day continues to have the majority support of members of the assembly; its importance lies in the normal convention that the government which loses a vote of confidence should resign.

Voting system – the arrangements by which votes are converted into seats on representative bodies.

Voting turnout – the number of citizens casting a valid vote expressed either as a percentage of those eligible to vote (adult citizens) or as a percentage of those on the electoral register.

W

Welfare state – not a form of state, but rather a set of public policies designed to provide for citizens' needs through direct or indirect provisions of pensions, health care, unemployment insurance and assistance to the poor and elderly.

Westminster model – a form of democracy based on the supreme authority of Parliament and the accountability of its elected representatives; named after the Parliament building in London.

White House Staff – special advisors to the president, part of the Executive office and similar to the Canadian Prime Minister's Office.

Wilderness preservationism – a form of environmentalism positing the intrinsic importance of wilderness for humankind.

World Trade Organization – an international organization created to provide and enforce ground rules for international trade and commerce.

Z

Zamindars – landlords who served as tax collectors in India under the British colonial government; abolished after independence.

Zionism – Jewish nationalist movement advocating the establishment of a Jewish nation-state.

Image Credits

Chapter 1

From its year of national independence in 1944 to 2014, Iceland experienced only a single police-shooting fatality.
Lögreglan 2007 Volvo S80 D5 Automatic, Reykjavík. Mr. Choppers. 2013. Wikipedia.

Churchill (left) and Roosevelt (center) meet with Stalin (right) at the Yalta Conference, marking one of the last moments of tentative cooperation before the Cold War saw democracy and communism enter into the hostile competition.
Big Three met at Yalta. National Archives and Records Administration. 1945. Wikipedia.

Swedish public housing built in Stockholm's Rinkeby district by the national government through their ambitious Million Programme implemented between 1965 and 1974. Approximately one million dwellings were built during the program's lifespan.
Rinkeby. Holger Ellgaard. 2009. Wikipedia.

Police forces are used by governments to enforce law and project sovereignty.
Police State. Kate Sheets. 2009. Flickr.

The indigenous ethnic Basque population (shaded) constitutes a nation (of peoples) without a state of their own.
Basque country location map. Eddo. 2010. Wikimedia Commons.

Map indicating the Croatian, Bosnian and Herzegovinian territory occupied by Serb forces during the Yugoslav Wars (March 31, 1991 to November 12, 2001).
Serbia in the Yugoslav Wars. Mladifilozof. 2010. Wikipedia.

2007 Brazilian protesters demonstrate the nation's continued skepticism and anti-U.S. sentiments.
Anti-US banner in a demonstration in Brazil. Nate Cull. 2005. Flickr.

Bolivian President Evo Morales initiated procedures necessary for a new national constitution to be drafted and ratified by January 2009.
Presidente Evo Morales Ayma. Eneas De Troya. 2013. Flickr.

Egyptian protesters gather in Cairo's Tahrir Square to demand Mubarak's removal from office in February 2011.
Tahrir Square. Jonathan Rashad. 2011. Flickr.

The United Kingdom is famous for its tradition of engaging in open, passionate and sometimes raucous political debates.
Passing of the Parliament Bill in the House of Lords. Samuel Begg. 1911. Wikimedia Commons.

1940s United States Housing Authority poster decrying the blight of slums.
Cross Out Slums. United States National Archives and Records Administration. c.1941-1945. Wikipedia.

Chapter 2

Map of Washington, D.C. indicating homicides by gun, knife or other means between November 2004 to November 2006.
Homicides in Washington, D.C. November 2004 – November 2006. Aude. 2006. Wikimedia Commons.

Former Mexican President Vicente Fox.
Vincente Fox podium. Gustavo Benítez, Presidencia de la República. 2005. Wikimedia Commons.

Nigerian police and military are deployed to keep the peace during the inaugural transfer of presidential powers after the 2015 election.
Security personnel hold hands to form human chain as Nigerian President Jonathan transferred power to President-Elect Buhari. U.S. Department of State. 2015. Wikimedia Commons.

Protesters in the U.S. capital demonstrate against the increasing influence of corporations.
Caution bribe coming through Washington D.C. Djembayz. 2013. Wikimedia Commons.

Euler diagram of European supranational organizations and their member states.
Supranational European bodies with NATO members. Perumalism. 2013. Wikimedia Commons.

World Social Forum rally in Brazil.
WSF 2003. Victor Soares, Agência Brasil. 2003. Wikimedia Commons.

Dubbed the "Tank Man," this iconic image shows an unidentified man non-violently blocking a column of tanks from deploying to the center of democracy protests in Tiananmen Square.
Tiananmen Square tanks protest. David Erickson. 2007. Flickr.

Zhou Yongkang, a former top Chinese domestic security official, was arrested in 2014 as part of an emerging anti-corruption movement.
Zhou Yongkang. Barry Bahler. 2006. Wikimedia Commons.

A 2013 anti-Putin procession marches towards Trubnaya Square in Moscow.
Moscow rally. Bogomolov. 2013. Wikimedia Commons.

A 1911 Industrial Worker (newspaper) illustration depicting their criticism of capitalism's hierarchy.
Pyramid of capitalist system. International Publication Company. 1911. Wikimedia Commons.

New Deal Era Social Security benefit poster.
Social Security poster. Franklin D. Roosevelt Library. c. 1930s. Wikimedia Commons.

Chart indicating the sharp decline in Russian male life expectancy.
Russian male life expectancy. Cold Light. 2009. Wikipedia.

Max Weber.
Max Weber. Elitenetzwerk Bayern. 1919. Wikimedia Commons.

Grand Ayatollah Sayyid Ruhollah Mūsavi Khomeini.
Ruhollah-Khomeini. Islamic Revolution Document Center. 2013.
http://www.irdc.ir/en/default.aspx

Axial chart of ideologies.
Accurate chart of ideologies and the relations between them. Program01. 2010. Wikimedia Commons.

Keith Ellison, elected to Minnesota's 5th congressional district in 2006, becomes the first Muslim congressman in the U.S. and swears in on a copy of the Quran owned by Thomas Jefferson.
Ellison. Michaela McNichol, Library of Congress. 2007. Wikimedia Commons.

Iranian revolutionaries take refuge behind makeshift barriers in 1979.
Iranian armed rebels during the Islamic Revolution in Iran in 1979. Q4233718. 2009. Wikimedia Commons.

Aftermath of a Boko Haram bombing.
Boko Haram bombing. Global Panorama. 2014. Flickr.

American Cold War propaganda.
American Propaganda during the Cold War. Magnus Manske. 2009. Wikimedia Commons.

CCTV surveillance cameras on Wall Street.
Surveillance. Jonathan McIntosh. 2009. Flickr.

Chapter 3

Euler diagram of the many overlapping relationships of the British Isles.
British Isles Euler diagram. T.W. Carlson. 2011. Wikimedia Commons.

Map indicating the five (named) autonomous regions of China.
China autonomous regions numbered. ASDFGH. 2012. Wikimedia Commons.

Map indicating the world's unitary states (dark) and federal states (light).
A map displaying today's unitary states. Lokal profil. 2007.

Québécois parade goers participating in Saint-Jean-Baptiste Day, a holiday increasingly expressing separatist instead of religious sentiments.
Fête nationale du Québec celebrations in Montreal. Montrealais. 2006. Wikimedia Commons.

Photograph of Russian Prime Minister Dmitry Medvedev (left) and President Vladimir Putin (right), dual executives of Russia in 2008.
Putin and Medvedev. Presidential Press and Information Office. 2008. www.kremlin.ru.

Two Iranian men attest their having voted in the 2013 presidential election by displaying their stamped index fingers.
Voter show stamped finger. Sonia Sevilla. 2013. Wikimedia Commons.

Israeli Prime Minister Shimon Peres reacts to the Knesset's plenary session no-confidence motion.
Peres responds to no-confidence motion. Harnik Nati, Government Press Office. 1986. Flickr.

World map indicating nations with bicameral legislatures (gray), unicameral legislatures (light gray) and no legislature (black).
Unibicameral map. Aris Katsaris, Canuckguy, SkyBon and Cerveaugenie. 2016. Wikimedia Commons.

Illinois Governor Daniel Walker greets Chicago constituents at the 1973 Bud Billiken Parade.
Illinois Governor Dan Walker greets Chicago constituents during the Bud Billiken Day Parade. John H. White, Environmental Protection Agency. 1973. Wikimedia Commons.

Japanese Prime Minister Ryūtarō Hashimoto faced a highly contended 1996 home district election, which, if he had lost, would have resulted in the selection of another head of state.
Ryūtarō Hashimoto. Robert D. Ward. 2002. Wikimedia Commons.

U.S. President Obama casts his 2012 ballot in Chicago.
Barack Obama votes in the 2012 election. Pete Souza, the White House. 2012. Flickr.

Washington D.C. canvasser collects signatures for the marijuana-legalizing Initiative 71.

DC cannabis campaign volunteer. Matthew Vanitas. 2014. Wikimedia Commons.

Occupy London sign demanding worldwide democracy and electoral reform.
A tent at the Occupy London encampment in the city of London. Neil Cummings. 2011.
Wikimedia Commons.

German ballot for the 2005 (proportional) federal elections.
Bundestagswahl 2005 stimmzettel. Schneelocke. 2005. Wikimedia Commons.

Nations that use first-past-the-post electoral systems (black).
Countries that use a first past the post voting system. Jiovigo. 2015. Wikimedia Commons.

Americans' affiliation by political party circa 2004.
U.S. party affiliation. JuWiki2. 2007. Wikimedia Commons.

First Minister of Scotland Nicola Sturgeon is the leader of the Scottish National Party.
Nicola Sturgeon. Christine McIntosh. 2015. Flickr.

*Logos for Mexico's Institutional Revolutionary Party (PRI), National Action Party (PAN) and
Party of the Democratic Revolution (PRD).*
PRI Party. Pueblo United. 2009. Wikimedia Commons. PAN Party. Pueblo United. 2009.
Wikimedia Commons. PRD Party. Pueblo United. 2009. Wikimedia Commons.

A Communist Party of the Russian Federation rally in Moscow.
Communist Party of the Russian Federation meeting at Manezhnaya Square. Bogomolov.PL.
2011. Wikimedia Commons.

Dwight D. "Ike" Eisenhower campaigning in Baltimore, Maryland.
Eisenhower presidential campaign in Baltimore, MD. Dwight D. Eisenhower Library. 1952.
Wikimedia Commons.

Bribery and interest groups can influence policy decisions that run contrary to public opinion.
Lobbying, blackmail, business. Pixabay. 2016. https://pixabay.com/en/lobbying-blackmail-
business-161689/

*Immigrant textile workers on strike in Lawrence, Massachusetts are surrounded by mobilized
National Guardsmen with fixed bayonets.*
Lawrence textile strike. Women and Social Movements. 2005. Wikimedia Commons.

Chapter 4

*Eleventh Night Protestant revelers in Newtownabbey, Northern Ireland signify their allegiance to
the United Kingdom by burning a Republic of Ireland flag on a bonfire.*
Ballycraigy bonfire. Shane Killen. 2007. Wikimedia Commons.

*A Mexican Zapatista rebel leader fighting for the rights of indigenous peoples of Mexico in the
Chiapas conflict.*
Sub Marcos horse from afar. Jose Villa. 1996. Wikimedia Commons.

*Cars burned in Liverpool during the 2011 England riots, which was incited by racial tensions
triggered by the police shooting of Mark Duggan, a member of the Black community.*
 Liverpool riots 2011 burnt cars. Andy Miah. 2011. Wikimedia Commons.

*1891 English political cartoon criticizing the differences in quality of life between the working
class and the middle class.*

Home life of peasants compared to the middle class. Wellcome Images. 2014. Wikimedia Commons.

A luxury cruise ship off the coast of Hainan, China.
Luxury, Hainan, China, Skyline. Pixabay. 2016.
https://pixabay.com/static/uploads/photo/2013/04/18/14/39/hainan-105596_960_720.jpg.

Slums of Ramos Arizpe, Mexico.
The other side of the tracks in Ramos Arizpe, Mexico. Codo. 2003. Wikimedia Commons.

1908 painting by Sergey Vasilyevich Ivanov depicting serf life in Russia.
S.V. Ivanov Yur's Day. Sergey Vasilyevich Ivanov. 1908. Wikimedia Commons.

Caxton Hall in Manchester, England hosts a suffragette meeting circa 1908.
Suffragettes, England. The New York Times. c. 1908. Wikipedia.

Mexico's lower house Chamber of Deputies.
Mexico Chamber of Deputies backdrop. Zscout370. 2006. Wikimedia Commons.

Rwandan parliament convening in December 2013.
Umushyikirano, Rwanda Parliament. Rwanda Government. 2013. Flickr.

The Sacred Heart Cathedral of Shenyang, China.
Sacred Heart Cathedral of Shenyang. Roscoe X. 2012. Wikimedia Commons.

Chinese police arrest a Falun Gong practitioner.
Woman arrested. Clearwisdom.net. 2003. Wikimedia Commons.

Zoroastrian fire temple in Yazd.
Yazd fire temple. Polimerek. 2005. Wikimedia Commons.

The Mandylion 12th century Russian icon.
Christos Acheiropoietos. Tretiakov Gallery. 2008. Wikimedia Commons.

MP Jim Murphy campaigns urges constituents to vote to remain part of the United Kingdom during Scotland's independence referendum in 2014.
Anti-Scottish independence campaigner. Thomas Nugent. 2014. Wikimedia Commons.

Reporters converge on U.S. Secretary of Defense William S. Cohen.
Secretary of Defense William S. Cohen talks with reporters. United States Department of Defense. 1999. Wikimedia Commons.

Protestors at the G-20 London summit.
Part of the crowd. Kashfi Halford. 2009. Flickr.

Street protestors of the Iranian Revolution confront armed regime soldiers.
Street clashes between protesters and Shah's regime in Iranian Revolution. Sajed.ir. 1978. Wikimedia Commons.

Mexican political graffiti reads, "They took them alive. We want them back alive. Solidarity with the 43 disappeared students."
Manifesto 43. Sortica. 2014. Wikipedia.

Anti-war protest in London against military intervention in Syria.
Bombing doesn't kill an ideology. Alisdare Hickson. 2015. Flickr.

Chapter 5

Egyptian police prevent protestors from advancing further during the Day of Anger protest on January 25, 2011.
Day of Anger riot police. Muhammad Ghafari. 2011. Wikimedia Commons.

A defiant Boris Yeltsin stands on top of a tank used in the attempted August Coup.
Boris Yeltsin. Kremlin.ru. 1991. Wikimedia Commons.

First-time South African voters register for the 2014 election, a multi-party contest which saw 249 of 400 National Assembly seats go to one party, the African National Congress.
Voter registration. Helen Online. 2014. Wikimedia Commons.

A mural in Portugal commemorating the military-led, civilian supported Carnation Revolution.
E preciso salvar Abril. Henrique Matos. 2008. Wikimedia Commons.

A disabled German World War I veteran begs on the streets of 1923 Berlin.
Berlin, bettelnder Kriegsinvalide. German Federal Archives. 1923. Wikimedia Commons.

A small town American gas station abandoned during the 1973-1974 winter fuel crisis.
Potlatch gas. David Falconer. 1974. Wikimedia Commons.

Agriculture commune workers, using lamps, toil the fields at night during the Great Leap Forward.
Xinyang working at night. Q4233718. 1959. Wikimedia Commons.

A homeless New York City resident sleeps on Broadway in affluent Manhattan.
Homeless person in New York City. Sony blockbuster. 2012. Wikipedia.

The Bengali community protests against the National Front and their racist supporters in East London in 1978.
Brick Lane. Alan Denney. 1978. Wikimedia Commons.

Mounted Argentinian police in Buenos Aires charge protesters.
Crisis 20 diciembre 2001. Arte y Fotografía. 2007. Wikimedia Commons.

A McDonald's restaurant in Buenos Aires offers kosher meals.
Kosher McDonald's, Abasto Shopping, Buenos Aires. Geogast. 2011. Wikimedia Commons.

Alter-Globalization Movement slogans displayed in Le Havre, France protesting the 37th G8 summit.
Manifestation anti-G8 au Havre. Guillaume Paumier. 2011. Wikimedia Commons.

Kenyan soldiers deployed in the African Union Mission in Somalia (AMISOM).
AMISOM Kismayo Advance. AMISOM Public Information. 2012. Flickr.

Competing French posters urging voters to either support or reject the drafted EU constitution.
Oui Non-Non Bourgogne. Justinc. 2005. Wikimedia Commons.

Sweatshops, such as this one in Indonesia, exploit cheap laborers.
Indonesian sweatshop. MyLifeStory. 2008. Flickr.

A Floating Production, Storage and Offloading (FPSO) vessel off the coast of Nigeria.
Mystras FPSO. Ciacho5. 2007 Wikimedia Commons.

Chapter 6

Police guarding the Charging Bull statue on the first day of the Occupy Wall Street, a protest movement critical of neoliberalism.
The Corporatist State. David Shankbone. 2011. Flickr.

Customers line up outside a Northern Rock bank branch during their liquidity crisis.
Northern Rock queue. Dominic Alves. 2007. Flickr.

Putin meets with Avtovaz automotive workers who were hard hit by the global recession.
Putin with Avtovaz employees in 2007. Presidential Press and Information Office. 2007. www.kremlin.ru

An Iranian soldier guards against Iraqi use of chemical weapons during the Iran-Iraq War, an eight-year conflict which claimed more than a million lives and cost an estimated USD 1.18 trillion.
Chemical weapons. Q4233718. Wikimedia Commons.

The National Health Service (NHS) is the publically funded healthcare system for England.
NHS NNUH entrance. Francis Tyers. 2006. Wikimedia Commons.

An Iranian woman begs on the streets of Tehran.
Street beggar with hijab. Kamyar Adl. 2008. Wikimedia Commons.

Many argue that the detention of non-military combatants at Guantanamo Bay represents the continued erosion of human rights.
Camp X-Ray detainees. Shane T. McCoy, U.S. Navy. 2002. Wikimedia Commons.

Chinese police detain a civilian during the 2012 crackdown in Tibet.
China's aggressive violence against Tibetan people. Students for a Free Tibet. 2014. Flickr.

Artistic depiction of King John signing Magna Carta.
Pictures of English history plate XXIV – King John and Magna Carta. Joseph Martin Kronheim. 1868. Wikimedia Commons.

Under Iran's judicial system that enforces Sharia, Iranian women are legally required to wear hijabs.
Two young women in Iran. Hamed Saber. 2007. Flickr.

Nigerians assemble in support of the Occupy Nigeria movement.
Occupy Nigeria rally in Ojota. Temi Kogbe. 2012. Wikimedia Commons.

Viktor Yushchenko, displaying visible signs of dioxin poisoning.
Viktor Yuschenko. Muumi. 2006. Wikipedia.

Heavy steel industrial pollution in Benxi, China.
Benxi steel industries. Andreas Habich. 2013. Wikimedia Commons.

Completed in 2005, Donghai Bridge connects Shanghai with the offshore Yangshan deep-water port.
Donghai Bridge. Zhang 2008. 2008. Wikimedia Commons.

Telmex cell phone tower in Mexico City.
Torre de teléfonos de Telmex. BlatZzz. 2014. Wikimedia Commons.

Anti-American mural in Caracas, Venezuela.
Anti-imperialismo Caracas. Erik Cleves Kristensen. 2011. Wikimedia Commons.